Leading Groups in
Stressful Times

Leading Groups in Stressful Times

Teams, Work Units, and Task Forces

JOSEPH A. OLMSTEAD

QUORUM BOOKS
Westport, Connecticut • London

Library of Congress Cataloging-in-Publication Data

Olmstead, Joseph A., 1921–
    Leading groups in stressful times : teams, work units, and task forces / Joseph A. Olmstead.
        p.   cm.
    Includes bibliographical references and index.
    ISBN 1–56720–610–7 (alk. paper)
    1. Teams in the workplace.   2. Leadership.   3 Organizational effectiveness.
    4. Stress management.   I. Title.
    HD66.O45   2002
    658.4'02—dc21   2002067912

British Library Cataloguing in Publication Data is available.

Library of Congress Catalog Card Number: 2002067912
ISBN: 1–56720–610–7

First published in 2002

Quorum Books, 88 Post Road West, Westport, CT 06881
An imprint of Greenwood Publishing Group, Inc.
www.quorumbooks.com

Printed in the United States of America

The paper used in this book complies with the
Permanent Paper Standard issued by the National
Information Standards Organization (Z39.48–1984).

10 9 8 7 6 5 4 3 2 1

To Burnelle and Rhonda

Contents

Preface

The overall purpose of this book is to present a coherent and useful analysis of groups at work, their principal dynamics, and the influences that impact upon their capabilities to perform effectively in organizations. The intent is to set out the factors that are critical for effective group performance—without all of the theoretical bells and whistles that sometimes get in the way of a useful understanding of material that could, by its very nature, sometimes appear to be exceedingly tenuous.

Throughout, there is an effort to avoid a simple listing of every extant reference on the topics of groups, organizations, and leadership. Especially important references, both recent and historical, have been cited; for those readers interested in the supporting literature, an annotated bibliography is included.

Many of these significant publications appeared years ago. Serious research on groups and application of its findings only began during and after World War II. For a number of years, research on groups flooded the journals. Recently, however, much of this work has been ignored.

But, to cite my first professor at the University of Texas, Harry Helson, "Good research never loses its value." I am firmly committed to the use of references that have had significance for the particular evolution of research and application concerned with groups. Many of the landmark references also contain useful information that still pertains but all too frequently has slipped through the cracks and been forgotten.

In effect, another purpose is to demonstrate that the "soft" variables of social psychology can be harnessed and organized in systematic application for useful purposes.

Another mentor at Texas, Robert Blake, drilled into my head that you can't go wrong in application when you use good research as the basis for your efforts. In this book, I have attempted to cite good research wherever possible. In the end, however, the pages herein are my own creation.

Finally, the material presented in the book is the product of many years of research and development conducted under the sponsorship of the former Social and Rehabilitation Service of the Department of Health, Education, and Welfare; the U.S. Bureau of Mines; the U.S. Army Research Office; the U.S. Army Research Institute for the Behavioral and Social Sciences; Defense Advanced Research Projects Agency; the Office of Naval Research; the Human Resources Research Organization (HumRRO); the Institute for Defense Analyses; and several proprietary business corporations.

PART 1

Groups in Organizations

Chapter 1

Introduction

Among all of the elements that can impact upon performance in organizations, probably the most compelling influences are the groups of which organizations are comprised and to which people belong (Olmstead, 2000; Vecchio, 1998). In just about any organization of any size, opportunities exist for groups to develop. Whenever people work together, groups are inevitable. Their impacts upon the effectiveness of organizations are substantial (Forsyth, 2000).

GROUPS AT THE CROSSROADS

Today, groups are at a significant crossroad. The choice is whether the excellence required of groups in most organizations can be maintained under the highly stressful conditions that are characteristic of the modern world.

The theme of this book is that groups constitute the fabric of organizations. It has long been known that the quality of its groups can make or break an organization. The performances of groups can result in either success or chaos. Frequently, the strengths of its groups will determine the capability of an organization for maintaining itself under conditions of high stress.

In organizations, the group is the meeting ground of individual (personality) and organization. Group relationships provide both solace and strength to individual members. Indeed, groups serve as both the citadels and bastions for members of organizations.

Concern for the performance of groups is important because groups constitute the connective tissues that unite the various elements within an organization, and their strengths can make a significant difference both for their performance and that of their larger organizations. At the same time, groups can be the most fragile elements in an organization. For this reason, the leadership, development, and maintenance of groups must be of genuine concern for executives of all types of organizations.

Today, organizations of all kinds face unprecedented challenges (Peters and Waterman, 1982). We are moving at break-neck speed into an information age and an information economy. The ability to rapidly accumulate, assimilate, and disseminate large quantities of information makes the present-day operating conditions of many organizations highly uncertain and unpredictable (Bellin, 1996; Kanter, 1983; Kirkpatrick, 2001). This is true for business corporations and government agencies, crisis-management organizations such as police departments and civil-emergency teams, as well as military units.

When these conditions are compounded by strong pressures generated by bottom-line management and frequent bureaucratic gridlock, organizational performance becomes highly important and extremely difficult. Under such conditions, leadership of groups is more critical than ever before. Leadership has always been an important element in organizational performance. Now, under present fast-moving, rapidly changing conditions, high-quality leadership at all levels, from executives to first-line supervisors, is essential for organizational success.

In addition to the changing performance requirements, increasingly complex technology, changed social values, and increased economic expectations make traditional organizational practices less effective. Indeed, changes in technology, society, and organizational practices are presenting numerous challenges that will require more skillful group members and more sophisticated leaders.

No matter where we may be living in the world of the 2000s, ours is an age of change to the point of no return. Confrontations between groups in competing and hostile relations, the alienation problems associated with a widening generation gap, and the fantastically rapid rate of technological change are reflected in problems that must be of serious concern to any manager or leader.

It is probably inevitable that the future will place even greater demands upon organizations than the present. Leadership requirements are based on the kinds of performance demanded of organizations. The kinds of performance required of most organizations are changing, and with the shifting demands, leadership will become both more complex and more important.

Whatever the purpose and mission of an organization, present-day operating conditions are characterized most often by the following:

1. high levels of turbulence within both the operating environment and the organization;
2. increasingly unpredictable events arising from highly turbulent conditions;
3. increasing rapidity of critical events; and
4. increasingly complex operations required to cope with threatening and uncertain events and their results.

In organizations, probabilities of success are increased only by taking relevant and appropriate actions. For organizations, whose very survival may depend upon the successful accomplishment of objectives, the actions require high levels of competence by numbers of people working together. The effectiveness of such an action system requires the coordinated efforts of individuals and groups performing parts of a total task so that the activities of each person and each group contribute in some fashion to accomplishment of the overall goal. Under these conditions, the quality of group performance becomes a paramount issue.

The pressing need for world-class organizations capable of coping with highly turbulent, complex conditions and unpredictable events places a premium upon the capabilities of organizations to address and respond to a more or less constant flow of new situations characterized by high levels of uncertainty. Overall, the view taken here is that the best approach would involve creating competent organizations capable of anticipating obstacles and overcoming them with a minimum of strain. Unfortunately, many organizations, including governments, only react to problems after crises have occurred. They only respond to yesterday. Accordingly, managers find themselves continually coping with one crisis after another, trying to overcome insurmountable odds created by their own fallibility.

All of these conditions have serious impacts upon the many groups that constitute most organizations. Groups can play conflicting roles in the life of an organization. The way in which they are led can exert serious impacts upon both the performance and the satisfactions of members.

The above emphasis upon organizational responses to problem situations points up the need for conceiving of organizations as problem-solving, decision-making systems in which the basic purpose is to take direct, unified action under frequently extreme pressures. In addition, there needs to be recognition of the intense requirements for organizations capable of functioning effectively in the new information age and information economy (Anderson and Anderson, 2001; Hite, 1999).

Leadership of the responsive organizations required for the future will embody a major responsibility for creative action. For such organizations to be effective, leading cannot be just passive reaction to problems as they occur; it must go beyond merely fighting fires that may arise. Instead, it will be necessary for leaders to strive actively to shape their groups and constantly push back the limitations that both human fallibility and system rigidity tend to place upon a group's capabilities for performing responsively.

Effectiveness under such conditions will require well-trained individuals who are knowledgeable about the fundamentals of leadership, thoroughly schooled concerning human factors that influence organizational performance, and skilled in applying this knowledge to the problems involved in guiding complex and, in some cases, highly ambiguous activities. Leadership can no longer be a matter of hunch or native ability, backed by a few elementary concepts and reinforced through the trial and error of experience. Instead, it must rest upon systematic knowledge and a rational and conscious application of sound principles and practices.

When these uncertain conditions are prominent, leadership becomes more important than ever before (Kanter, 1979; Kirkpatrick, 2001). Leadership has always been an important element in organizational effectiveness. However, under the present fast-moving, rapidly-changing conditions, high quality leadership at all levels is essential for organizational success (Olmstead, 2000; Peters and Waterman, 1982).

Without a doubt, the quality of available leadership at all levels determines the character of an organization and the effectiveness with which it accomplishes its objectives. Leadership has always been an important element in organizational effectiveness. Now, under present fast-moving, rapidly changing conditions, high quality leadership at all levels from executives to first-line supervisors, is essential for organizational success.

Many years ago, in his outstanding review of leadership theories, Warren Bennis (1959) stated: "Of all the hazy and confounding areas in social psychology, leadership theory undoubtedly contends for top nomination. And, ironically, probably more has been written and less is known about leadership than about any other topic in the behavioral sciences. Always, it seems the concept of leadership eludes us or turns up in another form to taunt us again with its slipperiness and complexity." Although Bennis made his statement over 40 years ago, it is still valid. Considerable progress has been made in understanding leadership; however, it remains a highly elusive element, especially where it involves leadership of groups within complex organizations.

PURPOSES OF THIS BOOK

The overall purpose of this book is to present an understandable analysis of groups at work in organizations, their dynamics, and influences that impact upon their capabilities to perform effectively. Groups in organizations can be made up of a variety of types, configurations, purposes, and personnel. Nevertheless, it is possible to identify the essential elements in group performance and to set forth principles for leading groups in organizations (Hare, 1976; Hinton and Reitz, 1971; Vroom, 1969).

Among the many kinds of groups that can be found in organizations are (1) work groups (work units, sections, departments, etc.), (2) teams (work teams, crisis-management teams, project teams), and (3) operating groups (task forces, operational staffs, and high-level decision-making groups). In this book, this variety of groups will be discussed in detail.

In addition to the overall purpose stated above, the book also has a number of more specific objectives:

1. to identify the essential elements in group performance within organizations,
2. to specify the particular essential elements that contribute to effective performance in the three major types of groups in organizations,
3. to propose a practical framework for guiding the management of the essential elements of performance,
4. to set out some principles for leading groups in organizations, especially for the three major types of groups,
5. to present a chapter devoted to analysis and critique of the present state-of-the-art of training for group leadership and to proposal of a detailed rationale for training leaders and potential leaders, and
6. finally, throughout the book, to reinforce the contention that groups are critical elements in organizational success and their leadership, maintenance, and development must be major concerns for managers and leaders.

GROUPS IN ORGANIZATIONS

For many people, the overriding concept of organization escapes any precise or all-inclusive definition. To some, an organization means something that is drawn on charts and recorded in manuals that describe jobs or specific responsibilities. Viewed in this way, organization takes on the aspect of a series of orderly cubicles contrived according to some rational logic. Such a view is useful for clarifying duties and responsibilities, but, taken alone, it is not sufficient for fully understanding a living, functioning system, which we call "an organization."

For this discussion, the term *organization* refers to the complex network of relationships among a number of people who are engaged in some activity for some reason, where the activity requires a division of work and responsibility in such a manner as to make the members interdependent. The clumsiness of this definition is only partly a matter of syntax. The fact is that only such a general statement can possibly embrace the varied forms of organizations encountered in the world today (Olson and Eoyang, 2001).

Two aspects of this definition warrant particular emphasis: (1) an organization engages in some activity for some reason—that is, it has goals which must be attained; (2) the pursuit of these goals establishes relationships between individuals and between subunits, which give the organization its bonds of identity and interdependence.

These aspects coincide with Bernard's (1938) classic distinction between effectiveness (goal achievement) and efficiency (internal working relationships). The rational, formal, task-centered aspect is mainly related to what is loosely called the *structure* of an organization—that framework of roles resulting from the allocation of authority, responsibility, and duties, as usually depicted in an organization chart and reflecting the formal bonds that tie the organization together. Closely related to structure are certain processes that function through it and make it viable, namely authority and influence. Since structure is the principal mechanism for channeling the activities of members in the direction required for organizational achievement, it is a critical component of the work context.

On the other hand, the relationship, motivational, maintenance aspect is related to the climate of an organization—that atmosphere which is peculiar to it and which reflects and determines its internal state and characteristic ways of working. Factors contributing to climate are such things as goals, policies, constraints, cohesion, leadership, communication practices, and relationships within and between groups.

The foregoing discussion suggests two critical strains that exist in many organizations. First, the requirement for coordination and control of activities often results in complex structures and high formalization, which are the most common causes of organizational rigidity. A second strain centers around the need to maintain a high level of motivation while exercising control over the actions of members. Although conflict between the two requirements may not be inevitable, it is common in many organizations (Kanter, 1979).

A series of seeming paradoxes confronts most organizations:

1. clear organizational lines are essential to effectiveness, but, if they become too fixed, they tend toward inflexibility;
2. well-defined goals focus the efforts and motivations of personnel, but they often make it difficult for an organization to change direction;
3. levels of authority assure control and coordination, but a complex hierarchy encourages rigidity;
4. clearly understood rules, policies, and procedures make for consistent and coordinated performance, but they circumscribe initiative and stifle innovation as they increase in number;

5. close supervision insures control, but it stifles motivation and forces decisions upward in the hierarchy;

6. the division of labor requires specialization of the functions of individuals and work groups, but specialization leads individuals and groups into a provincialism that may inhibit coordinated efforts toward common organizational goals.

Among all of the elements that contradict the logics of organization and impact upon performance in critical ways, probably the most compelling influence is the groups of which organizations are comprised and to which people belong (Tyler and Blader, 2000).

GROUPS AT WORK

In this book, a variety of groups will be discussed, ranging from low–level work units to teams of widely different types, and on to task forces, operational staffs, and high-level decision-making groups. At first, it might appear that the groups discussed here have little in common. However, such is not the case, because all are groups and, accordingly, all possess attributes found to be characteristic of groups. It can be asked legitimately what distinguishes between a mere collectivity of people and a group. The answer is that *a collectivity becomes a group when its members develop (1) common goals, (2) shared standards of behavior (norms), (3) differentiated roles, and (4) some degree of cohesion.* The leadership, or management, of groups must be devoted, at least minimally, to development of these attributes—if any level above minimum effectiveness is to be achieved. What defines effectiveness for this discussion is determined, in large part, by the fact that the groups under consideration exist in some sort of organization. Accordingly, the mission or goals assigned to a group by its organization will dictate what constitutes effectiveness.

Development of the above four group attributes would be exceedingly haphazard and difficult except for the saving fact that the groups discussed here, of whatever type, all occur in organizations. Whatever their specific nature, all organizations possess certain common properties that can be exploited, and, when a problem arises, its assessment in relation to basic organizational and group properties makes more insightful and lasting solutions possible.

Every organization has the following properties:

1. a structure of some sort, together with a set of either explicit or implied assumptions, premises, principles, or logics concerned with ways the activities of the organization and its constituent groups should be arranged and executed;

2. relationships among the personnel, some of which are based on work contacts, some on friendship, and some on group affiliation;

3. communication processes through which, to one degree or another, there is a flow of information about the internal state of the organization, its constituent groups, the environments within which it functions, and the relationship of the organization to its environments;

4. decision-making processes that guide the organization and determine its actions;

5. influence processes, usually centered in formally designated leaders, but sometimes based in individuals or groups not anticipated by the organization chart;

6. resources to carry on activities, such as personnel, money, equipment, and materials;

7. motivational and attitudinal characteristics, such as the forces drawn upon in mobilizing the efforts of personnel and the degree of favorableness and loyalty toward the work, the organization, its component groups, and its members.

Differences between organizations occur because of variations in the form and degree of the above properties and the specific configurations that evolve because of particular goals, tasks, and circumstances. However, every organization possesses the properties in some form and to some degree. Taken together, they constitute a foundation upon which assessment and developmental efforts can be based.

The development of effective groups within organizations can be highly rewarding but sometimes difficult. Group relations and the norms that regulate them are not static. They do not stay put permanently. Successes, failures, deprivations, changed environmental conditions, personnel losses, new leaders—all tend to bring about changes in the norms, functional arrangements, and operations of groups. Accordingly, developing and sustaining a highly cohesive and effective group constitutes a more or less constant maintenance activity for its leader.

High cohesion occasionally develops spontaneously. Because of some fortuitous experience, usually dramatic, a group may suddenly evidence at least a temporary sense of unity where none existed previously. This sudden rise in cohesion may be nothing more than a sort of emotional upsurge that will soon dissipate. If so, it serves little purpose except to provide the group with a temporary momentum. Under certain circumstances, such as entry into an extremely difficult situation—as for crisis-management teams or military units—such momentum may be desirable. However, temporary unity of this nature cannot be expected to resist disruptive forces of any consequence, unless conditions favorable to the development of high cohesion already exist in the group.

Those properties that enable a group to resist both internal and external stress are most often the result of careful and calculated developmental efforts on the part of a patient leader carried out over a period of time. Cohesion developed under such conditions provides a substantial foundation both for the resistance to disruptive forces and for unified actions of a more routine nature.

Developing sound cohesion in a group cannot usually be accomplished overnight. Neither can it be achieved by exhortation or gimmicks, no matter how colorful. The development of sound bonds of unity and strength requires a fine sensitivity to the constantly shifting currents of feelings and attitudes among personnel, attention to details and occurrences that might cause a negative shift in attitudes if not corrected, alertness to every event that might be used to reinforce feelings of unity and solidarity, and, most of all, recognition of the frailty and fallibility of the human individuals who are attempting to cope with all of the complexities of existing in group environments.

The good leader will analyze each specific situation calmly, patiently, and methodically. Most of all, he will not jump to conclusions. He understands that individual facts or actions cannot be interpreted except as components of a larger picture. This means looking at the event or action in relation to groups of people, their attitudes, and their codes of behavior. It means looking at the total group situation, including objectives, cohesion, morale, and discipline, to see, for example, whether the organizational climate is influencing the behavior of individuals as well as the entire group. It means looking at the operational situation to determine whether successes or failures, efficiencies or ineptitudes are exerting an influence upon behavior. It means taking into account previous experience and background of group members.

When all of the obtainable facts are viewed in relation to the total situation, their real significance will usually take more meaningful shape. Of course, it must be recognized that no one can reasonably expect to get all the facts about most situations. The important thing is to do some hard thinking about the facts that are obtainable, including both the feelings and attitudes of subordinates and those that the leader himself brings to the situation.

THE FUNCTION OF GROUP LEADERSHIP

For this discussion, leadership is *the process of influencing the actions of individuals and groups in order to obtain results desired by an organization.* According to this definition, leadership is exercised in the service of an organization and is usually a part of the managerial or supervisory function.

In most organizations, the managerial or supervisory function includes at least three broad activities, each of which makes an important contribution to effectiveness. The first activity involves decision–making. In virtually all organizations at virtually all levels, supervisors must make certain decisions regarding the technical aspects of the work for which they are responsible. These decisions are specific to the particular task to be executed, and although their effect must be taken into account, they are not primarily concerned with influencing people.

Another major activity involves *management*—the application of the proper procedures for allocating and using the human and physical resources of the organization. For example, a supervisor may make a judgment about a personnel assignment, or he may initiate a procedure designed to improve efficiency. These kinds of problems are related to management.

However, a supervisor is also responsible for the accomplishment of the work performed by others. Therefore, a third important aspect of supervision or administration is *leadership*. It is the function of leadership to stimulate and influence the activities of individuals and groups in constructive ways so that performance requirements will be met. Thus, leadership is concerned with human performance. *This emphasis upon human performance distinguishes leadership from other aspects of supervision or administration.*

It is apparent that, in practice, leadership activities can rarely be completely separated from the other aspects of administration. For example, skill in making work decisions may partly determine the ability of a supervisor to influence his personnel. If he consistently makes more right than wrong decisions, people will have more confidence in him. Conversely, his influence decreases if he consistently makes bad decisions. Leadership enters into every aspect of supervision; but, since it is concerned with influence and since supervisors differ in their capabilities for influencing their subordinates, it can be separated from the other elements and examined as a critical aspect of supervision or management, and, therefore, as a major determinant of the effectiveness of groups in organizations.

For most organizations, probabilities of success are increased only by taking relevant and appropriate actions. Furthermore, most actions require high levels of competence by numbers of people working together. The effectiveness of such an action system requires the coordinated efforts of individuals performing parts of a total task so that the activities of each person contribute, in some fashion, to accomplishment of the overall goals.

It is not surprising, in these terms, that the effectiveness of an organization should be so closely related to the effectiveness of the leaders at all levels. Regardless of the type or size of a work group, section, department, or entire organization, individuals who occupy positions of leadership must perform a variety of activities that will enable their groups to move toward accomplishment of their objectives.

This raises a series of questions about the abilities, or competencies, needed to function effectively in a leadership role. For example, how aware are leaders of the emotional and motivational conditions of their groups and of the individuals in their groups—conditions they must take into account in making decisions? Are leaders able to gather relevant and accurate information about the internal functioning of their groups? How competent are they in observing, talking with, and listening to the people with and through whom they must work? Are they able to translate their ideas for leading their groups into actions consistent with these ideas? How sensitive are they in determining whether to intervene in activities of their group members? Are they skillful in providing the necessary guidance to subordinates in such a manner that motivation and performance are not impaired? How well can they pick out the essential elements in leadership problems and then supply actions appropriate to the demands of the situations?

Answers to questions such as these have important bearing upon leader performance. Leaders become effective by understanding what is required of them, and how, in their particular groups, the human forces may be combined, balanced, and directed toward group goals.

The remainder of this book will be devoted to an analysis of groups at work and the leadership of such groups.

IMPLICATIONS

In the chapters that follow, the necessarily brief orientation and general statements presented in this chapter will be expanded, and the concepts will be developed. In proceeding through the remainder of the book, it will be helpful to keep two important points in mind.

The first is that, although it is sometimes treated simply, leadership has become a complex process. Recent technological developments have resulted in intricate organizations manned largely by highly skilled specialists. Under these conditions, leadership takes on greater complexity while simultaneously becoming increasingly important.

One of the gravest dangers in approaching leadership of groups is oversimplification. Successful leadership demands recognition that problems usually arise from multiple causes that are frequently complex, and that satisfactory resolution requires the manipulation and modification of numerous elements operating interdependently and simultaneously. In reading this book, it will be important to keep in mind that a relatedness exists between the various elements that are discussed. Clear understanding of group leadership requires explicit recognition that all are interrelated parts of a common system.

The second point is that there can be assurance that effective leadership is not a matter of supernatural qualities given only to a few accomplished individuals. A manager becomes an effective leader when he understands the organization of which he is a part and skillfully uses the forces by which his group is moved. Although leadership is complex, effectiveness results from knowledge and a rational and conscious application of sound principles and practices.

THE PLAN OF THIS BOOK

The effectiveness of an organization is, in part, dependent upon the conditions within it (Vaill, 1976). Its performance and the performance of the people who are members of the organization are the results of a reciprocal relationship between the actions of people and existing conditions within the organization. Groups within organizations are important parts of the members' environment.

Through examination of these essential aspects, it can be expected that a better understanding of both group and organizational performance can be achieved.

Part 1—Groups in Organizations

Part 1 is devoted to a general analysis of groups within organizations and the effects of organizational and environmental factors upon group performance. Chapters 1 and 2 introduce the book and discuss both the origins of groups in organizations and the impact of groups upon the performance and morale of members of a group.

Chapter 1 introduces the book and sets forth both its overall purpose and some specific objectives. A rationale is presented for the proposed approach to leadership of groups in organizations.

Chapter 2 opens with a discussion of the origins of groups in organizations. An important issue is concerned with the impacts that groups exert upon group members. The functions of group leaders will be examined, and some implications will be discussed.

In chapter 2, the special issue of groups that operate within organizations will be addressed. The very fact of organization results in opportunities for groups to develop. Whenever people work together, groups are inevitable and ubiquitous. The influences of such groups can be either positive or negative. Accordingly, leaders need to learn how to manage groups effectively. Chapter 2 sets out some basics for understanding groups at work. In addition, guidance is provided for developing groups as parts of an organizational system, and organizational conditions required for effective group performance are discussed.

Part 2—Major Types of Groups

Chapter 3 opens the discussion of specific types of groups with an analysis of work groups, the most common kind of group that occurs in organizations. *Work Groups* includes conventional work units, sections, departments, and so forth. Determinants of effectiveness of work groups will be discussed, and some pointers for leading them will be provided.

Chapter 4 is devoted to an analysis of teams and their leadership requirements. The label *team* refers to a group that is specifically designed to require the integrated and highly coordinated activities of several people. Within this requirement, teams may be as varied as *working teams*, which are task-oriented and, frequently, machine-dominant groups; *crisis-management teams*, such as police swat teams, fire department companies, medical emergency teams, and military combat teams; and, finally, *project teams*. Because teams, teamwork, and the components of team performance comprise a complex topic that can be subject to much misunderstanding, a conceptual model for thinking about teams will be proposed. Team types and skill requirements for different types of teams will be analyzed. Finally, planning for team training will be outlined, and the leadership of teams will be discussed.

In chapter 5, definitions and distinguishing characteristics of *operating groups* (task forces, operational staffs, and high-level decision-making groups) will be described. In contrast to work groups and teams, operating groups may have complex organizations, with numerous levels, broad missions, and many more personnel. Requirements for effectiveness of operating groups will be described. Of particular importance in chapter 5 will be a detailed discussion of decision-making within groups. Some of the difficulties specific to leading decision-making groups will be described. In addition, guidance for leading such groups will be included.

Chapter 6 is devoted to a discussion of actual groups, their essential functions, and some of the problems that may be encountered in leading them. Crisis-management organizations were selected as prototypes for illustrating groups in action. Required capabilities for crisis-management organizations will be discussed and some operational processes will be stipulated. Recommended procedures for improving real organizations will be presented.

Part 3—Leading Groups at Work

Part 3 is devoted to discussion of the development of effective groups and the leadership of all types of groups. Throughout part 3, human factors will be considered as major determinants of group effectiveness.

In chapter 7, the importance of human factors considerations will be emphasized. Some organizational conditions important for effective group performance and for performance in groups will be discussed. Five essential elements in organizations will be described, and their impacts upon both individuals and group performance will be demonstrated.

For the most part, the preceding chapters address issues involved with group performance, the attributes of particular types of groups, and specific ways of leading each type. In chapter 8, the issue of leadership in general will be addressed, and the discussion will identify and define the essential nature of leadership as an influence process. Some fundamental ideas for leading groups at work will be set forth. In addition, the nature of leadership skills will be examined.

In chapter 9, the substance of the discussion is that supervision and leadership are not the same. Supervision of groups becomes fully effective only when good leadership practices are superimposed upon the managerial techniques dictated by the kinds of jobs, the caliber of the personnel, and the work methods required by the mission or task. Some situational considerations are discussed, and the importance to group performance of the work context is emphasized. Finally, the difference between group leadership at high levels and leadership in first-line supervision is discussed.

Chapter 10 will examine the current state-of-the-art of leadership training. At present, the field is in considerable disarray. Some reasons for the lack of much effective training will be identified and discussed. Then, a rationale for effective leadership training will be proposed. Finally, some specific proposals for improving training for leaders will be presented.

Chapter 11 summarizes the significant concepts discussed throughout the book and also presents relevant conclusions about groups in organizations, group performance, and leadership of groups.

Chapter 2

Groups in Organizations

An organization of any size is a complex system of relationships between individuals in which each person has much contact with a few people, a little contact with some, and practically no contact with most of the other members. These relationships constitute the bonds that hold an organization together; they develop wherever people are thrown into contact with one another, and they exert potent influences upon attitudes and performance.

The interaction that occurs is not usually a matter of random contacts. Much of it depends upon the logical division of work and responsibility. Relationships arise from the necessary division of people into small work units, which become psychologically meaningful groups. Interaction results in the development of uniform and consistent points of view toward the group, the organization, the work, and other personnel. These uniform attitudes, or norms, exert strong influence on the behavior of every member, and the organization and its activities are evaluated in terms of them. They feed back into and affect—sometimes favorably, sometimes adversely—the official functions and relationships required by the formal organization (Altman, 1966; Bowers, 1969).

ORIGINS OF GROUPS IN ORGANIZATIONS

Much of the behavior of an individual in an organization is an expression of his place in the group to which he belongs. These groups tend to develop persistent patterns in their relations to each other. Because members identify with their own groups, they may express fairly uniform attitudes toward other groups. In some cases, well-developed patterns of antagonism are found between groups, with each being critical of the others and defensive toward itself. Thus, natural conflicts of interest exist even in the most wisely designed organizations. The formal structure typically establishes the basis for these conflicts by the way it differentiates its work units. With all of the diligence and understanding a manager can exert, differentiation across formal units and cohesion within each of them are the almost inevitable consequences of organizing for work.

From the foregoing discussion, a significant point becomes clear. An organization does not consist of an undifferentiated mass of people, all of whom have identical motives, attitudes, and loyalties. The very fact of organization means a network of smaller groups, each of which possesses its own values and standards of behavior. Because these groups have undergone certain common experiences as part of the larger organization, some of the values and behavioral standards will be similar. However, they have also undergone unique experiences that result in the development of values and standards that differ between groups. Through such values and standards, groups exert powerful influence upon their members and play an important role in the satisfaction and performance of all personnel.

EFFECTS OF COHESIVENESS

Central to an understanding of group relations and of their effects upon satisfaction and performance is the concept of *group cohesiveness* or *cohesion*. The term *cohesiveness* refers to the feeling of group pride and solidarity that exists among members; in individual terms, it is the attractiveness that a group has for each member. There have been numerous studies of the effects of cohesiveness, and, although some results have been mixed, there seems to be unanimous agreement that cohesiveness is central to any understanding of small groups and of group influence.

In a large-scale industrial study, Seashore (1954) found that member morale was related to group cohesiveness and that group influences were related to standards of performance. He concluded that groups of small size are more likely to have a high degree of cohesiveness than groups of larger size and that the degree of cohesiveness that develops is significantly determined by managerial decisions concerning the size of work groups and the continuity of membership in the groups. Gross (1954), in a study of small work groups within the Air Force, found that satisfaction with the Air Force and personal commitment to group goals were directly related to group cohesiveness. These findings have been supported by a long series of studies, summarized by Kahn and Katz (1953) and Likert (1961), which show that cohesiveness tends to be positively correlated with productivity, although the relationships are not always high nor consistent. On the other hand, studies by McCurdy and Lambert (1952), Albert (1953), Berkowitz and Levy (1956), Pepitone and Kleiner (1957), and Deutsch (1959) reported failures to find significant relationships between group cohesiveness and effectiveness.

Despite these mixed results, the predominance of findings favor cohesiveness as a major determinant of satisfaction and performance. At this point, an important distinction becomes necessary. After many years of research, it has become clear that no simple relationship exists between cohesiveness and group effectiveness. A group will not necessarily be outstandingly productive simply because it is highly cohesive. An additional factor to consider is the norms held by the group. Cohesive groups usually have strong norms; however, the important question that must be asked is "What are the norms?" It is possible for a highly cohesive group to possess strong norms for minimal productivity, in which case cohesiveness would not result in performance considered effective by the organization. On the other hand, if the norms of the group value high performance, effectiveness will usually result.

Therefore, three factors are necessary for effective performance by groups in organizations: (1) a group situation that is attractive to the members and that generates pride and solidarity; (2) strong group norms that value high performance; and (3) technical proficiency.

CHARACTERISTICS OF AN IDEAL GROUP

There can be no doubt that the primary, face-to-face group can exert a powerful influence upon an individual worker. However, from the standpoint of an organization, the influence is not always positive. One of the strongest forms of cohesiveness occurs when members of a group coalesce in order to defend themselves against what they perceive to be an oppressive supervisor. Similarly, a very high level of cohesiveness can develop when members perceive their group to be threatened by actions of the larger organization. In either case, a cohesive group may have negative effects upon both the aims of its supervisor and the goals of the organization.

On the other hand, groups can play very positive roles as potent means for influencing the effectiveness of individual personnel. For most administrators and supervisors, the problem is to develop and control the processes and interactions within work groups so that they function constructively and their activities are channeled by conscious design in directions most conducive to the achievement of organizational objectives.

Likert (1961) described some characteristics of the ideal work group:

Knowledge and Skills. All members are skilled in the technical requirements of their respective jobs and in the interpersonal and group functions required to serve as effective group members.

Attitudes. All members like the group and are loyal to the other members, including the supervisor. The supervisor and all members have a high degree of confidence and trust in each other. They believe that each member of the group can perform competently. These expectations help each member to realize his highest potentialities.

Motivation. The members of the group are highly motivated to meet group performance standards and to accomplish both group and organization objectives. Each member will do all in his power to help the organization and the group achieve its objectives. He expects every other member to do the same. He is eager not to let the other members down. He strives hard to do what he believes is expected of him. He is ready to communicate fully all information which is relevant and of value to the group's work, and is genuinely interested in receiving relevant information that any other member of the group can provide. This information is welcomed and trusted as being honestly and sincerely given. The motivation and ability of the members of the group to communicate easily contribute to the flexibility and adaptability of the group.

Working Relationships. Members of the group have developed well-established working relationships among themselves. The relationships are pleasant, and mutual assistance is the rule. When necessary, others will give a member the assistance he needs to accomplish his assignments successfully.

Atmosphere. Problem-solving and decision-making activities of the group occur in an atmosphere that is stable, informal, comfortable, and relaxed. There are no obvious tensions; it is a working atmosphere in which people are interested and personally involved. Respect is shown for the point of view of others, both in the way contributions are made and in the way they are received. There may be real and important differences of opinion, but the focus is on arriving at sound solutions, not on aggravating the conflict. Individuals also feel secure in making independent decisions that seem appropriate for their respective roles, because the atmosphere is one of clearly stipulated objectives and policies that provide each member with a solid basis for making decisions. This encourages initiative and pushes decisions down to the appropriate levels while maintaining a coordinated and directed effort.

These and other characteristics can usually be observed in effective groups. Every group will probably show some of these characteristics at one time or another; however, more effective groups will consistently demonstrate a preponderance of them.

GROUP COMPETENCIES

In recent years, the concept of "competency" has evolved as a powerful concept for use in assessing and developing the performance of both individuals and groups.

For individuals, a competency is *an individual's demonstrated knowledge, skills, and abilities.* Competencies go beyond traditional knowledge, skills, and abilities (KSAs); they are KSAs that are *demonstrated in a job context.* A cluster of demonstrated KSAs defines a competency and makes a real difference for organizational success. For example, planning is a competency. Rather than emphasizing a broad range of specific tasks and skills required for effective performance or attempting to establish the basic functions to be performed in a job, generic skills or competencies can be behaviorally defined and identified as basic to performance.

This approach asserts that, in daily job performance, an individual is faced with problem situations requiring decisions or actions. When the problems are routine or familiar, they are handled with little thought about the process. When problems arise that require conscious problem-solving, competencies are needed to structure the information, create ways of handling the problems, determine alternative solutions, and evaluate results of solutions selected.

The characteristics of competencies are:

1. they are abilities that have a unique hierarchy of component skills;
2. they are pervasive and recur across most job tasks;
3. the development of competencies is dependent on mastery of a knowledge and skill base;
4. integration of lower order knowledge and skills is required for demonstration of competencies;
5. when mastered, competencies can be applied in a variety of job contexts.

In numerous studies of a wide range of jobs, the job competency assessment approach has been found to identify superior performers. This applies to skilled workers, as well as supervisors, managers, and executives. The approach has an advantage over techniques based upon job dimensions derived by factor analysis or critical incident analysis, both of which usually provide only descriptive accounts of average performance in routine situations.

The fact is that many of the activities connected with work involve common elements or competencies. This is especially true for supervisors and managers, where the same competency may overlap many different tasks. An example is *communicating,* which may be necessary in many tasks performed by supervisors and managers.

Competencies are valuable in serving as bases for

1. assessing performance of personnel,
2. assessing training needs,
3. designing training or development programs, and

4. designing assessment centers.

Groups also have competencies. Like individuals' competencies, group competencies are the properties and characteristics of effective groups. Thus, competencies go beyond conventional performance elements. They are generic attributes that distinguish more effective from less effective groups.

Following Likert's characteristics of an ideal group, The Vanguard Research Group has identified seven group competencies that can be assessed and improved through systematic development and training (Olmstead, 1998). Following are the seven group competencies:

1. *Knowledges, Skills, and Proficiencies.* All members of the group possess the required knowledges and are skilled in the technical and role functions required to serve as effective members of the group.
2. *Attitudes.* All members like the group and the entire organization and are loyal to other members, including the supervisor. Furthermore, the supervisor and all group members have a high degree of mutual confidence and mutual trust.
3. *Motivation.* All members of the group are highly motivated to meet the performance standards and to accomplish the objectives of the group. Each member will do all in his or her power to help the group achieve its objectives, and expects every other member to do the same. Each group member is eager not to let other members down.
4. *Working Relationships.* Members of the group have developed well-established working relationships among themselves. The relationships are pleasant and mutual assistance is the rule.
5. *Objectives and Standards.* The steadying influence of objectives and values held in common by all members provides a stabilizing factor in the group's activities. All members endeavor to have the objectives and performance standards of the group in harmony with those of the larger organization.
6. *Working.* Problem-solving and decision-making activities occur in an atmosphere which is stable, informal, comfortable, and relaxed. It is a working atmosphere in which people are interested and personally involved. The climate is sufficiently constructive for subordinates to accept readily any criticism that is offered. Because the climate is one of clearly stipulated objectives and policies, individuals feel secure in making independent decisions that seem appropriate for their work.
7. *Leadership Climate.* The group's supervisor or manager attempts to lead in a manner that seems most likely to create a constructive climate and cooperative rather than competitive relationships among members of the group. The leader tries to establish a workable balance between necessary compliance and excessive conformity on unessential matters.

Another way of viewing competencies is to consider them to be a group's capabilities for coping with problems and requirements that arise within its operating environments. In short, they comprise the group's coping abilities.

A group can be assessed or evaluated on its competencies by (1) group members, (2) independent observers, or (3) supervisors or group leaders.

PROPERTIES OF EFFECTIVE GROUPS

Many groups that have the above internal characteristics, and their related competencies, have also been found to possess a number of performance attributes that are directly traceable to effective performance.

Many groups judged to be effective have been found to share a number of identifiable properties related to their performance.

Group Properties

- *Capacity to learn.* An effective group has the capacity to gather information relative to its actions and performance, analyze it, feed the information back to itself, and change according to what is learned either about situational demands or about the group itself. All of this makes possible continued development and improvement.

- *Open and efficient communication.* Effectiveness depends upon the ability to generate information about both external and internal conditions and to communicate it accurately and reliably. There must be a flow from one part of the group to the other of all relevant information important for each decision and activity. Members must exchange information and work at clearing up misunderstandings. Efficient communication enables members to achieve the common understanding of problems that is necessary for well-integrated action.

- *An atmosphere of confidence and freedom from threat.* There is a preponderance of favorable attitudes on the part of each individual toward other members, toward superiors, toward duties, toward the organization—in other words, toward most aspects of his work situation. Because of these favorable attitudes and loyalties, effective groups usually develop strong informal values and norms, particularly in relation to the more important aspects of performance. A poor atmosphere undermines communication, reduces flexibility, and encourages self-protection rather than commitment to the group.

- *Internal flexibility and innovative ability.* An effective group is sufficiently flexible that efficient shifting of both individual and group assignments is possible as changes in situations demand it. Thus, the group can adapt readily to unanticipated events. Procedures are not so rigid that adjustments to new situations become exceedingly laborious. Furthermore, over-formalization and strong dependence upon individual leaders do not exist to the extent that responsibility and authority cannot be easily shifted when situational demands change or leaders are lost.

- *A state of functional integration among subordinate units.* Functions and operations of the various parts of the group fit together so that they do not operate at cross purposes.

• *Operational proficiency.* This is essential in performance both of activities directly related to goal achievement and of functions required to support these activities.

Leader Resources

• *Leaders who arrive at valid decisions speedily and efficiently.* The energy of leaders and of decision-making staffs is not expended in interminable haggling or over-concentration on inconsequential details but, rather, is used to develop constructive solutions to critical problems.

• *Leaders who are skilled in identifying and using potential present among subordinates.* This means that talent is not wasted; the leaders of the group know how to locate, develop, and use the abilities of the personnel to best advantage.

• *Leaders who are skilled in mobilizing and guiding the efforts of personnel.* Every leader should be able to motivate personnel, coordinate activities, and to guide personnel to perform as a unified whole.

Personnel Resources

• *Commitment of the personnel to group and organizational goals and a high level of motivation to perform in accordance with the goals.* Commitment to goals leads to a willingness to work hard for achievement and to change when necessary. In the most effective groups, most members, but especially key personnel, accept the objectives and are committed to their accomplishment. Furthermore, there is a minimum of conflict about objectives or about the means for accomplishing them. This does not imply that divergent opinions may be present but not expressed; it means that if deep-seated differences exist, even though not expressed, unified action is not likely to result.

• *A sense of identity.* Personnel have knowledge and insight about what the group is, what it stands for, what its objectives are, and what it is supposed to do.

• *Technical competence.* Personnel know their jobs and are well trained to perform them. They possess the capabilities to cope with the tasks required of the group.

In demonstrably effective groups, properties such as these can be readily observed. It is important to note that many of these properties are only remotely related to the adequacy of organizational techniques, that is, techniques concerned with designing structures and developing operating policies and procedures. Good organizational techniques are essential for providing stability and channeling work activities. However, organizational techniques assume that people will behave in accordance with the logic of the system, and this is not always the case. People do not always carry out their duties in accordance with the assumptions made by the formal, rational system. Therefore, strains may develop in the group, causing loss of effectiveness.

Groups often encounter difficulties because personnel have not learned, or perhaps are not motivated, to function well together. For example, it is possible for a new group composed entirely of experienced personnel to exhibit operational problems until common habits of functioning have evolved. It is possible for highly trained administrators with records of individual success to be unable to work together. It is even possible for a group with a long history of accomplishment suddenly to develop functional difficulties because of internal problems arising from changed circumstances within it.

Effective performance by a group is a matter not only of technical and organizational proficiency but also of such factors as its objectives, its level of morale, the state of motivation, and the degree of functional integration among the various personnel and sub-groups of which it is comprised. The group most likely to succeed is a tightly knit, efficiently functioning system of people and activities composed of interlocking units effectively linked by capable leaders and served by an efficient communication system. The personnel are characterized by strong motivation and loyalty to the group, and there is mutual confidence and trust between personnel at all levels.

The attributes just described are characteristic of most effective groups. The problem is, How can leaders best determine what they need to do to adequately influence their groups so as to make them more effective?

Groups run a wide gamut of goals, sizes, missions, personnel, and geographical dispersion. The peculiar nature of each group will determine to some extent the specific problems encountered. Usually this requires that managers be concerned with particular cases and with diagnosing problems and taking actions to improve unique situations.

DEVELOPING EFFECTIVENESS

Carried to the extreme, this insistence on the specificity of problems would render hopeless any attempt to obtain a prior understanding of things that affect group functioning. The saving factor is that the problems all occur in organizations. Whatever their specific nature, all organizations possess the universal properties listed in chapter 1. These properties can be changed or improved. When problems in groups arise, the identification of their relations to relevant organizational properties makes possible more insightful and lasting solutions of the problems.

The task of developing effectiveness within an organization is one of making a functioning, operational system out of the human and material resources available to it. Viewed as a part of a system, a group must be capable of performing more or better than all of the resources that constitute it. It must be a genuine whole, different from the sum of its parts, with its total performance more than the sum of its individual efforts. A group is not just a mechanical assemblage of resources. To make a functioning work unit from a collection of people, buildings, and equipment, it is not enough to put them together in some logical form and then to issue a directive for work to begin. What is needed is a transformation of the resources. This cannot come merely from a directive. It requires leadership of a high quality.

The only resources within an organization capable of transformation are human resources. Money and materials can be depleted. Equipment can be used well or badly but can never perform more efficiently than it was originally designed to do. Humans alone can grow and develop. Therefore, it is essential that this resource be nurtured so that it can be used as fully and as effectively as possible. Effective utilization requires the organization of duties and functions so that they are the most suitable for the capabilities of personnel in the light of the group's goals and the organization of members so as to elicit the most effective performance from them. It requires recognition of the personnel as a resource, that is, as having properties and limitations that require the same amount of maintenance and attention as any other resource. It also requires recognition that the human resource, unlike other resources, consists of people who possess citizenship, legal status, personalities, emotions, and control over how much and how well they perform. Thus, they require incentives, rewards, satisfaction, stimulation, inspiration, and consideration.

Not to recognize these requirements can lead to serious interference with group effectiveness by creating such problems as failure to meet performance goals; breakdowns in communication; conflict, strife, and competition between individuals or groups; low morale; and poor discipline. The sources of such problems are likely to be diffuse and quite complex and may be traced to any or all of an array of factors, including working conditions, superior-subordinate relationships, communication, operational inefficiency, or just about any other condition related to life within an organization.

All of these facts lead to a fundamental conclusion. The essence of leading a group is not solely a matter of solving individual problems. In addition, it involves achieving some measure of integration among the many elements that the group comprises. Furthermore, leadership imposes a major responsibility for creative action. It cannot be just passive reaction to problems as they occur; it goes beyond merely fighting fires that arise within the group. It means taking action to make the desired results come to pass. A supervisor must take the necessary steps to shape his group: to plan, initiate, and carry through changes in it as required. He must constantly push back the limitations that human fallibility tends to place upon a group's capacity to perform more effectively.

Regardless of the type of organization, or the kind of group within an organization, a leader must make sure that objectives are established, plans are made, a structure is formed, personnel are assigned and trained, and policies and procedures are developed. Furthermore, the leader must establish areas of responsibility, set up mechanisms for co-ordination, delegate authority, direct subordinates, provide stimulation and inspiration for personnel, exercise control, maintain high levels of motivation and morale, and constantly adjust the activities of the group to broader changes in its programs and its environments. Fulfilling these and similar responsibilities is necessary regardless of the type of group being managed.

ORGANIZATIONS AS SYSTEMS

It is helpful to view a group as part of a system. The basic idea of a system is that it is a set of interrelated parts. Also implicit in the concept is a degree of wholeness, which makes the whole something different from, and more than, the individual units considered separately.

One of the most significant ways in which the system concept is useful to managers is in the consideration of subordinate units as parts of the system. This includes divisions, departments, sections, groups, and so forth, which appear on the conventional organization chart. Also in-cluded are ad hoc committees, boards, and other groups that have official status but are frequently not shown on the chart.

Thinking of an organization as a system offers at least two benefits: (1) it focuses on the relatedness of activities carried on by different in-dividuals and units; (2) it emphasizes the fact that, to meet the particular requirements for accomplishment of the organization's goals, each sub-unit must receive as careful attention in its development as does the overall organization. This is important because each part of a system affects, and is affected by, every other part.

A systems approach is especially useful in understanding the perform-ance of personnel. For example, it is often customary to consider such factors as goals, motivation, or communication as independent factors, each contributing to performance on the basis of direct cause-effect re-lationships. A supervisor who pursues the cause-effect approach tries to find one or more factors that can be taken as causes of certain occur-rences. He may conclude, for example, that a poor morale condition within a department is the cause of poor performance. Another manager might conclude that poor communication is the cause. Any number of such factors could be cited as causes, individually or in combination, of poor performance; yet, every presumed cause can be shown to have the given effect only under certain conditions and not under others.

A system view of organization recognizes the mutual dependence of various contributing factors. The formal structure affects, and is affected by, the objectives of the organization. Objectives affect, and are affected by, morale. Morale conditions affect, and are affected by, performance levels within the organization.

Thus, a change in a group's goals may be accompanied by changes in motivation and performance; a change introduced into morale will be accompanied by changes in performance and, perhaps, in goals. Similarly, a change introduced into the formal structure will have its effects upon goals, motivation, and performance. It is the interrelation of these elements that constitutes the total pattern of organization, which is what a leader should attempt to influence.

DEVELOPING A GROUP AS A SYSTEM

An organization needs a formal structure, with its concomitant procedures, in order to establish stability so that the activities of its personnel will be predictable. However, effective organizational performance is not made possible solely by definitions of authority and responsibility. Formal definitions can never anticipate all the actions of individual members, and the relations outlined in an organization chart only provide a framework within which fuller and more spontaneous human behavior takes place.

Leaders have the job of transforming an engineered, technical arrangement of people into a functioning system. A leader must know how to integrate this system of activities and relationships so that conditions will be most conducive to effective performance.

Probably the greatest impact will result from emphasis upon the interrelationships between structural and human aspects. There has been a decided tendency for theorists and researchers to stress either structure or people, usually while ignoring the other aspect. Yet, in reality, neither can be safely ignored.

Human factors must be considered in any reasonable understanding of group behavior. It also is unreasonable to consider people without recognizing the influence of the organization upon them. People function within situational contexts, and these contexts define and limit behavior. Within organizations, authority structures, policies, and procedures are important forces that circumscribe and channel activities. For this reason, both individual and group behavior within an organization is simply not the same as that outside of it. This fact can never be ignored.

CONDITIONS FOR EFFECTIVE PERFORMANCE

Research on leader effectiveness has found one recurring theme. Most leaders who are consistently effective recognize the fundamental purpose of leading and let it govern in all of their relationships with the people whom they are trying to influence. For any supervisor, the purpose of his relationship with subordinates is to promote effective performance among them by creating conditions in which they can function productively.

A supervisor can either provide or withhold a number of conditions that are necessary for capable people to perform effectively. These conditions are the basic components of a leadership climate and will be discussed under two broad headings: secure relationships with the superior and an optimum of independence.

Secure Relationships

In order to perform well, most people require a sense of consistent security in their relationships with their organizational superiors. Without such security, every task or problem occurs in an atmosphere of uncertainty. The subordinate is constantly harassed by the possibility of possible veto or reversal of his decisions or actions.

There are at least four elements in a work situation that affect the security of subordinates: mutual confidence between the superior and them, knowledge of their roles, consistent support, and clear performance expectations:

- *Mutual Confidence.* Research concerned with superior-subordinate relationships has uncovered a number of factors in the behavior and attitudes of supervisors that affect both the performance and the attitudes of subordinates. Many of those factors are related to the development of mutual confidence between the two individuals.

  Mutual confidence rests, in great part, upon the subordinate's belief in the integrity of the supervisor. A supervisor should be competent; subordinates cannot rely on a leader who is not. Similarly, a superior cannot have confidence in an incompetent, dishonest, or aggressively hostile subordinate. Nevertheless, the biggest determinant of confidence appears to be the subordinate's belief in the integrity of the superior. "Belief in integrity" refers to the subordinate's conviction that he will always get a fair break from the superior. The least suspicion that a superior cannot be fully trusted arouses anxiety. A supervisor creates this belief in his integrity through all of his daily actions, which creates a climate that subordinates will regard as compatible with them and their efforts.

  Subordinates must know that they have the full confidence and trust of their supervisors. If the climate is ambiguous or one of disapproval, they can have no assurance that their actions will meet with approval, regardless of what they do. In the absence of a genuine attitude of confidence, subordinates, no matter how competent, will feel threatened and insecure.

  It should be emphasized that the mere lack of censure does not constitute an atmosphere of approval. A positive leadership climate requires an active effort by the supervisor to communicate his confidence to his subordinates.

- *Knowledge of Role*. A second requirement for the security of the subordinate is knowledge of the precise role his supervisor expects him to play. Roles and role strains have been the sources of very costly problems. By far the largest number of problems encountered in organizations can be traced to role conflict and role ambiguity.

- *Consistent Support*. The third requirement for the security of subordinates is consistent support for their efforts, together with clear standards of performance that can serve as guides for action. In order to function securely, a subordinate needs to know that his supervisor is behind him. In addition, he needs to know what quality of performance will elicit continued support. He requires the strong and willing backing of his supervisor for those actions that are in accord with his mutually agreed-upon role.

  It is common to hear about superiors who fail to back up their subordinates. The insecurity bred by such failure leads subordinates to play it safe. Buckpassing and its resulting frictions and resentments become almost inevitable.

  With a clear understanding of his role, the subordinate needs also the firm assurance that he will receive the unqualified support of his supervisor, so long as his actions are consistent with directives and policies and within the limits of his responsibilities. Only under such circumstances can he develop the security and competence needed for effective performance.

- *Clear Performance Expectations*. Personnel need a clear explanation of the standards used in judging their performance. Everyone who must direct the activities of other people uses some frame of reference to determine whether their work is satisfactory. In certain instances, these standards are highly explicit; in other cases, the individual making the judgments cannot himself enunciate clearly the basis for the evaluations. Regardless of whether his ideas are hazy or clear, every supervisor uses some guidelines to judge whether performance is poor, satisfactory, or outstanding. The security of the subordinate depends upon his knowing what the performance expectations of the supervisor are.

  In addition, security requires that these performance standards be applied consistently. If a supervisor insists upon outstanding results on one assignment and settles for less than the best on the next, the effect upon the subordinate is obvious. He can never know for sure where he stands.

  Therefore, the security of the subordinate depends both upon assurance of the support of the supervisor and upon the consistent application of standards of performance. These must be applied and maintained in a climate of mutual trust and confidence; otherwise, public protestations of support will be viewed as insincere whereas high standards are seen only as pressure and harassment from above.

At every organizational level, a subordinate must know where he stands with his supervisor. Without such assurance, he can never know what to expect. He exists in an uncertain environment, where it is clear that he is dependent upon the evaluation of another person for advancement or even his job, but it is not clear what paths of action the supervisor will approve as satisfactory.

Optimum Independence

The second major component of an effective leadership climate is an optimum of independence. One of the most disturbing aspects of any job involves the written or unwritten constraints that may be imposed by superiors in the organization. The effect of these constraints is to require the subordinate to avoid certain actions or decisions that he may judge to be necessary for the best performance of his job. Excessive restraints block initiative and restrict the full exercise of capabilities.

Total independence is an organizational impossibility. Requirements for coordination and control do not permit complete freedom to anyone. For this reason, the term optimal independence appears to be the most accurate for describing this necessary condition for subordinate effectiveness. Independence rests upon three main requirements: the first, willingness to assume responsibility for one's own actions, must be met by the subordinate; the second and third, freedom to act and right of appeal, can only be provided by the superior in the relationship.

- *Responsibility for Own Actions.* From the standpoint of a subordinate, independence means that he must assume responsibility for his own actions and decisions. He must be willing to take the consequences for wrong actions, just as he is willing to accept rewards for correct ones. Willingness to assume responsibility depends upon confidence, experience, maturity, and a secure relationship with the superior. Thus, part of this willingness depends upon the personal makeup of the subordinate, part upon an adequate response from the superior. A climate of trust and confidence, knowledge of role requirements, and consistent performance standards all contribute to willingness of subordinates to assume responsibility for their actions.

- *Freedom to Act.* One of the most important requirements for independence is the freedom to act without fear of interference within the confines of assigned roles and responsibilities. An area of freedom may have strong boundaries, outside which the subordinate must always obtain approval for proposed actions, and its extent may vary for different individuals, different supervisors, and different situations. However, independence requires that there be some area within which capable and responsible people can operate without interference.

Freedom to act does not imply a lack of supervision. In granting it, the supervisor gives away none of his authority; he only permits the subordinate to act without restraints within clearly agreed upon boundaries. The real test of freedom is this: will the superior support the subordinate in carrying out the task in a manner different from that which he himself would have used, provided results are equally good?

Two points are important in this discussion. First, the supervisor does not relinquish any of his responsibilities for getting results. He can be as demanding in his standards of ultimate performance as he deems necessary, but he tries not to interfere in the methods of accomplishing the desired results. Second, freedom to act does not mean adopting a hands-off attitude. Leaving a subordinate to go his own way without providing support is likely to be construed as abandonment, which can have just as bad an effect as too much interference. What is needed is a realistic environment of freedom buttressed by supervisor support in the form of confidence, trust, and an adequate system of information and communication.

- *Right of Appeal.* The final requirement for independence is the right of a subordinate to appeal to the superior for a fair and unprejudiced hearing when he differs with the supervisor's decisions. This does not refer to a formal appeals procedure but to the subordinate's feeling of assurance that he can safely differ, even on important matters, without fear of retaliation and that his views will be considered. The supervisor does not have to yield his decision-making authority to the subordinate, nor must he change his decisions whenever the subordinate objects. However, he must be willing to listen.

    If the leadership climate is good and if sufficient communication occurs, the right of appeal may rarely be used. Nevertheless, the knowledge that he can safely use it when necessary gives a subordinate confidence.

A legitimate question is how much independence subordinates should be granted. No single answer is possible. Much depends upon the individual and the situation. However, one point is clear: the effective leader knows not only how to use his authority to get things done but also when to use it. The capacity to distinguish between situations that warrant constraints upon subordinates and those that do not is a critical aspect of leadership. The effective leader uses the power of his position selectively and responsibly to grant or restrict independence as appears necessary.

In the following chapters, three common types of groups will be examined. They are work groups, teams, and operating groups. Although vastly different, these three types constitute the great majority of groups in organizations.

PART 2

Major Types of Groups

Chapter 3

Work Groups

This chapter begins the discussion of different types of groups within organizations. Here, the discussion will be centered upon *work groups*, the most common kind of group found in organizations. *Work groups* include work units, sections, departments, and other types of conventional groups that occur because of ways that organizations are designed.

GROUP EFFECTS ON PERFORMANCE

When people work together toward mutual goals and undergo meaningful common experiences, the resulting interaction produces changes in their perceptions, emotions, thinking, attitudes, and actions (Sherif and Sherif, 1956). The distinguishing feature of these changes is that the individual comes more and more to identify his feelings, thinking, attitudes, and actions with the group (Thelen, 1954). Persisting personal relationships and values evolve and become stabilized, providing him with organized, enduring, and motivationally significant ties and rewarding experiences (Hinton and Reitz, 1973). These satisfactions may influence his attitudes toward other aspects of the work.

The opportunity for workers to interact with other personnel has been found to be important. Kerr, Koppelmeir, and Sullivan (1951) found that departments having the highest turnover rates provided the least opportunity for interactions among workers; and Richards and Dobryns (1957) found that the morale of a group of workers in an insurance company was lowered when rearrangement of their office resulted in a restriction of opportunities for social interaction. When an individual is able to maintain close relationships with a group in which he is highly accepted, his job satisfaction is usually higher. In a study of a child welfare agency, it was found that workers were more satisfied when they belonged to a group that they liked and whose members liked them.

Determinants of Effectiveness

In general, cohesiveness will be increased by conditions that cause group members to develop common perceptions of problems, to evolve shared perspectives of themselves and their group, and to become consistently and harmoniously involved with the activities and goals of the group (Savell, Teague, and Tremble, 1995). On the other hand, cohesiveness will be disrupted by conditions that encourage tendencies opposite to these. Following is a discussion of several general factors that may influence effectiveness:

Tasks and Task Organization. The kinds of tasks assigned to a group, and the organization that results, can exert a decided influence upon cohesiveness and effectiveness. Where a task requires the tightly coordinated efforts of all personnel, with each individual's activity fitting closely into the total endeavor, higher cohesiveness is more likely to result. Where the task dictates independent actions by different individuals or where the individuals must be separated in space and type of activities, cohesiveness will be more difficult to maintain.

Superordinate Goals. Superordinate goals are those objectives that are equally compelling for all and cannot be ignored but that cannot be achieved by the efforts and resources of one individual alone. They require the coordinated efforts and resources of all the individuals involved. This does not mean that every objective of every individual in every group must be identical. However, there are usually one or more goals that are central within a group, and these weigh heavily in determining the kinds and quality of activities that will result. Therefore, a maximum degree of compatibility should exist between those overall objectives that are important for the continued effectiveness of the group and the goals of individual group members. The goals and needs of individuals that have no relation to the activities and welfare of the group or the organization need not harmonize with these overall objectives.

Similarity of Personnel. Similarities among personnel have long been recognized as an important element in cohesiveness. When people perceive themselves to be alike in certain characteristics, a greater potential exists for mutual understanding, for the development of common attitudes, and, in general, for greater consensus on many matters that are of significance for the members. It is important to recognize that similarity can exist along many dimensions. For example, cohesiveness tends to be greater when members of a group are similar in level of experience.

Individuals with like abilities are more attracted to each other than are people with widely divergent abilities. Similarly, uniformity of age and educational level will be positively associated with cohesiveness. To generalize, high cohesiveness in a group is facilitated by perceived similarity or uniformity among its members. The conviction of similarity makes it possible for members to believe they understand one another, and they are more attracted to other personnel and to the group. Homogeneity is not conducive to cohesiveness unless members are aware that similarities exist. Leaders can sometimes enhance cohesiveness by efforts to increase this awareness.

Common Experiences. Groups are held together by stable relationships (functional integration) and common attitudes (normative integration) among their members. Persisting relationships and common attitudes evolve and become stabilized only when people undergo significant experiences together. Shared experiences thus serve two important functions. First, they permit members to become familiar with one another, to learn each other's characteristic ways of behaving and through this familiarization process to develop stable expectations relative to performance and ways of working. Second, shared experiences provide members with a common frame of reference. Because they have undergone the same experiences, members view things from similar perspectives. They are bound together by having experienced unique events to which others have not been exposed.

Success Experiences. Of particular significance here are experiences of success. Probably nothing contributes so greatly to cohesiveness as successful action. Success operates to confirm the validity of the group's ways of operating and gives the individual confidence in himself and in the group. A long tradition of success appears to make for much greater cohesiveness. As a secondary effect, tradition of success is likely to provide the group with greater prestige, thus encouraging more ready identification by members. Success is effective, however, only as it is experienced, and it is experienced only in relation to the objectives perceived by the personnel. An action by a group is deemed successful only if the members become aware that their efforts have actually resulted in achievement of the group's objectives. Administrative control of this factor is possible through such measures as setting realistically high objectives, insuring clear recognition of them by personnel, and furnishing adequate evaluation of the results of group efforts.

Just as success tends to enhance cohesiveness, experiences that are perceived by members as failures of the group are disruptive. Severe or consistent failure usually results in loss of confidence, bickering, and recriminations. The amount of disruption that will occur depends upon both the level of cohesiveness reached prior to the failure and the severity of the failure. High prior cohesiveness, together with mild failure, may result in nothing more than minor loss of confidence, which may be rapidly recovered. At the other extreme, low prior cohesiveness and strong failure may result in severe disruption. It should be clear that failure alone does not necessarily result in disruption of cohesiveness. The critical factor appears to be whether failure causes personnel to lose confidence in their leaders, the organization, or in themselves.

Organizational Stability. Cohesiveness requires sufficient organizational stability for emotional and social bonds to develop. Both integration of task functions and the development of strong norms require that people work together long enough for common perceptions and values to evolve. Neither can reach a very high level when there is a great deal of instability in the organization. Replacement and transfer policies that result in frequent movements of personnel into and out of work groups are not conducive to high cohesiveness.

Communication. It should be self-evident that cohesiveness is related to communication. Those norms that give rise to cohesiveness are the products of interaction between people. These interactions must take the form of communication. Therefore, cohesiveness is strongly dependent upon communication. In general, the principle can be set forth that increased communication between members will heighten cohesion—unless the communication is unpleasant, critical, hostile, or otherwise divisive. Any official communicative acts that emphasize membership in the group or focus attention upon group values and standards of conduct will heighten cohesiveness. This especially applies to those communications of an informal and personal nature that emanate from a supervisor.

Anything that interferes with the communication process contributes to a disruption in cohesiveness. For example, blockages in the formal communications channels can lead to the opening of informal channels that carry rumor, innuendo, and so forth. These distortions create disruption because they tend to breed suspicion and hostility among group members. Cohesiveness may also be disrupted because of communication restrictions arising from the geographical dispersion of members. When members of a group are widely separated, the likelihood increases that only essential information will be communicated. It becomes difficult for members to maintain identification with the group. Because of lack of information about the activities of other members, feelings of common effort and solidarity are absent. This is disastrous for unity and cohesiveness.

Interpersonal Conflict. Particularly vicious kinds of disruption derive from conflicts that may develop between influential individuals within a work group. Conflicts between senior members, supervisors, or other individuals who occupy sensitive status positions may easily spread throughout the group. Cohesiveness is affected because of the tendency of people to take sides in such conflicts or because superiors may expect to be supported. The resultant cliques, splinter groups, and so forth, block unity and solidarity. When there are two or more strong or influential members competing and forcing other members to align themselves into cliques, the result is divided loyalties and discord. Such alignments often spread throughout a group. Conflicts of this sort sometimes arise because differential and preferential treatment of personnel by supervisors creates competition, jealousy, and rivalry. Regardless of the cause, conflicts between individuals who occupy influential positions carry with them the seeds of disruption of solidarity.

Cooperation and Competition. When members of a group engage in activities that are competitive and reciprocally frustrating, such that the achievement of a desired objective by one individual results in defeat or loss for other individuals, unfavorable attitudes develop that result in additional competition between them. As used here, "competition" refers to something more intense than friendly rivalry. It concerns a situation in which important interests and/or welfare of an individual or group are at stake and success by one results in a serious loss by another. The essence of a truly competitive situation is that one individual must win and others must lose. When important stakes are involved and the goal of each individual in a group is to win, the consequences for cohesiveness are disastrous. Personal reputations assume greater importance. Certain members, more aggressive than others, or for whom the thought of victory carries particular appeal, may begin to try to exercise more weight in group affairs than has been previously customary. Actions may begin to be aimed more and more toward belittling the competitors' position. Members may develop more negative attitudes and express more hostility toward others. The negative attitudes thus generated usually intensify the conflict and further erode mutual respect and confidence within the group. When attitudes of this nature become predominant within a work group, actions designed to protect self-interest and enhance personal aspirations are likely to take precedence over those that would contribute to the common objective.

On the other hand, when cooperation is the rule, members tend to view the group as a whole and other members individually in a favorable light. Members try to get along well in their interpersonal relations and tend to work with others in order that mutual objectives may be better accomplished. Communication is used to reduce conflict rather than aggravate it. When individuals pull together, favorable information about other members is seen in a positive light, and the probability of information being used effectively is enhanced. When members of a group are committed to cooperation, a manager or supervisor is in a position to take bolder steps toward bringing about understanding and mutually supportive actions. He can take concrete action to enhance cooperative endeavors, and he can more freely delegate responsibility. Decision processes can proceed more effectively, and decisions reached are more likely to receive whole-hearted support from group members.

Reward System. Cooperation is most likely to develop when members can receive significant satisfactions from behaving cooperatively and when competitive behavior is not rewarded or is punished. The system of rewards is an important determinant of group effectiveness. The satisfactions available to members of a work group are not limited to formal rewards such as promotions, salary increases, and so forth, although these are highly useful devices for motivating people to behave cooperatively. The reward system in a group includes all of the means by which a member may receive satisfaction or recognition from behaving in a particular manner. This may be a word of approval by the supervisor, recognition from fellow members, satisfaction from a job well done, and so forth.

The critical factor in determining cohesiveness is whether or not members of the work group can receive satisfaction of their personal needs only when they contribute to group effort. In a cooperatively organized group (one in which the more significant rewards are given for group effort), no individual can move toward his personal goals without also furthering the progress of other members and of the group, whereas the reverse is true of a competitively organized group (one in which rewards may be obtained for efforts that further individual interests without contributing particularly to group efforts). Formal group incentive plans have been found to be highly effective in this regard.

Administrative Practices. No matter how high the motivation to cooperate, effectiveness within a work group will not result unless members' efforts are effectively channeled. Therefore, an additional requirement is efficient and effective administrative practices that provide the means through which activities of the group members can be integrated. The term *administrative practices* refers to those procedures and practices used to perform such functions as exercising direction, assigning responsibilities, exchanging information, making decisions, organizing, coordinating, and so forth, within the work group. They include formal policies and procedures but go beyond them to encompass the various means of a less formal nature by which the activities of members are integrated and coordinated. Effective group operations require administrative practices that will ensure that, consistent with their goals, tasks, and responsibilities, members are provided with all the information, decisions, guidance, and assistance necessary to perform effectively and to contribute appropriately to the group effort. More specifically, the practices must function in such a manner that

- each member of the work group is provided tasks and goals that he will be motivated to accomplish and that, when accomplished, will contribute to the goal of the group;
- the techniques, procedures, and plans developed by the work group are such that members will be motivated to use them to their maximum potentiality;
- the activities of group members fit together and are mutually supporting;
- individuals who make decisions use fully and capably all information available within the group;
- opportunity is provided for contacts between members sufficient for mutual trust and confidence to develop (Likert, 1959).

EFFECTS OF GROUP SIZE

Conceptually, the size of the basic work group should be one aspect of organizational configuration; however, it is of sufficient importance to be treated separately. Among all of the structural properties of organizations, work unit size stands out as one of the strongest influences upon job satisfaction, performance, absenteeism, and employee turnover.

There can be little doubt that work group size is significantly related to the attitudes of personnel. Consistently, workers in small groups have been found to display greater job satisfaction than those in larger groups. Higher satisfaction among members of small groups has also been suggested as the reason for less absenteeism and turnover. In general, larger work units have been found to have higher absence rates. Similar findings have been reported for turnover.

It is important to note that most of the studies were concerned with blue-collar workers and that there is some indication that size of work group may be less influential with white-collar workers (Porter and Lawler, 1965). This fact may have special relevance for the organization of paraprofessionals. If they can be said to be similar to blue-collar workers in their attitudes and preferences, placement in smaller units might enhance satisfaction and reduce turnover and absenteeism.

With regard to job performance, the evidence is not as clear-cut. Some studies have found that smaller work unit size leads to higher productivity (Katzell, Barrett, and Parker, 1961), whereas others have found tendencies for larger groups to be more productive (Argyle, Gardner, and Cioffi, 1958), and some have found that middle-sized groups produce better (Herbst, 1957). These mixed findings suggest that the kind of work in which the group is engaged and the way the group is organized may be important modifiers of the effects of size. At least one study has found this differential effect in comparing work groups within different companies. Indik and Seashore (1961) found no relationship between size and productivity in automobile dealerships but did find that productivity was higher in small groups within a package-delivery organization.

It begins to appear that, for some types of work, organization into smaller groups will lead to improved performance; for other kinds of work, size of the group may be irrelevant for productivity. It can be conjectured that in highly structured, machine-dominant systems, size of work group may not be critical for productivity, although smaller groups will still be important for job satisfaction, absenteeism, and turnover. On the other hand, in loosely structured, man-dominant systems, such as professional organizations, division into small work groups may be highly conducive to both performance and attitudes.

Why should small work groups be conducive to satisfaction and performance? The reason is clear. The most critical determinants of the attitudes and behavior of people in organizations are their experiences in their day-to-day work situations. Much of the situation is created by fellow workers. When people work together and undergo common experiences, the resulting interaction produces changes in their perceptions, emotions, attitudes, and actions. The distinguishing feature of these changes is that the individual comes more and more to identify his feelings, thinking, attitudes, and actions with those of his fellow employees. Personal relationships and values evolve and become stabilized, providing each individual with organized, enduring, and motivationally significant ties with his primary group. In addition, he receives numerous satisfactions from interactions with the group, which exercises a strong influence upon his attitudes and behavior.

For this discussion, the critical point is that strong bonds are difficult to develop within a large work unit because interaction between more than a few members is impossible. Under such conditions, genuine group relationships that include all members cannot develop. This is the reason why small units are more satisfying and, when work permits interaction, frequently more productive.

The optimal size of a work unit has never been established and probably differs according to both type of work and other properties of the parent organization. Nevertheless, it is probably safe to say that the maximum should never be more than 20 members and that greater cohesion will result from even smaller units, down to a minimum of six or seven individuals. It is also worth noting that, in work organizations, optimal group size must in part be determined by the number of personnel one supervisor can direct (span of control).

LEADING WORK GROUPS

In general, the principle can be applied that group co
be increased by anything that heightens the awareness o
that he is a functioning member of one specific group a
obtain significant satisfactions from his membership in it _____., 1998).
At all times, everyone of us identifies himself with some group or organization. However, these so-called *reference groups* are not always those
of which we are, at the moment, members. Therefore, the problem of
developing work-group cohesiveness is basically that of changing an individual's identification from other groups to the principal work group
of which he is a member (Leonard, 2000).

Sound cohesiveness in a work group cannot be accomplished overnight, nor can it be achieved solely by exhortation. The development of
sound bonds of unity and strength requires a fine sensitivity by a leader
to the constantly shifting currents of feelings and attitudes among personnel, attention to numberless details and occurrences that might cause
a negative shift in attitudes if not corrected and alertness to every event
that might be used to reinforce feelings of unity and solidarity. Developing and maintaining high cohesiveness is a constant activity.

Whether effective relationships will develop within a group depends
largely upon the nature of the leadership available to it. If a supervisor
adopts a style of leadership that encourages competition in the advancement of individual interests, he is not likely to develop a very high order
of group effectiveness. On the other hand, high cohesiveness may result
if he adopts practices capable of making cooperation effectively serve the
best interests of the group and the organization.

This raises an important question. What should be the relationship of
the supervisor to his work group? The answer is straightforward. The
supervisor is a part of the group he directs. Like his subordinates, he
responds to what he assumes, feels, and perceives things to be, and since
his behavior can either facilitate or jeopardize the effectiveness of the
work group, he cannot treat it as something apart from himself. He both
affects and is affected by it.

Only by being aware of this involvement can a supervisor perform his
functions effectively. A supervisor who can accept and handle his own
personal involvement with some skill is likely to do a better job. Such a
leader does not deny his feelings of involvement with his work group;
neither does he give these feelings priority. Through the awareness of
his own subjectivity, he becomes more objective.

In attempting to manage and cope with his involvement, effectiveness
will be enhanced if the supervisor recognizes that his own behavior is
the dominant influence in the group. He must be aware that his attitudes,
skills, and actions are critical in establishing the character of the work

group. He must see a subordinate as a unique personality but also as a contributing member of an integrated group. He has to recognize all of the varying viewpoints within the work group, not that of just one segment. He has to respond to many different perceptions and ideas, not just a selected few.

Practice of this orientation constitutes the real skill of group leadership. It requires the capacity of a superior to respond to the feelings and ideas of others, as well as the capacity to communicate his own feelings and ideas to others in such a fashion as to promote cooperation and effective contribution to a common task.

The development of a cohesive group begins with the effective direction of individual subordinates. A genuine regard for the worth, capabilities, and trustworthiness of subordinates is necessary to equip the supervisor with the capacity for developing effective cooperation among his personnel. When this regard for subordinates is coupled with skill in group leadership practices, the supervisor is relieved of much of the necessity for masterminding events that occur within the work situations of individuals. When the supervisor is freed of this burden, he can devote more of his attention to developing group relationships between these individuals.

Dangers of Over-Control

One of the most common barriers to effective collaboration is over-control. Individuals and groups are frequently so bound by the limits imposed upon them, that true collaborative teamwork is often beyond their capabilities. Therefore, a principal function of a supervisor is to remove obstacles from people who are trying to work together—to uncover and clear away conditions that limit efforts to work cooperatively.

There are many specific ways a supervisor can aid subordinates to develop effective group relationships. Some are simple, routine functions of administration. Others require rather complex leadership skills. In either case, most of the ways will involve attending to matters that are related to the three principal determinants of effective group work: goals, rewards, and administrative practices. Some of the ways for achieving work group effectiveness follow (Olmstead, 1997):

- *Subordinates must be kept aware of group objectives.* As he goes about his daily activities, the supervisor must strive to keep both the goals of the work group and the objectives of individuals constantly before the members. It is assumed here that the basic task—the group's reason for being—is obvious and self-evident to all members. The problem for the supervisor and his subordinates is to establish and work toward the accomplishment of concrete goals whose achievement will result in execution of the basic mission or task of the group.

Effectiveness requires that members keep these goals constantly in the forefront of awareness. As he works with subordinates, the supervisor should use every opportunity to stress the group's objectives and the best means for their achievement. Through constant emphasis, the supervisor must strive to stimulate individual involvement with the common goals of the group.

- *A cooperative atmosphere must be developed in the group.* The supervisor must also strive for genuinely cooperative relationships between him and his subordinates and among the members themselves. He will not try to impose cooperation on people but will simply work toward the development of mutual respect and support among the members of the group. He will rely upon his own cooperative attitude to filter gradually through the group until, in time, individual members begin to function more cooperatively, to communicate more among themselves, and to exchange dependence upon the supervisor for interdependence among all the members, the supervisor included.

- *Adequate communication must be established.* The problem of who should communicate what to whom, when, and by what means is one of the most important problems in group relationships. Effective group performance will be maximized only when there can be established common terminology; common definitions of goals, problems, and situations; and common agreements (either explicit or implicit) concerning modes and channels of communication. Most such understandings develop in the course of frequent and free association between group members. An important task of the supervisor is to encourage such contacts and to ensure that the limiting conditions present in every organization do not create barriers to communication.

- *Common understandings must be developed concerning standards of performance and behavior.* Agreement on appropriate standards of performance and behavior is intimately related to development of an effective work group, because the system of standards serves as a means of quality control. When an individual accepts the standards of a group, he belongs. When he belongs, he coordinates his actions in accordance with the common needs. The supervisor can influence the development of common understandings by publicly and officially expressing the standards he deems desirable and, even more important, by subjecting both his own performance and behavior and that of his subordinates to evaluation against these standards.

- *Control must be exercised on cooperative efforts within the work group.* An important aspect of group functioning is agreement (implicit or explicit) concerning the amount of control to be exercised by the supervisor, the degree of authority and responsibility to be delegated, areas of responsibility to be assigned, and the limitations to be placed upon individuals' freedom to act. The control exercised on cooperative effort is one of the functions more commonly associated with supervision. Whenever a supervisor undertakes to define, interpret, or clarify the autonomy extended to individual subordinates, or the limitations imposed upon them, he is influencing the performance of the work group and is at that time giving direction and leadership to its members.

Probably the most significant aspect of this supervision by control is the degree of autonomy or discretion to be granted subordinates. The issue involves restriction of freedom of action, or, more simply, the control of alternatives open to subordinates for making decisions.

This particular point has long been a bone of contention in discussions of group leadership. The positions have ranged from retention of total control of all actions and decisions by a single leader to wide diffusion of responsibility throughout the group members. The fact is, however, that from the beginning neither of these extremes has been at all effective. Group performance is effective when subordinates are provided sufficient latitude to exercise responsibility within their own assignments, while supervisors or leaders simultaneously exercise the guidance and control necessary to coordinate the activities that contribute to the accomplishment of the larger group's goals. This can be achieved through common understanding concerning areas of authority, responsibility, freedom to act, and so forth, and through explicit policies that establish clear criteria as to which decisions should be made by group members and which should be referred to the supervisor.

• *Rewards must be distributed fairly and equitably within the group.* The distribution of rewards and other satisfactions can encourage group effectiveness, or it can splinter the group. Members' perceptions of who gets the credit or their detection of the odor of exploitation—regardless of whether it actually exists—is the problem involved here.

Because of the distribution of function and responsibility in most organizations, it is almost inevitable that some assignments will seem to have more status than others, that some individuals will have jobs more satisfying to them, and that the contributions of all personnel will not seem equally valuable and will not be equally rewarded. Reactions to differences are particularly subjective when the issue seems to be reward expressed in status, favor with the supervisor, and so forth. Disgruntlement and competition arising from such perceptions can be especially destructive for work group effectiveness. A supervisor must be alert for such problems and must exercise extreme care that misconceptions in this area do not develop within his group.

Numerous elements influence the development and effectiveness of a work group. Usually because of his position as the link between many related activities and individuals, the supervisor is the only person who can wield sufficient influence to pull the various elements of his group into an integrated whole. He may encourage subordinates to share this responsibility through their own contributions, but he can never lose sight of the fact that, as supervisor, his behavior will set the tone. He must constantly strive, in contacts with subordinates, to provide the example of behavior conducive to effective group functioning. If he is successful in these efforts, effectiveness should be the result. A group in which effectiveness is the norm is likely to be a strong group, which makes the supervisor's job both easier and more satisfying.

Chapter 4

Teams

In the consideration of groups in organizations, teams are a special case. In the daily vernacular of many organizations, *team* is a common term referring to the fact that a number of people work together toward the same goals. Frequently, the meaning stops at this point.

However, in many other organizations operating in the high-tech world of today, *teams* take on special significance as groups that are specifically designed to require the integrated and highly coordinated activities of several people. Within this broad requirement, teams may be as varied as *working teams*, which are task-defined and frequently machine-dominant groups; *crisis-management teams*, whose activities may determine life or death; and *project teams*, which may be more loosely structured than working teams. In this chapter, special consideration will be given to working teams, crisis-management teams, and project teams. The general discussion, however, will apply to all types of teams.

TEAM TYPES

Teams may have innumerable purposes, goals, and activities. However, despite its particular purpose or configuration, every true team is a role system, driven and controlled by operational (task) demands and maintained by shared values and norms.

A role system is a set of specific, interrelated activities that are generated by interdependent tasks. Role and performance requirements derive from system requirements (task or mission demands). The forces that maintain the role system are the task (mission) demands, shared values, and the observance of team norms.

Since teams are driven and controlled by tasks, the nature of the task dictates a team's configuration and its activities. Because tasks may vary widely in their requirements and complexity, teams may also differ considerably.

Here, three quite different types of teams—working teams, crisis-management teams, and project teams will be considered. It should be noted, however, that some organizations can consist of both teams that serve operational purposes and task forces that direct the activities of operational teams. The crisis management organizations discussed in chapter 6 are of this combined type.

Working Teams

The term *working team* refers to teams that are most often task-controlled and machine-dominant. That is, the activities of members are dictated by input requirements of a mechanical system and by outputs of the same system. Accordingly, working teams operate in *established situations* where the stimulus-response model applies. In short, working teams function where all input activities can be predicted, programmed, and practiced. Stimuli can be predicted, and responses can be practiced until they become almost automatic. Examples are certain operations in auto and aircraft assembly plants, military gun crews, and some ship-handling activities.

The most significant characteristics of working teams are that they operate in established situations, perform programmed tasks, and engage in mutually exclusive but mutually supportive task performances and, thus, may be summed to produce a single team product. Such activities are specific to and defined by the roles of the individual members within the team.

In working teams, the predominant skills are role-specific individual skills—the skills required to perform those activities specific to the respective team roles and which are performed by individuals independently but in support of other team members. In addition, some degree of team performance skills is usually needed, although the amount may vary with different team tasks.

Crisis-Management Teams

The term *crisis-management team* applies to a wide variety of teams that must make prompt and usually vigorous responses to situations that may threaten life, property, or even survival of an organization such as a military unit. This type of team includes (1) police teams, such as swat teams, riot squads, disaster control teams, and so forth; (2) fire department companies; (3) medical emergency teams; and (4) military teams of varying types ranging from infantry fire teams to air defense tracking and fire control centers. Military teams also include small independent action forces, which may operate independently in extremely hostile environments.

Crisis-management teams are most often involved in highly *emergent situations*. Although team performance in emergent situations depends upon the practiced skills of individuals who function in coordination, task activities and sequences cannot always be specified. Similarly, the probable consequences of some actions cannot be fully predicted because full information is not always available.

Crisis-management teams are usually faced with situations characterized by lack of structure and high levels of turbulence and uncertainty. Therefore, task situations are much more complex than those for working teams, and effective performance requires a greater variety of skills, with special emphasis upon team performance skills. Furthermore, since emergent situations allow for unanticipated behaviors to emerge, greater adaptability is required for team members, even though their roles may be strictly defined and clearly differentiated.

Project Teams

A *project team* is a work group that is formed to accomplish a specific purpose and that comprises personnel deemed to possess qualifications that will contribute to achievement of the objectives. Because many project teams consist of personnel selected to provide a variety of qualifications, such teams may be quite diverse in their make-up. This diversity can create difficulty in achieving a desirable level of team integration.

Project teams may be formed merely to obtain information and submit a report (study groups) or to plan and execute activities to accomplish assigned goals, or both. Whatever the reason and purpose, the clear attributes of a project team are as follows:

1. there is an assigned goal,
2. membership may be diverse,
3. members have assigned roles, which may be diverse,
4. members' activities must be coordinated, and
5. activities must be integrated into a single result (report, plan, or physical product).

Although project teams have, or should have, clear goals and concrete guidance, they still must cope with emergent situations, because tasks and activities can be specified only in general terms, all information is not available, and both information and actions depend upon preceding activities. Thus, intervening activities and final outcomes cannot be predicted in advance.

The typical project team is an information processing system that has a large storage capacity, part of which comprises plans and procedures that coordinate the behavior of individual members or sub-teams. These plans may be given to the team at its inception, or they may be generated by the team itself. The evolving task situation determines how the plans will be used. The performance of the team depends on how good the plans are and how well they are executed.

A CONCEPTUAL MODEL

The literature on teams and team performance is a morass of claims and counterclaims, conceptual confusions, and aborted attempts to bridge the gap between scientific analysis and real-world application. Fortunately, there have been published in recent years a number of excellent analytic reviews (Brannick, Salas, and Prince, 1997; Dyer, 1985; Hall and Rizzo, 1975; Knerr, Berger, and Popelka, 1979; Knerr, Nadler, and Berger, 1980; Nieva, Fleishman, and Rieck, 1978; Parsons, 1972; Thorndyke and Weiner, 1980; Wagner, Hibbits, Rosenblatt, and Schultz, 1977). Taken together, these reviews have defined the field and its issues reasonably well.

On the other hand, even though the issues have now been well defined, many of the practical problems raised by them have remained cloudy. Whereas teams and the elements of team performance are better understood, the practical application of this knowledge to the problems of team development and team management has remained in a relatively unsystematic state until now.

There can be little doubt that it is extremely difficult to derive sound procedures for team development from even the best research-based concepts. The individual charged with responsibility for designing a team development program finds himself faced squarely with some very complex problems. As he sets out to design procedures for developing or improving a team, he encounters the question of the team attributes he should develop. Indeed, as he goes about identifying desired team attributes, he must resolve the deeper problems of the nature of *teamness*, how this rather nebulous concept can be translated into something meaningful and concrete, and how *teamwork* can be developed. Is the result of development to be the acquisition of individual technical skills performed by each member; the learning of team skills, which, though performed by individuals, fit together interdependently to produce a collective product; perceptual and attitudinal changes, which produce a *team perspective* among the members and, accordingly, influence joint behavior—or all of these? Answers to questions such as the above are essential before sound team development procedures can be specified.

In the discussion which follows, a systematic framework for addressing the above issues will be proposed. It is the product of an intensive analysis of all of the reviews listed earlier, study of many of the publications mentioned by them, and a survey of 250 additional publications covering the period 1940–1997. However, it is not the intention here to present just one more comprehensive recitation of all of the literature concerned with teams and team performance. Rather, the purpose is to set out a meaningful, research-based framework for understanding group integration, how it affects team functioning (teamwork), and how it may be developed in various types of teams.

Such an analysis seems to be needed. As far back as 1977, Collins concluded, after a study of military team training, that team training technology is underdeveloped and that few advances had been made within the preceding ten years. Some of the specific deficiencies Collins cited were absence of a theory of team behavior; lack of population data on teams; limited analytical techniques and criteria for the study of teams, their training, and their performance; few assessment, evaluation, and feedback systems for use by operational military units during team training; lack of an instructional system development (ISD) model for teams; and absence of team training guidelines for use in the design of large, complex, team training devices. Collins might have added also a lack of acceptance by military trainers of innovative team training strategies.

Nieva et al. (1978) concurred with Collins concerning the lack of understanding of team performance and went on to conclude that a principal reason is that insufficient attention is focused upon understanding the nature of group performance itself. In other words, Nieva et al. concluded that inordinate attention has been given to the identification of group attributes (taxonomies) and their impacts and not enough has been devoted to the dynamics of group performance. Then, they presented a conceptualization of team, or group, performance which differentiates between the individual and interactive components of performance. Thus, Nieva et al. had a concept and a methodology for analyzing the interactive concepts of team performance.

This is a most useful approach. The products of most writers have been purely descriptive, that is, in terms of taxonomies or of classification schemes. Although every reviewer and many researchers have been careful to mention the essence of *teamness* or *teamwork*, most have given short shrift to these aspects and have moved on to some classificatory scheme that would appear to offer a more immediate and concrete product. The dynamics of teams and of team performance have been passed over rapidly. Those aspects that appear to offer the most promise for team training and development rarely receive the attention they deserve.

Team integration is closely related to, if not identical with, teamness and teamwork. In fact, teamness may be the generic concept for integration within groups. Accordingly, it would seem most practicable to develop an approach to team integration within the context of teamwork.

From the above discussion, it should be apparent that a team is more than just a simple, straightforward work group. As considered here, teams possess very special and specific attributes. Furthermore, some teams have highly complex configurations.

A variety of models have been devised to describe teams. However, most researchers have concluded that a systems approach best captures the dynamic nature of teams and, further, that a simple input-process-output paradigm is most useful for understanding the relationships between environment, team, and performance.

Although some of these systems models are complex (Roby, 1968), most are simple paradigms illustrating the straightforward effects of inputs and internal conversion processes upon outputs. Such simple models are useful in identifying variables and determining where relationships exist.

Unfortunately, these simple models tell us little about the nature of factors that influence the performance of processes and, thus, about how team integration can be achieved. This was recognized by McDavid and Harari (1968) who defined a team as "an organized system of two or more individuals who are interrelated so that the system performs some function, has a standard set of role relationships among its members, and has a set of norms that regulate the function of the group and each of its members."

Role Systems

Apparently, a more complex version than a simple conversion-output model will be required if team integration is to be thoroughly understood. One concept that provides a valid stepping stone to team integration is that of *role system* (Katz and Kahn, 1966).

A *role system* is an open *social system* whose structure consists of a set of roles that are defined by *task demands*. The system is maintained by *norms* and *values* held in common by all or most of its members.

As the patterned interdependent activities of human beings, social systems are defined mainly by roles, which are the patterns of behavior associated with the various positions in each system. A role consists of (1) the formal duties of the position as defined by the system and (2) the expectations held by all other members about how the role should be performed. A role is the set of perceptions and expectations held by both the position occupant and other people about how the duties of the position should be performed. In theory, role enactments are dictated by and appropriate to task demands and system requirements. They are not necessarily appropriate to the personality expression of the individual. However, it should be apparent that there is great potential for instability in roles and for discrepancies in role perceptions and role expectations, depending upon the degree of integration in the system. With greater integration, there should be less discrepancy between the role perceptions of position occupants and the role expectations of other members.

Social systems are characterized also by a set of *norms* and *shared values*, which, when functioning properly, integrate rather than differentiate; that is, they are held in common by all, or many, members of the system and produce common attitudes that constrain deviation and ensure required uniformities in member behavior.

Social norms, or group standards, *are expected uniformities of behavior held in common by all or most of the members*. Norms serve two functions: (1) they provide standards against which members may evaluate the situations they encounter, and (2) they serve as standards which guide the respective role performances of members. Norms refer to the expected behavior sanctioned by the system and thus have a specific *ought* and *must* quality. Although in organizations norms refer mainly to role performance, they may also apply to other than role-related behaviors.

Shared values provide the rationale, or justification, for the constraints and requirements dictated by norms. They are beliefs about what behavior is *right* or correct and what is *wrong* or incorrect with respect to performance of both one's own and others' roles.

System norms and values have the general function of tying people into the system so that they remain within it and carry out their role assignments. This function is what is referred to as "integration." The more specific functions are (1) system norms and shared values provide cognitive maps for members which facilitate their performance of their roles, and (2) norms and values provide the moral or organizational justification for system activities both for role occupants and for people formally outside the system. The result is cohesion, or integration.

Of particular importance is the fact that an organization or team can exist only as long as people can be induced (1) to be members or role occupants and (2) to perform as such. Katz and Kahn (1966) recognized an essential dichotomy between *operational* (production) inputs and processes and *maintenance* inputs and processes. Operational inputs and processes are the materials, energies, and activities directly contributory to the mission-related activities of the team. Maintenance inputs and processes are the energy and informational contributions necessary to hold the people in the system and persuade them to carry out their role-prescribed activities as members of the system. No organization or team can exist without (1) the more or less continual acceptance by its members of organizational expectations concerning performance of required activities and (2) the motivation to engage in that performance.

Thus, a role system is a set of functionally specific, interrelated behaviors generated by interdependent tasks. Role and performance requirements derive from system requirements (task or mission demands). The forces that maintain the role system are the task (mission) demands, shared values, and the observance of norms. Accordingly, *a team is a role system driven and controlled by operational (task) demands and maintained by shared values and norms.*

What is being discussed here is team integration and the commitment of members to the team and the parent organization. Integration occurs when members are committed and hold shared values and common norms about the performance of their respective roles. As one illustration, Greenbaum (1979) concluded, after an extensive study of small military units in combat (World Wars I and II, Yom Kippur War, Korean War), that:

1. properly led individuals in combat units will develop strong bonds of identification with one another; these bonds are functional, serving to control individual fear and helping the individual to be effective in his work;
2. individuals will use others in the unit as a standard of comparison for competence, values, emotions, and a sense of well-being; such comparisons are a product of pressure toward cohesion in the face of stress; and
3. the processes of affiliation and comparison contribute to the powerful influence that the small group exerts on the individual.

In a similar way, teams can serve as reference groups for their members. *A reference group is a group with which an individual identifies and to which he refers for standards to guide his behavior and against which to gauge the situations that he encounters* (Merton and Kitt, 1950). If a team is a strong reference group for an individual and a standard of the team is for coordinated actions, that is, teamwork, he is much more likely to value coordinated behavior and will be much more likely to coordinate his actions with those of other members.

George, Hoak, and Boutwell (1963) concluded that coordinate response behavior becomes habitual in effective teams. Response coordination is learned by trial and error when team members are individually competent in their roles, and it becomes habitual when members are task-oriented because the resultant improvement in team performance is reinforcing to each person.

To summarize, teams are best described as *role systems*. The roles in the system are the official positions occupied by members of the team. Integration is the force that melds the activities of members, and it derives from norms and shared values held by members of the team. The strength or degree of integration that exists in the team is dependent upon the level and nature of cohesion within the team and the parent organization and is manifested by the integration of team structure and function.

Definitions

1. A team consists of
   (a) at least two people who
   (b) are working toward a common-goal/objective/mission where
   (c) each person has been assigned specific roles or functions to perform, and where
   (d) completion of the mission requires some form of dependency among the group members.

The above definition of team is Dyer's (1985) and, as noted by Dyer, it is quite similar to the widely used definition by Hall and Rizzo (1975), except that it does not include their requirement for a formal team structure. This permits application of the concept to more widely different types of groups.

2. Teamwork is activities performed by team members in such a manner that each activity is coordinated with every other one and contributes to the goals of the team and supports the activities of other members.
3. Team integration is the force that melds together the roles, attitudes, and activities of members and is manifested by the integration of team structure and function and, hence, by team cohesion.
4. To be effective, a team must perform as a unified role system that executes competently all of the activities and group functions needed to enable the team to accomplish its tasks and achieve its goals.
5. Maximally effective performance of a team as a unified system requires full integration of members' roles, attitudes, and activities.

COHESION AND ITS EFFECTS IN TEAMS

When people work together toward mutual goals and when they undergo meaningful common experiences, the resulting interaction produces changes in their perceptions, emotions, thinking, attitudes, and actions. The distinguishing feature of these changes is that the individual comes more and more to identify his feelings, thinking, attitudes, and actions with his group. Persisting personal relationships and values evolve and become stabilized providing him with organized, enduring,

and motivationally significant ties and rewarding experiences. These satisfactions may influence his attitudes toward other aspects of the work.

When an individual is able to interact with and maintain close relationships with members of a group in which he is highly accepted, his
job satisfaction is usually higher (Van Zelst, 1951; Zaleznik, Christensen,
and Roethlisberger, 1958). Similarly, workers are more satisfied when
they belong to a group that they like and whose members like them.
Greenbaum (1979) also found similar results in his study of small military units discussed earlier.

Central to understanding of group relations and of their effects upon
satisfaction and team performance is the concept of *group cohesiveness* or
cohesion, discussed earlier. The term *cohesion* refers *to the feeling of group
pride and solidarity that exists among members*. It has also been defined as
"the extent to which group members share the same norms" (Coch and
French, 1948).

In individual terms, cohesiveness has been defined in a variety of
ways. One popular definition (Festinger, Schacter, and Bach, 1950) refers
to cohesiveness as the attractiveness, or valence, of a group for its members, or in Lewinian terms, as the resultant of all of the forces acting on
all of the members to remain in the group. Cartwright and Zander (1960)
described cohesiveness in terms of willingness of group members to
work together toward a common goal, to overcome frustration or endure
pain to accomplish that goal, and to readily defend the group against
external criticism or attack. They have postulated that cohesiveness depends upon two categories or factors: (a) the properties of the group,
and (b) the needs of the members. Although the definitions in this par-
agraph can be made operational for research purposes, ease of discussion
makes the definition of Sherif and Sherif (1956) preferable. Here, *cohesion
will be defined as group pride and solidarity*.

There have been numerous studies of both the effects of cohesiveness
and the conditions necessary for its development. Although some results
have been mixed, there is almost unanimous agreement that cohesiveness is central to any understanding of groups, teams, and group influence.

As a result of a review of research on group effectiveness, Mills (1967)
concluded that cohesive groups are more productive than less cohesive
groups. Cohesiveness was manifested in the more effective groups
through greater commitment to goals, more open communication,
greater coordination, and more friendly interpersonal relations. However, of even more significance for training and team development, Mills
found that a *circular relationship* exists between group effectiveness and
solidarity. That is, as the group becomes more successful, it also becomes
more cohesive. In short, experiences of success while a group is working
together make the group more cohesive. Gill (1977) went even further

by maintaining, on the basis of his research, that the predominant causal direction is from performance to cohesion, rather than vice versa. According to Gill, effective performance produces greater cohesion, rather than cohesion producing more effective performance. For training and development, the implication is clear. The provision to teams of success experiences should result in improved cohesion.

The conclusions from this discussion of team cohesion are important. As stated earlier for work groups, two factors appear to be essential for effective team performance—in addition to technical proficiency:

1. A group situation that is (a) attractive to the members and (b) that generates pride and solidarity (cohesion), and

2. Strong group norms that value high performance.

CONDITIONS NECESSARY FOR COHESION

Besides leadership, one of the few areas that has been investigated with any degree of thoroughness is concerned with the effects of group properties upon performance. Much of this work was summarized by Likert (1961).

When organizational incumbents work together over time, norms, status structures, and patterns of interaction develop. These group attributes exert lasting influence upon the ways members go about their tasks and the levels of motivation that are achieved. The development of such properties is most pronounced in small, face-to-face, primary groups (e.g., squads, crews, etc.); however, even at levels above the basic unit, there exists the potential for the development of genuine team properties. Likert considered the development of group properties to be especially desirable among those individuals who "link" the various levels and groups within the larger organization. Linking functions are performed by group leaders, supervisors, and managers.

Group relations influence execution of system process activities in at least two ways. First, group relationships influence the motivation of members to perform their role-prescribed activities and, under high cohesion, to perform beyond the requirements of their official roles. Second, group relations determine the extent to which members share perspectives concerning organizational requirements and expectations.

There is little doubt that cohesiveness is the critical attribute in team effectiveness. Accordingly, it becomes important to examine certain underlying conditions that are necessary for the development of goal-oriented cohesiveness within teams.

The analysis in this section follows the classic analysis of Sherif and Sherif (1956). In general, cohesiveness will be increased by conditions that cause team members to develop common perceptions of events and problems, to evolve shared perceptions of themselves and their group, and to become consistently and harmoniously committed to the activities and objectives of the team. On the other hand, cohesiveness will be disrupted by conditions that encourage tendencies opposite to these.

The general conditions necessary for the development of cohesion are

1. common objectives conducive to cooperation,
2. shared experiences,
3. a stable and efficient organization, and
4. shared norms of performance and behavior.

Common Objectives Conducive to Cooperation

The development of a unified team occurs through the interaction of personnel who possess common objectives and, hence, common motives. When people share objectives that require cooperative action to achieve, they will work together.

The phrase *conducive to cooperation* is especially important. All objectives experienced by a number of people at the same time and in the same place are not necessarily conducive to cooperation. On the other hand, *superordinate goals* always require the coordinated efforts and resources of all the individuals involved. Superordinate goals are those objectives that are equally compelling for all and cannot be ignored but that cannot be achieved by the efforts and resources of one individual alone. This does not mean that every objective of every individual in every group must be identical. However, there are usually one or more goals that are central within a group and these weigh heavily in determining the kinds and qualities of activities that will result.

It is not sufficient that a team merely possesses objectives. Each member must perceive, even though dimly, that other people also face a set of circumstances or a problem that can be solved, escaped, ignored, or dealt with in some fashion by cooperating with one another. Therefore, it is equally important for every member to consciously perceive that such objectives exist and that cooperative effort is required to achieve them.

Shared objectives serve the essential function of generating cooperative interaction between individuals. Only when this interaction occurs is it possible for stabilized relationships and shared norms (values and standards of behavior) to develop. Stable relationships and shared norms are necessary for teamwork. Accordingly, common objectives are an essential condition for team development and the development of team cohesion.

Shared Experiences

When people work together toward common objectives and undergo common experiences, each individual becomes a part of a functioning system that exerts a major influence upon his experience and his actions. Close identification with other personnel and with the group that symbolizes this relationship rarely occurs unless members have undergone common experiences. Similarly, uniform standards of performance and behavior have their foundations in the shared experiences of team members.

Groups are held together by stable relationships (functional integration) and common attitudes (normative integration) among their members. Persisting relationships and common attitudes evolve and become stabilized only when people undergo significant experiences together.

Shared experiences serve two important functions. First, they permit personnel to become familiar with one another, to learn each other's characteristic ways of behaving, and through this familiarization process to develop stable expectations relative to performance and ways of working. Second, shared experiences provide personnel with a common frame of reference. Because they have undergone the same experiences, members view things from similar perspectives. They are bound together by having experienced unique events to which others have not been exposed.

Of particular significance are experiences of success (Mills, 1967; Gill, 1977). Probably nothing contributes so greatly to cohesiveness as successful action. Success operates to confirm the validity of the group's ways of operating and gives the individual confidence in himself and in the group. A long tradition of success appears to produce much greater cohesiveness. As a secondary effect, tradition of success is likely to provide the team with greater prestige, thus encouraging more ready identification by members.

Success is effective, however, only as it is experienced, and it is experienced only in relation to the goals perceived by the members. An action by a group is deemed successful by members only if the members become aware that their efforts have actually resulted in achievement of the group's goals. Leader control of this factor is possible through such measures as setting realistically high team objectives, ensuring that team members actually recognize the objectives, and furnishing adequate evaluation of the results of team efforts in relation to the objectives.

Just as shared experiences of success tend to enhance cohesiveness, experiences that are perceived by team members as failure of the group are disruptive. Severe or consistent failure usually results in loss of confidence, bickering, recriminations, and deterioration of cohesion. The amount of disruption that will occur depends upon both (1) the level of cohesiveness reached prior to the initial failure and (2) the severity of the failure. High prior cohesiveness, together with mild failure, may result in nothing more than minor loss of confidence and a slight lowering, if any, of level of aspiration, which may be rapidly recovered. At the other extreme, low prior cohesiveness and strong failure can result in severe disruption of cohesiveness.

It should be clear that failure alone does not necessarily result in disruption of cohesiveness. The critical factor appears to be whether failure causes team members to lose confidence in their leaders, the organization, or in themselves.

A Stable and Efficient Organization

High cohesion requires sufficient team stability for emotional and social bonds to develop. Both integration of role and task functions and the development of strong norms require that people work together long enough for common perceptions and values to evolve. Neither can reach a very high level when there is a great deal of turbulence and instability in the team. Replacement and transfer policies that result in frequent movements of members into and out of teams are not conducive to high cohesion.

Coordinated action requires that each individual be able to predict with a reasonable degree of accuracy how other relevant members will behave, and furthermore he must know what others expect of him. In short, organized effort requires a system of stable expectations in terms of how each member should and will perform.

The state of team affairs commonly referred to as *solidarity, cohesion,* or *integration* is largely a consequence of a stabilized structure of relationships in which the various members meet expectations that define their particular roles and functions. When a team reaches a level in which all members have clear expectations of how each relevant person will perform and, more important, have strong confidence that every individual can be relied upon to fully meet these expectations, high cohesion can be said to exist.

Stable expectations evolve from stable relationships. It is impossible for people to know with any degree of certainty the requirements for their own or others' behavior if relationships are superficial, temporary, or inconsistent. Where relationships are unstable, ambiguity and lack of confidence are likely to be prevalent.

The formal team structure serves as the basic framework for the development of stable relationships and expectations. The formal organization provides general definitions of the duties and responsibilities of each position in a team. When people with common goals work together over a period of time, informal expectations may also become stabilized.

These may not necessarily be in full agreement with those definitions put forth by the organization.

The extent to which there is agreement between formal job requirements and informal role expectations is a potent determinant of system (team) effectiveness. Where wide discrepancies exist, control and coordination may be exceedingly difficult. The efficiency of the organization's communication, authority, and decision processes determine whether such discrepancies will exist. Where these processes function effectively, leaders are able to ensure that their definitions of desired behavior are the ones accepted by the team.

Shared Norms of Performance and Behavior

Norms are attitudes and codes of behavior held in common by all or most members of a group. In small-group contexts, they are also referred to as "group standards." A team may develop norms relative to what constitutes a fair day's work, what level of performance is desirable, the amount of coordination that is needed, how hard and how fast a team ought to work, and so forth. In short, norms can be developed around just about anything having to do with the life and work of the team members.

From the team's standpoint, norms are important because of the strong influence they exert on the actions of personnel. Norms regulate the behavior of members in matters of relevance to the team. When people have an emotional investment in a group or organization and have internalized its values, norms provide them with a basis for governing their behavior and for evaluating the actions of others. The more integrated and cohesive the organization, the more strongly do norms exert influence.

It should be self-evident that cohesion is also related to communication. Those norms which give rise to cohesion are the products of interaction between people. These interactions must take the form of communication of some sort. Therefore, cohesion is strongly dependent upon communication. In general, the principle can be set forth that increased communication between members will heighten cohesion—unless the communication is unpleasant, critical, hostile, or otherwise divisive.

TEAMWORK

Teamwork depends upon team integration. If a group is not integrated, teamwork is likely to be minimal—regardless of efforts to develop it. On the other hand, where integration in a group is high, there is greater potential for the development of teamwork. It does not necessarily follow that good teamwork automatically will also be present.

High cohesion is a necessary ingredient for the development of teamwork, but not the only one. In order for teamwork to be developed, a number of other elements are essential.

The Nature of Teamwork

Many factors operate to encourage the development of team relationships. Common membership in a particular group, the possession of a common terminology, the sharing of a common doctrine, common problems with regard to the current operational situation of the team, and common understandings of its significance, the possession of common means and channels of communication, the fact of frequent association, and shared values regarding the necessity for working as a team—these are all factors that enhance the development of teamwork.

Nonetheless, the presence of the above factors alone will not assure effective teamwork. In addition, the development of a closely knit team requires each member to possess a frame of reference that embraces cooperation and coordination as operational requirements.

Cooperation and Competition. When people act at cross purposes, it is because they are impelled by individual, rather than common, motives or by motives that are incompatible and irreconcilable. On the other hand, teamwork develops through the efforts of individuals who possess motives that require cooperative activities for their attainment.

As discussed in chapter 3, when members of a group engage in activities that are competitive and reciprocally frustrating, unfavorable and protective attitudes develop between the individuals, which result in additional competition and reduced cooperation between them. As used here, *competition* refers to something more intense than so-called "friendly rivalry." The essence of a truly competitive situation is that one individual or group must win and others must lose.

When such conditions prevail, the urge to win may become primitive and basic. Therefore, the consequences for teamwork are substantial. When attitudes of this nature become predominant within a team, actions designed to protect self-interests and enhance personal aspirations are likely to take precedence over those that would contribute to a common objective.

On the other hand, when cooperation is the prevailing attitude, members tend to view the team as a whole and other members individually in a favorable light. Members tend to work with others in order that mutual objectives may be better accomplished. Furthermore, communication is used to reduce conflict rather than to aggravate it. When individuals pull together, favorable information about other members is seen in a positive light, and the probability of information being effectively used is enhanced.

Determinants of Teamwork

The development of closely coordinated teamwork requires

1. superordinate objectives that are meaningful, clear, and desired by all;
2. a system of potential rewards for contributing to team effort;
3. an organizational system that provides effective operating procedures and efficient patterns of communication among the members.

Clear superordinate objectives and a meaningful system of rewards focus efforts upon common aims and motivate members to cooperate and coordinate. The organizational system channels the motivation to cooperate into effective actions.

Clear Superordinate Objectives. As discussed earlier in this chapter, with regard to cohesion, *superordinate objectives are those goals that are equally compelling for all and cannot be ignored but that cannot be achieved by efforts and resources of one individual or group alone. They require the coordinated efforts and resources of all the individuals or units involved.* Teamwork depends upon the recognition, acceptance, and commitment to team and organizational objectives by every member of the team, to include especially the leaders and senior personnel.

Among other things previously discussed, cohesion depends upon commitment to superordinate objectives; however, in addition, teamwork depends also upon the clarity of such objectives. Probably the most significant characteristic of effective objectives is that they are clear. To steer activities and to mobilize coordinated effort, an objective must be specifically formulated in concrete terms and carefully communicated so that every relevant person understands it.

The most obvious effect of unclear objectives is poor coordination among units and among personnel. Coordinated effort requires that everyone understand missions and objectives in the same way. Lack of clarity leaves room for each member to place his own interpretation upon objectives and, equally important, upon the kinds of activities to be derived from them.

The importance of clear objectives is obvious. The principal function of objectives is to provide group members with concrete and specific targets toward which to work and with specific standards against which to evaluate activities. Accordingly, it is essential for leaders to insure that the objectives are clear and unequivocal.

Reward Systems. Cooperation is most likely to develop when members can receive significant satisfactions from behaving cooperatively and when competitive behavior is not rewarded or is even punished. The system of rewards in a team is an important determinant of teamwork.

The critical factor appears to be whether or not members of the team can receive satisfaction of their personal needs only when they contribute to team effort. In a cooperatively organized group (one in which the more significant rewards are given for team effort), no individual can move toward his personal goals without also forwarding the progress of other members and of the larger organization. The reverse is true of a competitively organized group (one in which rewards may be obtained for efforts that further individual interests without contributing particularly to team efforts).

An Efficient Organizational System. No matter how high the motivation to cooperate and coordinate, teamwork will not result unless members' efforts are effectively channeled. Therefore, teamwork also requires an efficient organizational system that provides a means through which activities of team members can be integrated and coordinated.

The term *organizational system* refers to those practices and procedures used to perform such functions as exercising direction, assigning responsibilities, exchanging information, making decisions, organizing, coordinating, and so forth within the team. The organizational system includes the formal organization and its procedures; but it goes beyond them also to encompass the various less formal means by which the activities are integrated and coordinated. These interdependent processes constitute an overall system that channels and guides the activities of the team. For this reason, it has been deemed more appropriate to refer to the organizational system rather than merely to organization as a determining factor.

Effective teamwork requires an organizational system that will ensure that, consistent with their tasks, objectives, and responsibilities, members are provided with all of the information, decisions, guidance, and assistance necessary for them to perform their roles effectively and to contribute appropriately to the overall team effort. In short, effective teamwork requires a system capable of providing all elements with the guidance, support, and coordination needed for them to perform their respective roles effectively.

TEAM TYPES AND SKILL REQUIREMENTS

In a comparison of individual and team training, Briggs and Johnston (1967) concluded that the relative value of individual and team training depends upon the complexity of the task situation. Here, "complexity" referred to the array of stimulus inputs, control operations, the level of uncertainty in the task as a whole, and the degree of structure in the task situation. Briggs and Johnston concluded that team training becomes more valuable as task situations become more complex.

Boguslaw and Porter (1962) devised a scheme for classifying task situations, based upon the nature of the team task and the context in which the task must be performed. According to Boguslaw and Porter, an *established situation* is one in which (1) all action-relevant *environmental* conditions are specifiable and predictable, (2) all action-related *states of the system* are specifiable and predictable, and (3) available research, technology, or records are adequate to provide statements about the *probable consequences* of alternative actions. An *emergent situation* is one in which (1) all action-relevant environmental conditions have *not* been specified, (2) the state of the system does *not* correspond to relied-upon predictions, (3) analytic solutions are not available, given the current state of analytic technology.

The *ultimate established situation* would involve a machine-dominant task in which inputs to and outputs from a machine, computer, weapons system, and so forth fully control the activities of team members. At one extreme, working teams, as discussed earlier, participate in established situations, although situations may vary in the degree to which team members' activities are dictated and constrained by task requirements.

Emergent situations may also vary widely. The ultimate may be *emergency* or *crisis-management* situations such as military operations, civil disasters, police activities, and fire department operations. In business affairs, certain project teams may function under emergent conditions.

When an emergent situation arises, the coordination demands placed on a team increase and may influence performance. As Knerr et al. (1980) noted, the emergent nature of military operational settings "increases demands for coordination, communication, and cooperation within the team." These demands tend to complicate team functions. According to Meister (1976) and Olmstead et al. (1973), they also tend to degrade team performance. This same can be said for emergent situations in the civilian world.

Team Types

There is no question that many teams operate in the emergent situations described by Boguslaw and Porter, and, accordingly, also follow the *organismic* team model, devised by Alexander and Cooperband (1965) to contrast with a *stimulus-response* model. The stimulus-response model applies to teams operating in established situations like those described earlier.

Since organismic teams function in emergent situations, the requirements for effective functioning become more complex. In contrast to stimulus-response teams, organismic team functioning requires not only a greater variety of skills, but, in addition, other complex attributes. Because the task situations are complex, *team training* becomes more valuable.

Skill Requirements

The effective functioning of teams in the modern world requires at least the following:

1. role-specific individual skills
2. team performance skills
3. integration

Role-Specific Individual Skills. Individual skills refers to activities that could be or are performed by individual members. Such activities are specific to and defined by the roles of the individuals. Although, in simple team tasks, individual task performances may be mutually exclusive and thus may be summed to produce a simple team product, there may be considerable overlap among the complex role requirements of some team members. Accordingly, more complex processes of combination may occur.

Nevertheless, *role-specific individual skills are the skills required to perform those activities specific to the respective team roles and which are performed independently of other team members.* Although an element of all team role definitions, coordinative skills are not individual skills.

Team Performance Skills. Team performance skills refers to the skills needed to execute activities/actions that are performed in response to the actions of other team members or that guide/cue the actions of other team members. Although they are the skills of individual members, they contribute to the performance of team functions. Whereas many people view team functions and team processes respectively as operations of the team as an entity, team performance skills remain the skills of individual team members. They are required by individual members in order for them to contribute to the collective execution of team functions or team processes. *In effect, these are the skills of coordination. They are skills that must be performed by the various team members to ensure that everyone is kept informed and that all activities mesh efficiently.*

Integration. As defined earlier, *team integration* is the force that *melds the roles, attitudes, and activities of members.* In the terminology of group psychology, integration refers to the cohesion, or cohesiveness, of the team as a group. Cohesion produces a coincidence of the psychological fields of members. This shared perspective results in team integration. Through its influence upon the norms and values held by members, it enhances unity within the system and focuses individual and team skills upon the task requirements of the system. Thus, the effective performance of team functions requires

1. role-specific individual skills,
2. team performance skills, and
3. integration of the team.

TEAM TRAINING

After an analysis of the state-of-the art of team training, Wagner et al. (1977) put forth a set of premises that should be considered in any effort to develop training for teams. They apply to all types of teams. The premises follow:

1. teams are created or designed to accomplish certain goals or missions;
2. the relationships among team members are meaningful only to the extent that they are involved in attainment of the goals;
3. before any team training is undertaken, an in-depth analysis of the system should be performed; the task characteristics should be identified and training objectives derived;
4. the members of the team should be made aware of the team's goals and objectives;
5. exercises and instructional materials should be structured with respect to the objectives;
6. the training situation should be made as similar as possible to the actual operational situation; and
7. the quality control components of the system should provide feedback data to trainees and trainers for the purpose of improving the training system and team proficiency.

Following are a number of recommendations that apply to team training (Dyer, 1985). It should be clear, however, that relative applicabilities may vary according to the type of team.

1. *Team training should be preceded by individual training.* Individual proficiency is necessary for team training to be successful. Furthermore, cross-training of team skills is not effective until individual expertise has been acquired. The relative emphasis given to each form of training should depend upon the team task, with tasks that demand little member coordination requiring less team training than those high on coordination.
2. *Team training should be sequenced in terms of increasing complexity and degrees of teamwork required.* The most complex form of team training involves situations

that include emergent (unexpected, new) tasks. Cross-training can be used in team training to increase both individual and team proficiency.

3. *Team training should be conducted periodically.* Repetition of training increases long-term retention of skills. Periodic training should be conducted with different tasks/situations to enhance both proficiency and ability to adapt to new or different situations.

4. *Insofar as possible, teams should be trained in conditions that approximate those situations in which they will be expected to perform.* If a team is expected to perform under stress, members should train under stress. If a team is expected to work as a coordinated unit, members should be trained under conditions that force coordination. The need for realistic training settings has been proven repeatedly.

5. *Team goals should be clear and explicit.* Team objectives should be spelled out in every way possible. Illustrations should be presented to show the consequences of errors to the team's performance.

6. *Interdependencies among team members should be emphasized.* Members of teams cannot and should not act independently of each other. Lack of coordination can often lead to serious team errors. The ways in which one member's actions impact upon other members and the team as a whole need to be illustrated and stressed.

7. *Team training should include training individuals to analyze their own errors, to sense when the team or team members are overloaded, and to adjust their behavior when overloads occur.* In a team, it is easy to blame someone else, the group as a whole, or a piece of equipment for one's own errors; but such actions are done at the expense of not learning how to avoid the error in the future. A team member should be able to sense when any member, including himself, is overloaded.

8. *Team members should receive performance feedback.* Training situations that provide feedback during the training exercise, as an automatic consequence of team and/or individual actions, as well as trainer feedback after the exercises, are preferred. For some tasks, team members can immediately observe the consequences of their actions. However, other tasks do not provide such intrinsic feedback. Although feedback in the form of debriefings or after-action reviews is important in both situations, it is especially critical in the latter situation since that is the only feedback members may receive. During initial training, feedback by the trainer should not be too detailed or voluminous because individuals cannot absorb and may even misuse such information. At later stages of training, feedback should be more refined. Feedback should be provided on all important aspects of team functioning because individuals tend to maximize performance on the aspects about which they receive feedback.

To summarize, it can be concluded that

1. team training is a necessary addition to individual training for tasks that require interaction and other team skills;

2. effective team training can occur only if team members enter the tr
   situation with the individual skill competencies that are required;

3. the team context is not the appropriate location for initial acquisition of
   by individuals; and

4. performance feedback is essential to team as well as individual acquisition of
   skills.

LEADING TEAMS

It is the function of leadership to define the goals for a team and to make them operational as the purposes of team existence, to create a viable system distinctively adapted to these objectives, and to ensure that the team's energies are channeled in the required directions. The team leader's role usually involves at least four broad activities: (1) formulating goals and purposes for the team and roles for its members; (2) developing and maintaining the team as a viable system; (3) promoting team performance to include training; and (4) representing the team to other groups and higher organizational levels.

Depending upon the type of team, leaders may vary from the lead person, group leader, or first-line supervisor of working teams to what may be a highly trained professional serving as project director or manager of a project team. The specific qualifications of the leader will depend upon the task demands and requirements. In general, it can be said that a team leader must serve two functions: (1) oversee the work of the team and exercise quality control, and (2) represent the team to higher levels and other teams. In some types of teams, it may be a leader function also to conduct training.

A number of skills essential for leading teams have been identified. They are

1. team-management skills,
2. communication skills,
3. problem-solving skills,
4. technical skills, and
5. goal-setting (tactical) skills.

Training in the above specific skill categories should equip leaders to supervise the teams discussed here.

High-level leaders are limited in the extent to which they can directly influence the actions of most of their subordinates. On the other hand, first-line supervisors, such as team leaders, are in a position to translate the larger objectives, intents, and purposes into action, and through their daily contacts can directly influence the attitudes, motivations, and performance of even the lowest-ranking personnel.

Elements of Team Leadership

There are four basic elements involved in supervisory leadership: (1) behavior that enhances someone else's feeling of personal worth and importance (support); (2) behavior that encourages members of the group to develop close, mutually satisfying relationships (interaction facilitation); (3) behavior that stimulates an enthusiasm for meeting the group's goal or achieving excellent performance (goal emphasis); and (4) behavior that helps achieve goal attainment by such activities as scheduling, coordinating, and planning, and by providing resources such as tools, materials, and technical knowledge (work facilitation).

These four classes of activities encompass most of the leadership behavior of team supervisors.

Support. In general, anything that contributes to insecurity or feelings of being threatened will tend to reduce the effectiveness of subordinates. If, in contacts with personnel, the supervisor communicates attitudes of distrust, hostility, or lack of confidence, influence attempts will not be effective, because the members will be too busy protecting themselves. Similarly, people who, because of insecurity, are forced into yes-man roles with supervisors cannot contribute with maximum effectiveness.

A sense of personal worth rests on a base of personal security. In responsible and capable individuals, it also requires the opportunity for them to participate in the solution of meaningful and worthwhile problems, to discuss decisions that may affect them, to assume responsibility when they are ready for it, and the right to appeal. Opportunities to contribute, to be heard, to be active members of an important activity are what most team members like. Supervisors who provide such opportunities will have personnel who display greater motivation, higher morale, and greater involvement with the work and with the organization.

Interaction Facilitation. It is probably true that the greatest barriers to effective performance are interpersonal—emotional relationships between people who feel threatened in some way by the presence of other people whom they dislike or whom they do not understand. Pleasant relationships reduce threat and permit members to shift their attention from interpersonal problems to work goals.

When a team is so led that some of its members are communicationally peripheral to others, these individuals are likely to become disheartened, frustrated, and unproductive. A team that is organized or led so that contacts between all members are restricted is not likely to become very cohesive. The effective leader organizes the work so that the fact of a common task to accomplish gives team members valid reasons for interacting. He coordinates activities in such a way that his personnel have adequate opportunities to consult on problems, and he ensures participation in a wide range of assignments so that all members get a chance to know each other closely.

Goal Emphasis. One of the most consistent findings in leadership research is that the effective leader emphasizes goals and goal accomplishment rather than becoming immersed in the details of minute tasks. This is probably the most difficult point for a supervisor to accept. He is responsible for making sure that his personnel accomplish their tasks and frequently feels compelled to become deeply involved in the details of the work. Instead of becoming deeply involved in the details of task accomplishment, a more constructive approach for him is to continually provide subordinates with performance goals to which they will be committed, adequate training, and performance standards that clearly specify his expectations.

Most people will strive to reach performance goals to which they are committed and will exercise self-discipline and self-control to the extent of this commitment. The best results can be obtained by actively promoting excellence through continual stress upon high performance. In this way, a supervisor can add new dimensions to his subordinates' views of their roles. He can stimulate new avenues for achievement, new opportunities for development, and new endeavors for reaching all sorts of goals that can stir even the most settled of workers into renewed activity. Any action that excites enthusiasm for meeting both team and individual goals and for achieving excellent performance is part of this behavior.

Work Facilitation. There can be little doubt that employees value a supervisor who helps them accomplish work objectives. In addition to directing activities and training, the supervisor must also contribute to the efficiency of the group (e.g., through planning and good management) and minimize inefficiency (e.g., by eliminating problems and disrupting influences within the work situation).

Much of the time of effective supervisors is spent in planning, coordinating, scheduling, and mobilizing resources. They work on activities that assist their personnel to move toward the team's objectives without lost motion and wasted effort. This implies that a supervisor must think ahead, anticipate difficulties, and take whatever actions are necessary to forestall problems. The important conclusion is that an effective supervisor takes a larger perspective than his subordinates and adjusts his activities to that perspective.

Performance of the above four classes of leader activities contributes to all of the conditions for effectiveness discussed earlier. In general, it can be concluded that the supervisor who provides support to subordinates but still permits autonomy, who encourages interaction among subordinates and works at developing team solidarity, who emphasizes goal accomplishment and high performance standards rather than detailed task execution, and who provides whatever actions are necessary to help team members do their jobs, including planning, scheduling, coordinating, and so forth, will be the more effective supervisor in terms of both member satisfaction and member performance.

Chapter 5

Task Forces, Staffs, and Decision-Making Groups

Work groups and teams are usually small, compact groups whose members have clearly delineated roles and perform specific duties and functions. Although such groups are found most often in large organizations, their boundaries are frequently so tightly circumscribed that a work group or team will take on an identity that sets it apart from all similar groups. In addition, most such groups have very simple structures, with a supervisor or a team leader and subordinate members.

OPERATING GROUPS

In contrast, operating groups (task forces, operational staffs, and high-level decision-making groups) may have complex structures, with numerous levels. Furthermore, their missions may be quite broad, the roles of members may vary widely, and the groups may consist of many more personnel than work groups or teams.

Despite these differences, task forces, operational staffs, and high-level decision-making groups all possess the fundamental group attributes discussed in earlier chapters. Accordingly, they can be managed and led by addressing these same properties.

Definitions

Task Force. The term task force refers to a group of individuals that has been constituted to accomplish an assigned mission. The mission may be to obtain information, to assess some situation, or to accomplish a specific operational objective. Although the term originated in military usage, it is now current in various civilian environments as well. It may be used to refer to an organization of whatever size that is tasked to accomplish an objective by a parent organization.

A task force is organized and staffed so as to best accomplish the assigned objective. Ideally, it will be staffed with selected, highly qualified personnel at all levels. The distinguishing characteristics of task forces are

1. they are semi-autonomous but are accountable to a higher authority;
2. usually, the organization is the conventional pyramid, although shapes may vary somewhat, depending upon the purpose;
3. in addition, there may be numerous committees (either advisory or functional) and an operating staff within the task organization;
4. the organization will consist of several hierarchical levels; and
5. the upper levels will be staffed by high-level and, hopefully, highly qualified personnel and, frequently, the entire task force will consist of highly qualified professional personnel.

Although a task force may be of any size, this discussion will be limited to small- and middle-sized units (under 100 people). Larger task forces take on the structure and complexity of a conventional organization.

Operational Staff. Operational Staff refers to a group consisting of senior command and control executives of an organization and their supporting staff personnel. Normally, an operational staff would not consist of more than two executive levels plus senior supporting staff.

The most typical operational staff occurs in military organizations, where a battle staff may consist of the commander, his principal staff officers (personnel, intelligence, operations, and logistics), and his immediately subordinate commanders. The distinguishing characteristic of an operational staff is that executives make decisions and staff personnel contribute to the decisions through the acquisition of information, making recommendations, and overseeing execution of the decisions. It should be apparent that, under these circumstances, staff personnel can wield considerable influence, although only the executive personnel may legally make the decisions. Classic examples of operational staffs are congressional and legislative committees. Many large corporations also use operational staffs.

Regardless of the nomenclature, operational staffs operate according to the principles of group functioning described earlier in this book. However, many are loosely structured, and members may represent conflicting interests, thus resulting in potential for considerable inefficiencies and reduced effectiveness.

High-Level Decision-Making Group. The final type of group to be considered is the *high-level decision-making group*. These groups are mainly boards and committees, which may govern or may recommend, but which do not oversee execution of their decisions or recommendations. In many instances, however, the decisions may be binding.

Basically, these groups consist of people who occupy high levels in companies, communities, or other organizations but who just consider problems, recommendations, or issues, and make decisions. They do not normally get involved in oversight or execution of decisions, although individuals who must execute may be members of the group. Frequently, a small support staff will also be assigned.

COMMON GROUP ATTRIBUTES

At first glance, it may appear that task forces, operational staffs, and decision-making groups are different from work groups and teams. In fact, they are different in certain aspects. However, they still function as groups and possess group attributes discussed earlier in this book.

Task forces, operational staffs, and high-level decision-making groups are all role systems, driven by tasks, and maintained by norms and shared values related to performance. Similarly, cohesion plays a central role in their effectiveness. (See discussion of cohesion in chapters 3 and 4.)

Accordingly, the same following conditions necessary for the development of cohesion apply:

1. common objectives conducive to cooperation,
2. shared experiences,
3. a stable and efficient organization, and
4. shared norms of performance and behavior.

It can be seen that the underlying attributes are the same as for other types of groups. On the other hand, task forces, operational staffs, and decision-making groups may have certain characteristics that make them distinctive, such as the following:

1. they may be, and usually are, multi-level;
2. they frequently have a single mission, usually important;
3. depending upon their charter, they may be assigned a mission; however, within the mission, they most often develop their own objectives;
4. there is a division of responsibilities;
5. the group may be devoted to problem-solving, or execution of a particular project, or both;

6. the group usually includes a number of high-level people; and

7. its organization may be more loosely structured, but it is still a group.

These distinctive characteristics can make the development of operational effectiveness more difficult than for conventional groups. Especially, the fact that such groups may have broadly defined missions, high-level personnel, and divided responsibilities can result in considerable difficulties for leaders.

REQUIREMENTS FOR EFFECTIVE OPERATING GROUPS

Effectiveness in accomplishing missions depends upon a group's ability to cope with and control its operational environment. For a group to be successful, it requires

1. *Capacity to evaluate reality*—the ability to search out, accurately perceive, and correctly interpret all elements of the operational situation, including conditions both internal and external to the group,

2. *Adaptability*—the capacity to solve problems and to react flexibly to changing demands of the operational situation, and

3. *Operational proficiency*—the technical competence to successfully execute the tasks arising from the demands of the mission.

Essential Properties

To meet the above requirements, effective operating groups usually develop the properties related to performance that were identified in chapter 2. Here, all of the properties will be listed again; then each will be discussed as it relates to operating groups:

Group Properties

1. capacity to learn
2. open and efficient communication
3. climate of confidence, trust, and so forth
4. internal flexibility and innovative ability
5. a state of functional integration among subordinate units
6. operational proficiency

Leader Resources

1. leaders who are able to arrive at valid decisions speedily and efficiently
2. leaders skilled in identifying and using potential present among subordinates
3. leaders who are skilled in mobilizing and guiding the efforts of personnel

Personnel Resources

1. commitment of personnel to group objectives
2. a sense of group identity
3. personnel who possess the proficiencies necessary for mission accomplishment

Group Properties

1. *Capacity to learn.* An effective operating group has the capability to gather information relative to its actions and performance, analyze it, feed it back to itself, and change according to what is learned either about situational demands or about the group itself. All of this makes possible continued development and improvement.

2. *Open and efficient communication.* An operating group must have the ability to generate information about both external and internal conditions and to communicate it validly and reliably within the group. There must be a flow from one part of the group to the other of all relevant information important for each decision and action. Members must exchange information and work at clearing up misunderstandings. Because of efficient communication, members are able to achieve the common understanding of problems necessary for well-integrated action.

3. *A climate of confidence, trust, and freedom from threat, especially among key personnel.* There must be a preponderance of favorable attitudes on the part of each member toward duties, toward superiors, toward the group—toward most aspects of his situation. Because of these favorable attitudes and group loyalties, effective groups usually develop strong informal values and standards of behavior, particularly in relation to the more important aspects of performance. Thus, each member will do all he reasonably can to help the group achieve its objectives, and he expects every other member to do the same. A poor climate undermines communication, reduces flexibility, and encourages self-protection rather than commitment to the group.

4. *Internal flexibility and innovative ability.* An operating group must be sufficiently flexible that efficient shifting of both individual and group assignments is possible when changes in situations demand it. The group should be able to adapt readily to unanticipated events. Procedures are not so rigid that adjustments to new situations become excessively laborious. Furthermore, over-formalism and strong dependence upon individual leaders do not exist to the extent that responsibility cannot be easily shifted when situational demands change or leaders are lost.

5. *A state of functional integration among subordinate units.* Functions and operations of all parts of the group must fit together so that the parts do not operate at cross purposes.

6. *Operational proficiency.* This is essential in performance both of operations directly related to mission accomplishment and of activities required to support the operations.

Leader Resources

1. *Leaders who are able to arrive at valid decisions speedily and efficiently.* The energy of leaders, and of decision-making staffs, cannot be expended in interminable haggling or over-concentration on inconsequential details but must be used to develop constructive solutions to critical problems.

2. *Leaders skilled in using potential present among subordinates for mission accomplishment.* This means that talent is not wasted; the leaders know how to locate, develop, and use member abilities to the best advantage.

3. *Leaders who are skilled in mobilizing and guiding the efforts of members.* This is the ultimate leadership skill. Every leader should be able to motivate their members, coordinate activities, and guide members to perform as a unified whole.

Personnel Resources

1. *Commitment of members to group objectives and a high level of motivation to perform in accordance with the objectives.* Furthermore, there must be a minimum of conflict in the group about basic objectives. There can be no effective coordinated action if there is conflict among influential members about objectives or about means for accomplishing them. This does not imply merely that divergent opinions may be present but not expressed; it means that, if deep-seated differences exist within the key leader group, even though not expressed, unified action is not likely to result. From commitment to objectives comes willingness to work hard and to change when necessary.

2. *A sense of group identity.* Members must have knowledge and insight about what the group is, what its objectives are, what it is to do, and what it stands for.

3. *Personnel who possess the proficiencies necessary for mission accomplishment.* Every member of the group should possess the technical knowledge and skills needed for outstanding performance of his/her assigned role(s).

Because of the above properties, performance standards are high and dissatisfaction may occur whenever achievement falls short of objectives. This highly constructive orientation toward the group and its objectives is achieved by mobilizing all the major motivational forces that can exercise influence in an organizational setting. These forces, with bases in both the formal and informal areas of organizations, are exceptionally potent sources of leader effectiveness.

THE ANATOMY OF AN ORGANIZATION

Most operating groups follow what have been called "the logics of organization." The logical derivation of an organized structure is almost universally based on the distribution of responsibility. In fact, the very foundation of organization is a basic system of stable expectations regarding differential responsibilities and relationships among the members. Without this system, there would be little possibility of coordination or of directed action (Smith and Tannenbaum, 1971).

The distribution of responsibility usually results in a structure characterized by specialization of function and strict lines of authority. The large organization is broken down into smaller components, each having a fairly independent identity. The components are, in turn, usually divided into even smaller identifiable elements. This authority structure is laid out so as to create a precise format in which each unit is clearly charted and its missions assigned. The system is designed to prevent duplication of effort, and, through control along the lines of authority and responsibility, to ensure that each person knows exactly what he is supposed to do and will perform in accordance with expectations.

Organization derived along the lines of distribution of responsibility carries with it a number of principles intended to maximize effectiveness through controls. They include such principles as the following:

1. *Unity of command.* In each organization and at each level, there must be only one source of authority.
2. *Chain of authority.* There should be a clear-cut line of responsibility.
3. *Standardization of functions.* There must be standardized procedures for most operations. This standardization includes uniformity in the performance of every activity, regardless of the person executing the activity.
4. *Specialization of function.* In addition to standardization, activities should also be specialized with each individual learning a particular task.
5. *Clarity of job specification and responsibility.* Effective standardization and specialization requires detailed specifications for each position in the organization with explicit descriptions of duties and responsibilities.
6. *Line and staff functions.* To provide for flexibility in operations and to give full information to executives about the way the group is functioning, staff positions are created at numerous organizational levels.

The rationale of formal organization is clear. The structure and the logic upon which it rests are directed toward the influence and control of units and personnel. This is accomplished through communication and decision systems outlined by the chain of authority that specifies who communicates with whom and at which levels certain kinds of decisions will be made.

The structure and principles just discussed refer to the so-called formal organization. It is formal in the sense that it can be planned and set down on paper. It is the inevitable result of division of responsibility and is essential to effective coordination of large numbers of people. Emphasis upon the formal structure and principles is important for two reasons.

First, proper observance of organizational channels and principles is essential for operational efficiency. Second, an inefficient system tends to create frustration and conflict among personnel, which, in turn, affect performance.

With regard to the first reason, it is necessary that the system function as designed if efficiency of operations is to be achieved. When circumstances dictate deviation from these general principles of organization, difficulties often arise.

The second, and equally important, reason for concern with organizational principles is that an ineffective system tends to create frustration and conflict among personnel. Excessive interference with work activities due to breakdowns in the organization can be as devastating to motivation as inadequate working conditions or poor personnel policies. This is important because of the multiplying effects on attitudes. People get frustrated and angry at one another when they have difficulty doing their jobs.

The Leadership Dilemma

The considerations just discussed force recognition of the special difficulties involved in leading an operating group. Many of these problems derive from the numbers of competent people whose activities must be influenced and coordinated. The necessity for obtaining smoothly functioning, well-integrated performance from them can create some critical strains in the operating group (Kanter, 1979; Porter, 1973; Tyler, 2000; Vaill, 1976).

First, there exists a deep source of strain because the mission necessitates organizational complexity and formalization, which are the most general causes of rigidity. There is likely to be a direct relationship between the size of a group and its tendencies toward inflexibility. There are, of course, exceptions to the general hypothesis that size begets rigidity. Some small groups are quite inflexible, while some very large ones are highly responsive to change. However, where these latter exceptions occur, they are usually due to skilled leaders who know how rigidity develops and are constantly on guard against it.

These same problems may carry over into the information-processing system, into the development of methods and procedures, and into virtually every aspect of performance. In each case, the high degree of formalization made necessary by organizational complexity can result in rigidity and overcontrol, both of which serve as first-class impediments to effectiveness.

A second organizational strain centers on the continuous effort to maintain a high level of motivation while also exercising control over the actions of personnel. Size and the hierarchical arrangement of the group increase every person's distance from people who influence his actions, his welfare, and sometimes even his fate. Although close superiors have a great deal to do with determining a group member's actions, decisions beyond the immediate superior, or even beyond the immediate supervisor's superior, set limits on the nature and direction of their activities. Direct communication with these distant leaders is almost impossible. Accordingly, the individual's anonymity increases and so does his uncertainty about what will become of him—a phenomenon that is most important because of its effect upon motivation and morale.

The moral of this discussion is that a leader of an operating group, working within exacting requirements for coordination and control, must rely upon formal structures and organizational principles to obtain much of his results. However, he must also strive simultaneously to combat negative motivational forces that are, in part, created by the very system that is intended to make performance more effective (Gellerman, 1998; Green and Butkus, 1999; Porter, 1971). This contradictory interplay of procedures required for coordination and control and of practices designed to stimulate performance creates a conflict that constitutes one of the central problems of group leadership.

Necessary Conditions

The fundamental problem is How can the leader of a high performance group consisting of a diverse membership with varied responsibilities develop his group into the integrated system described earlier? Many practical actions can be taken (Bellin, 1996; Savell, Teague, and Tremble, 1995). Some of these will be discussed in later paragraphs of this section. First, however, it is important to, once again, examine the underlying general conditions that are necessary for the formation and effective functioning of a group. These conditions are necessary because they are the means for reconciling the conflict between the formal and informal areas of organization. When properly developed, they provide the motivational forces for melding diverse individuals and units into an effective functioning entity (Forgas and Williams, 2000; Hogg and Abrams, 2001). Regardless of the specific techniques used, most of the development efforts of leaders are devoted to creating such conditions.

The general conditions essential to the formation and functioning of an effective group are common objectives conducive to cooperative action among personnel and units, shared experiences in the pursuit of common objectives, a stable and efficient organization, and shared norms of performance and behavior. These conditions have been addressed before in this book. Here, they will be examined from the special standpoint of operating groups.

Common Objectives Conducive to Cooperation. The development of a unified group occurs through the interaction of people who possess common objectives and, hence, common motives (Leonard, 2000). When people share objectives that require cooperative action to achieve, they work together.

The phrase "conducive to cooperation" implies that members must perceive, even though dimly, that other people also face a set of circumstances or a problem that can be solved, escaped, ignored, or dealt with in some fashion by cooperating with one another. Therefore, it is not sufficient that a group merely possesses objectives. It is equally important for every member to consciously perceive that such objectives exist and that cooperative effort is required to achieve them.

Common objectives serve the essential function of generating cooperative interaction between individuals and between groups. Only when this interaction occurs is it possible for stabilized relationships and shared norms (values and standards of behavior) to develop. Stable organizational relationships and shared norms are necessary for teamwork. Accordingly, common objectives are an essential condition for organizational development.

Shared Experiences. When people work together toward common objectives and undergo common experiences that are meaningful, the resulting interaction produces changes in their perceptions, emotions, thinking, attitudes, and actions (Hinton and Reitz, 1971; Sherif and Sherif, 1953). The distinguishing feature of these changes is that the individual comes more and more to identify his feelings, thinking, attitudes, and actions with the group. Furthermore, persisting personal relationships and values evolve and become stabilized. These provide each individual with organized, enduring, and motivationally significant ties with the group. Thus, over time, the individual becomes a part of a functioning system that exerts a major influence upon his experience and his actions.

The critical factor is *shared experiences.* Close identification with other members and with the group that symbolizes this relationship rarely occurs unless members have undergone common experiences. Similarly, uniform standards of performance and behavior have their foundations in the shared experiences of members.

The development of an effective group requires that members be exposed to a variety of opportunities to work together, solve problems together, and train together. Anything is useful that provides opportunity for personnel to have meaningful experiences that they can hold in common and that can tie them closer to the group.

A Stable and Efficient Organization. Coordinated action requires that each individual be able to predict with a reasonable degree of accuracy how other relevant members will behave and, furthermore, he must know what others expect of him. In short, organized effort requires a system of stable expectations in terms of how each member should and will perform.

That state of affairs commonly referred to as "solidarity," "cohesion," or "unit integrity" is largely a consequence of a stabilized structure of relationships in which the various members meet expectations that define their particular roles and functions. When a group reaches a level in which all members have clear expectations of how each relevant person will perform and, more important, have strong confidence that every individual can be relied upon to fully meet these expectations, high cohesion can be said to exist.

Stable expectations evolve from stable relationships. It is impossible for people to know with any degree of certainty the requirements for their own and others' behavior, if relationships are superficial, temporary, or inconsistent. Where relationships are unstable, ambiguity and lack of confidence are likely to be prevalent.

The formal organizational structure serves as the basic framework for the development of stable relationships and expectations. It provides general definitions of the duties and responsibilities of personnel. However, when people with common objectives work together over a period of time, informal expectations may also become stabilized. These are not necessarily in agreement with those definitions put forth by the formal organization.

The extent to which there is agreement between formal requirements and informal expectations is a potent determinant of effectiveness. Where wide discrepancies exist, control and coordination may be exceedingly difficult. The efficiency of the group's communication, authority, and decision processes determine whether such discrepancies will exist. Where these processes function effectively, leaders are able to influence the way expectations develop and can ensure that the group's definitions of required behavior are the accepted ones.

The effective operation of these processes depends almost completely upon those individuals who occupy linking roles in the organization— the managers of each group at each level. At every level, groups must be supervised by competent personnel who effectively link their units to the next higher level and, eventually, to all other units in the larger group.

This linking function is critical. When an individual who occupies a linking role fails to perform his functions adequately, the unit(s) under him will not be an effective part of the group. When not so linked, subordinate units experience substantial handicaps in performing their missions.

The linking function is more important at high levels than at low ones, because the problems are more important to the total group and affect more people. For this reason, failure of the linking function at higher echelons has even more serious effects than failure at lower levels.

The linking function will be performed best when personnel at each level also function effectively as a group. When people at each level work together as a group over a period of time, they also come to have uniform understandings of how things should be done, and they develop customary ways of working together that permit them to function smoothly without constant intervention.

A senior leader who develops subordinates and relevant staff members into a cohesive group, of which he is an actively functioning member, lays the foundation for well-integrated action throughout his organization. Since these people occupy key positions, their influence on performance is great. When they function as a group, they learn the leader's expectations, his preferred ways of operating, what his performance standards are, and how he desires the group to be led. Because of their key positions, they are able to infuse the leader's viewpoints into the next lower level. When, therefore, each level is linked to succeeding levels in similar ways, influence from the highest echelons can permeate the organization. In effect, this is how an organizational climate is developed.

The effectiveness of the organization and its capacity to deal with difficult problems depend upon the effectiveness of the linking groups of which the structure consists. The more effectively the linking function is performed, the more integrated and better coordinated the total organization will be.

Shared Norms of Performance and Behavior. As people work together to develop an effective group, by-products of their activities begin to emerge. Such things appear as catchwords, jargon, customs, traditions, nicknames for significant figures, and so forth. Similarly, routines, rules of conduct, standards of performance, and values emerge. This superstructure of customs, rules, standards, and values is referred to as the "norms" of the group.

Norms are attitudes and codes of behavior held in common by all, or most, of the members. A group may develop norms relative to what constitutes a fair day's work, what level of performance is desirable, what kinds of conduct are good or bad, and so forth. In short, norms can be developed around just about anything having to do with the life and work of the members.

From the leader's standpoint, norms are important because of the strong influence they exert on actions of group members. Norms regulate the behavior of members. When people have an emotional investment in a group and have internalized its values, norms provide them with a basis for governing their behavior and for evaluating the actions of others. The more cohesive the group, the more strongly do norms exert influence. For these reasons, it behooves any leader to do everything possible to create conditions that will result in norms that will be constructive for the performance of his group. Norms that are counter to official objectives are exceedingly difficult to change.

DECISION MAKING IN GROUPS

Problem solving and its corollary function of decision making are commonly said to be the heart of high-level group activities. Yet, it is doubtful whether the main body of problem-solving and decision-making theory does, in fact, provide a realistic account of problem-solving in high-level groups operating in complex situations. Most such theory approaches problem-solving as a rational process carried out by an individual. This rational process goes somewhat as follows:

(a) an individual is confronted with a number of different, specified alternative courses of action;

(b) to each alternative is attached a set of consequences that will result if that alternative is chosen; and

(c) the individual then ranks all sets of consequences according to preference and chooses the alternative that has the preferred consequences.

If this framework is used to describe how real groups solve problems in a real world, it soon becomes apparent that it does not advance understanding of the process very much. This is true for the following reasons:

(a) in group functioning, an individual rarely solves the entire problem alone;

(b) the alternatives are not usually given but must be searched for;

(c) which consequences are attached to which alternatives is seldom given or obvious; they must be searched for, and absolute certainty of consequences is rarely possible; and

(d) the comparisons among alternatives are not usually made in terms of a single, simple criterion. There are often important consequences that are so intangible as to make evaluation in terms of a single objective criterion impossible. Accordingly, operating groups cannot always search for the one best alternative. Instead, they are frequently confronted with finding a satisfactory alternative that will attain a specified goal, and will, at the same time, satisfy a number of auxiliary conditions.

Operating groups usually face situations that involve problems that are nonrepetitive and often involve long-range questions about the operations of a complex organization. The problems arise initially in very loosely defined form. Furthermore, they require an extensive search for alternatives, consequences, and so forth.

Even more important for the present discussion, group problem solving involves individual problem solving, *but much more*. The thinking done by a member of a highly coordinated group occurs in a different context from that done by the isolated thinker. Decisions that will govern the actions of a complex organization are processes involving many elements. Each organizational component carries partial responsibility for overall problem solutions. Interests of all components must be considered in the final outcome. Accordingly, individuals rarely solve problems in isolation. Reaching a group solution requires an agreement process that affects the total outcome but that is partly a result of the unique relationships within the group. Because the process occurs in communication and interaction among group members, the products of such joint effort may be quite different from that obtained by isolated individuals.

Factors That Affect Group Decision Making

Factors that affect decision making in operational groups are both numerous and complex. Group morale and efficiency are easily disturbed. Relationships shift within the group and between members and others. Understanding of the factors operant in group relationships is necessary if leadership is to increase group effectiveness. Of the many factors that may influence coordinated effort and the group problem-solving process, the more important ones are singled out here for elaboration.

The Work Environment. A most obvious characteristic of group problem-solving is that the individuals concerned work in a social environment—either in immediate physical proximity to one another or with the knowledge that others are working on parts of the same task and will, in the near future, react to their products. Since this social context can be shown to affect a person's work and mental processes, it constitutes an important factor in effective group functioning.

The general atmosphere that exists within the group is the result of the attitudes of all the group members toward their work, toward other members, and toward their leaders. Groups vary greatly in this regard, and the atmosphere that exists within a particular group can become rapidly apparent to even the most casual observer. This environment can exert a definite influence upon the performance of individual members as well as the group as a whole. Where members feel close, competent, and strong, stress both from within and from without can be taken in stride. However, when the atmosphere within a group is insecure or antagonistic, it can create paralysis or confusion. An insecure group fears that it may lack unity and ability. Therefore, each problem it faces becomes fraught with danger.

One of the more common forms that insecurity within a group may take has been called "fear of consequences." Many examples of poor group problem solving can be traced to fear of the consequences of contemplated actions. One very real example is fear of failure. As work proceeds, numerous questions can arise in the thoughts of group members. Will the solution later prove to be the wrong one? Do we have enough facts and information to recommend this decision? What happens if the information is incorrect? What will happen to the entire group? A confident, smoothly functioning group will assess the possible outcomes of various alternatives while it is in the process of reaching agreement on a solution. But, this weighing procedure can bring disagreement, division, and paralysis to insecure groups.

Another fear of consequences concerns anticipated reactions of the leader to solutions derived by the group. Realistically, any group must consider not only the objective implications of its problem solutions but also the way the leader will receive its recommendations. A confident and united group will encounter no problem in this regard. Its relations with the leader will enable recommendations to be made with confidence that they will be judged solely on their merits. A poorly functioning group, however, is likely to be unclear as to the expectations of the leader, and its operating effectiveness may be seriously impeded by fear of the possible consequences. The emotions generated by such anxieties interfere with the productive work of individuals and, more seriously, they impede coordination and agreements. Each person is so concerned with protecting himself that cooperation becomes difficult.

The working atmosphere within a group may exert potent influence upon both individual and group performance. Where the atmosphere is one of confidence, good will, and optimism, work will be harmonious and efficient. However, where the climate is filled with distrust and insecurity, disagreements and inferior performance may be the principal results.

The major determinant in the creation of a constructive environment is the behavior of the leader. Those leaders who are most successful at developing effective groups create conditions that enable their members to maintain a sense of both personal security and personal worth. In brief, the basic conditions necessary for a sense of personal security are a climate of trust and approval; knowledge of role, what is expected of an individual and how well he is living up to these expectations; and consistent support and discipline, both in the form of backing when a person is right and in the form of correction when he is wrong.

A sense of personal worth rests on the base of personal security. However, in responsible individuals, it also requires (in addition to security) opportunity to participate in the solution of meaningful and worthwhile problems, opportunity to discuss decisions that may affect them, opportunity to assume responsibility when one is ready for it, and the right to appeal.

Effective managers lead their groups in such a way that there is no threat to the self-esteem of members. An effective leader develops a constructive environment by instilling feelings of security and personal worth among his personnel.

Group Member Interdependence. Effective group functioning requires that each member has sufficient ability to handle his responsibilities and that he has sufficient maturity and skill to promote satisfactory relationships with other members. In addition, he must have sufficient motivation to fulfill his responsibilities.

In considering motivation for group problem solving, the most significant point is that each individual not only works in close proximity to others, he also works with them on common tasks. Typically, in generating plans and solving operational problems, he and his associates work toward a single solution or end product. In short, there exists a group objective and most group members work in a relationship where success or progress by one person contributes toward progress by the entire group toward its objective. This relationship fosters the development of interdependence.

In an organization whose work does not require interdependence or cooperation, subordinates are dependent solely upon the leader for decisions, assignments, objectives, rewards, punishments, and directives regarding most critical actions of the group. The members exert relatively little influence upon one another. But, in group work, cooperation is essential. As people work with and learn from one another, they begin to see one another as resources and as people upon whom one can depend for support. As group members become aware of their associates as resources, a role system develops. Certain stabilities appear with regard to preferences for whom to contact in the different sections. Preferences begin to develop for those individuals who find it easy to initiate action and to propose ideas acceptable to the group. Consistencies occur in patterns of influence, patterns of talk, and patterns of viewpoint. As members develop interdependencies, the group begins to function as a team.

Some indicators of dependence and lack of cooperation in operating groups are the following:

1. overdomination by one or more favored members;
2. dependence upon certain members always to initiate ideas or actions;
3. nonparticipation among the majority of the group during conferences or problem discussions;

4. covert resistance to the leader or other members; and

5. disruption and breakdown of communication within the group.

Some indicators of the development of cooperation and interdependence are

1. spontaneous interaction and communication between members;

2. sharing of leadership or initiative among members of equal status;

3. high commitment to agreements made by members;

4. strong feelings of member responsibility toward group actions and recommendations; and

5. a feeling of ease and comfort in group conferences and in relations with the leader.

Standards of Behavior. As a group continues to work together, an observer can note the rise of what appear to be shared expectations concerning what members should do, perhaps even what they should think and how they should feel. These standards of behavior become stabilized over time and become powerful determinants of the behavior of group members: As a member becomes inducted into the life of a group, he will become increasingly aware of forces that tell him how to deal with the leader, how to get prestige from other group members, how to get rewarded by the leader, how to prepare presentations, how to conduct a staff study in the preferred way, and so forth.

Behavioral standards can and should cover a variety of work situations. For example, standards may be set regarding expected levels of group performance, mutual concern for overall performance, degree of member concern for the effectiveness of procedures, appropriateness of reactions to others' work products, methods of giving and receiving assistance, the extent to which information should be coordinated among members, and so forth.

Members of a group may be more or less aware of the standards that influence them. For example, in one group there may be a great deal of surprisingly accurate talk among members as to various and subtle ways of influencing the leader in his decisions. In another group, members may be almost completely unaware of the effects of their behavior in contacts with the leaders. For a behavioral standard to be an effective determinant of behavior, there must be some degree of awareness of it. This awareness develops through communication.

All groups set standards affecting the behavior of members. However, too frequently, standards about work evolve informally and are uncontrolled by leaders. Uncontrolled standards may be unfavorable to group effectiveness. For example, a few hostile or insecure members having influence with other members can very rapidly develop standards for mediocre performance. Under such conditions, efforts of the leader to set high performance goals for the group and to support them with extrinsic reward and punishment systems will be only partially successful. At best, the result will be a continued clash between the organization's goals and group standards. If a leader hopes to effectively exercise influence upon his group, he must understand and, to some extent, control the way standards develop among its members.

The Communication System. One of the more important factors in effective group functioning is the communication system. Poor communication is a symptom of all the other problems encountered by people in their attempts to work together. An individual's attitudes and his motivations determine his verbal and nonverbal communication with others. Conversely, the amount and kind of communication he receives from others will partially determine his viewpoints and his motivations with regard to his duties, other members, and the work problems. Thus, the content and distribution of communication within a group has important implications for its functioning (Reid and Hammersley, 2000). For example, it is difficult to build cooperation if 90 percent of the total communication within the group takes place between the leader and individual members on a private basis. Perception of consensus deriving from communication between group members tends to increase involvement in problems and gives the communicators some stake in the final product. Furthermore, communication exposes ideas to more public scrutiny and provides the group as a whole with more complete information relative to work problems.

As a group matures and learns to work as a problem-solving team and as it develops interdependence, members begin to communicate with each other easily and well. When members have little need to defend themselves and when they feel sufficiently secure to freely expose their ideas and viewpoints to others, the communication level in the group is becoming deep enough to permit the development of a valid team spirit.

Coordination. An efficient system of coordination is a necessary condition for effective group functioning. Within that system, there is the necessity for using both formal and informal methods. Sole reliance upon formal procedures makes group operations overly cumbersome and slow. Consequently, these formal methods must be supplemented by informal coordination. On the other hand, overreliance upon informal procedures usually results in confusion and inability to tell what has actually occurred in the handling of a problem. Some middle ground seems to be the most desirable.

Either lack of coordination or overcoordination can create problems within a group. Lack of coordination results in duplication of effort, failure to use all available resources in solving problems, and loose ends—

failure to consider all relevant factors in making decisions. Furthermore, lack of coordination tends to produce in the individual group member a feeling of isolation, of being out of touch, of loss of group support.

On the other hand, overcoordination results in the member feeling overburdened, under pressure, bogged down in paper work or conferences. Overcoordination results from much the same factors as undercoordination—a lack of knowledge of whom to communicate with and a lack of systematic procedures for monitoring the communication channels to see that they do not become clogged with irrelevant information. The principal difference between these two kinds of difficulties is that undercoordination most likely develops from a motivation to get things done in a hurry or a lack of motivation to work cooperatively in a group setting. Overcoordination is more likely to result from a desire to play it safe—the feeling that if you miss anything, you'll miss everything—and inability to delegate authority.

Interpersonal Relations. There is in everyday experience considerable evidence that a leader and his group can all be capable individuals with histories of successful performance in different organizations and yet be unable to work together effectively. The fact that a set of individually capable and well-trained people may not necessarily form an effective group points to the importance of interpersonal relations as a factor in group performance.

Positive relationships may lead to better communication and wider interaction between group members. In a group composed of friends, it would be expected that communication channels would be more open and more numerous. This, in turn, would be expected to exert facilitative effects on problem solving because it might lead to greater interchange of viewpoints and information and to more wide-spread contributions to problem solutions. In addition, the sense of mutual support and the active cooperation created by friendly relations will enable the group to deal more confidently with its tasks and with the environment, including the leader.

In all groups, personal differences occur. In the give-and-take of group work, differences can occur that provoke feelings that may be either momentary or relatively enduring. Some of these differences serve useful functions, others can be highly destructive. One problem for the leader of a group is to identify those that are destructive to unity and to cope with them in such a manner that their negative effects will be dissipated.

Differences over both objectives and the means for accomplishment of objectives are inevitable and healthy as part of the decision-making process. A decision usually means a choice between alternatives. If the choice were simple and clear-cut, there would be little need for joint effort. Accordingly, differences concerning the basic issues and the means for tackling them are desirable when they occur prior to the time a decision is made. After such time, of course, the effective group closes ranks to execute the decision regardless of its nature.

The opportunity for predecision differences to be brought into the open should be protected. To be highly effective, a group should always strive to maintain itself as a forum where all sides of important issues can be examined. The problem is to recognize and accept valid differences of opinion and to recognize as more destructive the conflict that springs from interpersonal hostility. The first kind of difference can be healthy and strengthening. The second is destructive of cohesiveness and team spirit and leads toward poor and uncoordinated staff work. Here is a point where leadership can play a crucial role. Unless personal conflict can be dissipated and gradually turned toward more productive effort, not only the present task of the group but future undertakings may be endangered.

Personal conflict does not remain dormant. If it persists, the hostility between the central individuals will be increased. In turn, they are likely to search for allies among other members. Before long, the group can be split into hostile camps with all individuals forced to choose sides, even though they may really want neither side. Even if division of the group does not occur, personal conflict among the few individuals may grow until every undertaking becomes distorted by it. Nonfighting members, feeling dominated by the conflict of which they are not a part, may become apathetic. Thus, a team effort is turned into a perpetual war.

Whether differences are concerned with genuine issues or with personal conflict, it serves no purpose to bury them or ignore their existence. A more effective approach is to try to develop a climate where differences on issues are welcomed as part of the problem-solving process and where personal hostility can be recognized and dealt with as seems most appropriate.

A somewhat less dramatic, but equally troublesome, problem in interpersonal relations occurs as the result of conflicting loyalties arising from the various other groups to which members may belong. Each individual is a member of the central group. However, each may also be a member of his own department. This membership in various groups can create problems of divided loyalties. The way each member acts as he works with other group members may be partly determined by loyalty to his own department and only partially by the objective issues facing the present group. If the common problem deeply concerns his department, two important questions arise for him: What will the members of my department think of me when they learn of our decision here? and What position do, or would, the members of my department want me to take on this issue?

Such conflicts are inevitable in problem-solving groups, but they are not without solution. The best solution is to develop a climate within the group where it can be publicly recognized that each member is naturally concerned with the interests of his own department while still remaining loyal to the leader and the overall group. In such an atmosphere, each individual who bridges two groups can realistically test whether differences are genuinely deep or merely surface problems that can be compromised.

Many successful groups develop an awareness of the importance of interpersonal relations and exhibit much initiative in developing constructive relationships among the members. However, in addition, the leader must be able to encourage cooperative relationships among members, to recognize conflicts when they occur, and to deal with these conflicts appropriately (Bellin, 1998; Tyler and Blader, 2000).

LEADING OPERATING GROUPS

Given the complexities of group functioning, leadership assumes particular significance. In general, the leader of an operating group has to persuade its members to move simultaneously in two contrary directions. He has to ensure the intricate coordination necessary to establish and maintain effective procedures and routines. He must also stimulate the ideas and imaginativeness that are the life of good group work but that are often disturbing to routine. Where the two can be successfully blended, a strong and effective group will be the most probable result (Beckhard, 1972; Bellin, 1996).

For operating groups, problem solving is a primary endeavor. Where problem solving is considered to involve collecting information, analyzing it, selecting alternatives, and coordinating the actions that follow decisions, task forces, operating staffs, and high-level decision making groups are clearly problem-solving groups, even though the actual decision that finally resolves the problem may be made by one person— the leader. This is best exemplified by the concept of *completed staff work* where, ideally, the staff studies a problem, evolves a single recommended solution, and presents it to the leader, who then has only to approve or disapprove the solution.

Underlying these activities is a single, unified process, which, for want of a better term, is simply a shorthand way of stating that the members of a group have confronted and solved a common problem. In brief, group problem solving involves the *psychological* and *social* processes whereby individual solutions are created, communicated, and eventually assembled into a product that represents the group.

The most important single factor affecting group functioning is the character and competence of that person who serves in an actual leadership capacity. It is clear that the leader, by actions and through explicit policy, is able either to promote or limit performance of the group members and, thus, he exercises great influence upon group effectiveness.

The leader of a group must be able to hear the music as well as the words in group behavior. In addition to the technical and procedural aspects of group work, the effective leader must be aware of the less tangible, but equally important, social and interpersonal influences that affect performance. Furthermore, he must be adept at exploiting these factors for greater group effectiveness.

Several aspects of leadership are especially relevant. First, group work usually involves the continual exploration and reformulation of problems. All activities cannot be planned to the smallest detail with absolute certainty because no one can ever be sure of all the factors that may become involved as an operation proceeds. Therefore, activities often have to be studied or planned on the basis of less than complete information or in anticipation of many possible eventualities, some or all of which may or may not ever occur. Even to select the particular facts that are relevant from all the data that are available is no easy matter. Much of group work involves exploring a wide range of data to find possible alternatives that will yield desirable consequences.

Much of the dislike that some people have for operating group work is due to the inability of these individuals to tolerate the necessary uncertainty about recommended actions. If a person's confidence requires that a proposed action be the only right action, then he is on thin ice, indeed, in high-level group work. Even for those personnel who are able to tolerate ambiguity, the instability of the conditions with which groups must deal can sometimes make life difficult. One important function of group leadership is to guide this exploring process. By providing structure in the form of guidance and problem definition, the leader keeps ambiguities to a minimum.

A second leadership function involves the provision of appropriate methodological assistance as needed by the group. The leader may suggest relevant concepts, and techniques that will aid in problem solution. In addition, he must guide the group along lines that will provide a happy compromise between the procedural rigidity and laxity that can develop in connection with coordination. Failure to provide this methodological help may be a genuine source of unsuccessful group functioning.

A third function of group leadership involves the discovery and coordination of member resources. Attention must be paid to finding and maintaining conditions that will enable each person who can make a needed contribution to make it. This function requires awareness of the different abilities that people can bring to bear on problems. It also requires defining members' assignments in each undertaking in such a way that the most useful people will feel most called upon to contribute. In this connection, a leader may encounter difficulty if he does not make himself aware of the motivations and behavioral standards of his particular group.

These statements concerning the functions of group leadership are presented as a general introduction to the problem. It will be worthwhile, however, to discuss in some detail just how these general functions may be performed. It is helpful to think of the problem as one of analyzing the factors that inhibit cooperative performance and the ones that help it. These factors were examined earlier. From them, it is possible to derive several principles of group leadership that may be applied to a variety of situations.

Principle one. The effective group has a leadership climate conducive to effective performance and is so organized as to permit maximum contribution by all members.

In general, anything that contributes to insecurity or feelings of threat on the part of members will tend to reduce effectiveness. For instance, if, in contacts with group members, the leader communicates attitudes of distrust, hostility, or lack of confidence, joint performance will not be effective, because the members will be too busy protecting themselves. Similarly, people who, because of insecurity, are forced into yes-man roles with leaders do not contribute to the best group performance.

Opportunities to contribute, to be heard, to be an active member of an important organization are opportunities that most people like. Consequently, leaders who provide such opportunities tend to develop groups that display greater cohesiveness, higher morale, and greater involvement in the work. On the other hand, membership in a group where one's contributions are negligible and where members feel threatened and insecure can be frustrating. The performance of the group will suffer accordingly.

Principle two. The effective operating group is so organized and led as to permit maximum interaction between the members.

It is probably true that the greatest barriers to effective group problem solving and performance are interpersonal—emotional relationships between people who feel threatened in some way by the presence of other people whom they dislike or whom they do not understand (Ashkanasy, Hartel, and Zerbb, 2000). Pleasant relationships reduce threat and permit members to shift their attention from interpersonal problems to work objectives.

In any group, there is, initially, a certain amount of jockeying for position among the members who are trying to appraise one another. Each wants to know how he can best relate to the others and what to expect from them. Each person wants to learn the status system in this particular group and, if possible, to influence it in his individual favor. Each person needs to feel the others out, to discover whether it is safe to talk freely, to openly express new ideas or genuine feelings about the group and its work. Each person usually affiliates with a few other compatible individuals and, from those affiliations, definite cliques may emerge. Each individual needs to learn what the leader is like for the purpose of determining how best to relate to him.

The effective leader recognizes that all of this is neither good nor bad. Rather, it is inevitable. Therefore, he tries to channel the process in such a way that it will least interfere with the group's functioning. He organizes the work so that the fact of a common task to accomplish gives personnel valid reasons for interacting. He coordinates activities in such a way that members have adequate opportunities to consult on problems. He ensures participation in a wide range of assignments so that various members get a chance to know each other well.

Here, the real problem is the integration of individual motives with group objectives. The problem is not so much whether individual motives differ or conflict with the objectives of the whole group—they usually do to some degree—but whether the group is able to resolve such differences. Most research suggests that groups whose members can communicate with one another will probably proceed to resolve differences and, thus, simplify the accomplishment of common objectives. Difficulties are encountered in groups where, for whatever the reason, individuals cannot communicate with each other.

When a group is so organized that some of its members are communicationally peripheral to others—that is, when a particular person is out on the fringe, perhaps communicating regularly with only one other member—these particular individuals are likely to become disheartened, frustrated, and unproductive. And a group that is organized so that contacts between all members are restricted is not likely to become very effective.

Efficiency in problem solving and performance increases with increased communication. It is often possible to get increased communication through appropriate design of the group's coordination procedures and through establishing an atmosphere of informality in contacts both within and outside the group.

Principle three. Explicit formulation of objectives increases group cohesion and member involvement with group missions.

A group's operating effectiveness improves when the group's objective is clearly understood and accepted by all the members. This is obvious. Yet, it is surprising how easily a leader can think he has communicated objectives adequately when he has failed utterly to do so. Because of such failures, groups sometimes are forced to spend many useless hours discussing the leader's real desires, speculating about purposes, and attempting to reformulate assignments into manageable problems. Although necessary, such activities may cause members to lose involvement with unit problems. A major consequence of loss of involvement is conflict, which results in reduction of cohesion within the group.

On the other hand, when leaders explicitly formulate objectives or problems, clearly indicate necessary activities, and designate desired outcomes, cohesion and high member involvement are likely to be the results.

Principle four. Provision of clear policies and procedures reduces uncertainty; but these guides to action should be kept flexible.

One of the principal sources of frustration in group operations is uncertainty—uncertainty of objective, uncertainty of progress, uncertainty about the appropriateness of projected actions. Clarification of areas of uncertainty through provision of guidelines in the form of policies and procedures can be expected to contribute to more effective functioning.

Policies and procedures should be provided routinely. Furthermore, at the beginning of each new undertaking, it should be determined whether special guidelines or limits should be imposed for the duration of that operation.

On the other hand, the leader must be ready to discuss and modify existing policies and procedures if this becomes necessary to meet the new demands of changing situations. *The crux of effective group functioning is flexibility—the provision for change when change is needed.* Many aspects of group work can be controlled through procedure, but it is highly important that the procedures do not get in the way of operations. Procedures should exist to help the group to function and not to hinder it. Thus, policies and procedures cannot be regarded as sacred. They should be looked upon as tentative guides to be modified when needs arise.

Principle five. Close coordination is a necessary condition for effective group functioning.

The purpose of coordination is to keep the group working on tasks in a reasonably objective and rational way. By coordination is meant the mobilization of members' activities in such a way that the group moves toward its objectives without lost motion and wasted effort. This is achieved by the continual modification and channeling of activities to meet the changing needs of the problem situation.

Effective groups have been found to use some of the following more or less formal coordination procedures:

(a) regular staff meetings in which there is an orderly and systematic procedure for review of current work and for discussion of new problems;

(b) use of coordination sheets or routing slips indicating with whom a staff paper should be coordinated and with whom it has been coordinated;

(c) assignment to a specific project officer of direct responsibility for coordination of a project with appropriate group members;

(d) constant monitoring of the coordination process by the leader or a deputy to ensure that there are no mix-ups;

(e) special conferences among relevant personnel whenever special problems arise; and

(f) daily diaries of ongoing activities.

IMPLICATIONS

From the standpoint of a leader, the effective direction and stimulation of group performance requires a blend of commitment, understanding, and determination. These elements come together to produce the skills a leader must use in obtaining the results needed to accomplish the group's missions.

Excellence as an operational ideal requires that the leader of an operating group be a realist. Just as with technical problems, the fundamental consideration in leading a group has to be results. Accordingly, those actions taken to improve or maintain group performance can be evaluated only in terms of the final consequences they evoke. This emphasis upon final consequences deserves more than casual consideration in any study of high-level group leadership. One of the major responsibilities of the skillful leader is the avoidance of opportunism. The term *opportunism* refers to the pursuit of immediate, short-run advantages in a way inadequately controlled by considerations of principle and ultimate consequences. It is good to take advantage of opportunities, but a leader must look to the long-run effects of his actions instead of present advantage alone.

This is nowhere more relevant than in attempts to direct and stimulate a group's performance. Where, on first impulse, a leader may be tempted to take rapid and direct action in order to immediately correct a group's direction, consideration of the ultimate consequences of such action may lead to the conclusion that more deliberate and careful direction will produce infinitely greater benefits in terms of performance. The leader's job is to get results from his group, and only those actions can be correct that, *in the long-run*, lead to the best performance of the group.

Chapter 6

Groups in Action

Whatever its mission, the effectiveness of an organization depends upon its ability (1) to assess realistically the operational situation with which it is confronted and (2) to adapt flexibly to the requirements of these situations. These are the classical functions of all organizations, and performance of them has always been essential for organizational success.

After years of research (Olmstead, 2002), it is now clear that functional proficiency and the integration of command and control systems play very important roles in the performance of all groups and organizations. This is especially true for organizations and groups whose purposes are to cope with and overcome emergencies and crisis situations. Such organizations and groups include (1) police teams (swat teams, riot squads, disaster control teams), (2) fire department companies, (3) medical emergency and disaster teams, and (4) military teams of varying types. It should be noted that a military tactical unit (ground, naval, air) is the example *par excellence* of a crisis-management organization. Accordingly, this discussion applies to both civilian and military organizations.

In this chapter, an analysis of crisis-management teams and organizations will be used to illustrate some of the more important aspects of group performance as applied to real-life situations.

CHARACTERISTICS OF PRESENT-DAY CRISES

- A loaded oil tanker hits an Alaskan reef. It takes 48 hours for the first company damage-control personnel to reach the scene of the accident.
- Hurricane Hugo approaches the coast of South Carolina and aims directly for the city of Charleston. Three days ahead of the predicted landfall, the governor

orders 100 percent evacuation of coastal areas and strictly enforces the order. Accordingly, despite enormous damage to property, prompt and decisive action by the governor's office resulted in only 17 fatalities in remote rural areas.

• Organized state emergency relief personnel did not reach the devastated areas until three days after Hugo passed, and FEMA (U.S. Government) personnel did not begin activities until three weeks later.

• Seven cars of an AMTRAC passenger train jumped the track near a southern suburban community, resulting in numerous casualties and eight fatalities. It took rescue personnel 28 minutes to reach the wreck, despite the fact that it occurred within sight of a large plant of a major chemical company. Local emergency personnel were finally notified by a telephone call from an AMTRAC dispatcher in Jacksonville, Florida, who had learned about the wreck by radio from the train crew.

• A small private airplane crashed in the outskirts of a medium-sized, city, damaging three occupied houses. Responding to "911," the first ambulance arrived within 8 minutes, but fire and police units did not arrive not arrive until 22 minutes after notification. Two fatalities occurred in the airplane, one fatality and three injuries occurred in burning houses.

Each of the above events was a crisis demanding the organized efforts of numbers of people for its control. Outcomes varied, depending upon the capabilities of responsible organizations to assess a situation and its requirements, make decisions about appropriate responses, and execute the required activities.

Present-day crises are most often characterized by

1. highly unpredictable events preceding and during the crisis,
2. increasing rapidity of critical events,
3. increasingly complex operations required to cope with threatening events and their results, and
4. high levels of turbulence within both the environment and the organization.

The necessity for coping with highly turbulent, complex environments and unpredictable events places a premium upon the capabilities of crisis-management organizations to address and respond flexibly to a more or less constant flow of new situations characterized by high levels of uncertainty. The ability of such organizations to cope with crises effectively is the outstanding indicator of their capabilities.

Ideally, the process for organizations to cope with uncertainty situations involves handling an operational cycle that flows up and down the chain-of-authority and consists of situation—information—decision—action—altered situation—new information—supplementary decision— and so on. Through its command and control function, the organization seeks to regulate this cycle without becoming inflexible in its responses.

In practice, however, the operational cycle is not usually so straightforward as described above. For one thing, although the logical starting point for the cycle should always be a specific situation, there are, in reality, no concrete boundaries for many situations. Thus, situations may overlap, or one may flow into another. Furthermore, there is no specific mechanism for recognizing a situation. Sometimes, information will reveal a situation. Sometimes, action taken in one situation creates another situation elsewhere. Frequently, one organizational level, by decision or action, creates a situation for another higher or lower level. Thus, the cycle tends to operate erratically.

In addition, the process whereby information, decisions, and actions are brought into conjunction involves a complex interplay between and among levels. For example, as information flows upward in the chain of authority, parts are siphoned off and bits are added. The flow of directives downward is similarly affected. At the same time, decisions and actions from intervening levels enter into the flow of information and directives.

This constant interplay that occurs is the essence of dynamic organizational process, and the extent to which it is dealt with competently is a major determinant of organizational effectiveness. The ability to control and direct the processes that drive an organization determines, in large part, the capability of the organization for coping with the pressures imposed by operational environments.

To be effective under such conditions, organizations must possess capabilities to

1. search out, accurately identify, and correctly interpret the properties of operational situations as *they* develop;
2. solve problems *as they occur* within the context of rapidly changing situational demands;
3. generate *flexible* decisions relevant to changing situation; and
4. cope with *shifting situational demands* with precise appropriateness.

The necessity for flexible, unified responses to changing events creates some major difficulties for many organizations. Some general problems or areas of difficulties encountered by many organizations follow;

1. *Failure of the organization to sense changes in the environment and/or incorrectly interpret what is happening.* This problem is clearly concerned with failure of the organization to obtain all relevant and current information and to apply the correct meaning to the information obtained.
2. *Failure to communicate all relevant information to those parts of the organization that can act upon it or use it.* This potential failure refers to both the upward and downward communication of information. No organization can adapt to

changes effectively and rapidly without continuous updating of information about the ongoing situation and of operational requirements.

3. *Failure of the headquarters staff to ensure that all personnel and smaller units make the changes and adjustments indicated by new information or changed plans.* Research has shown that obtaining internal change in an organization requires more than merely the recognition or the announcement that such changes are necessary. A major omission is failure of a headquarters staff to oversee and verify the implementation of required changes during ongoing operations.

4. *Failure to consider the impact of changes upon all parts of the organization and failure to obtain information about the effects of changes.* The pitfall is failure to follow-up on the effects of actions taken so that everyone in the organization can learn from the results.

The above are common pitfalls that may occur in all types of organizations. They were presented here to demonstrate that many of the problems that are encountered are not the results of individual errors or bad judgment, or of poor execution, but, rather, their sources may lie in deficient organizational functioning—in failure of the organization, as a system, to adequately perform the problem-solving, decision-making, action-taking functions that are common to all organizations but take specific forms within particular types, for example, crisis-management organizations. These functions are essential for developing the unified systems necessary for coping with the intensive pressures and problems encountered by emergency organizations.

This emphasis upon organizational responses to complex problem situations points up the importance of *the organization* as problem solver, decision maker, and action taker. Although individual members may actually perform the problem-solving and decision-making activities, either singly or jointly, the necessity for global organizational responses makes it useful to conceive of the organization as a problem-solving and decision-making unit. Thinking of actions as the product of an organization rather than of individuals makes it possible to analyze situations more understandably and consequently to develop more effective means of coping with problem environments.

ORGANIZATIONAL ATTRIBUTES

Over the past 50 years, extensive research has identified certain attributes that constitute the underpinnings for organizational effectiveness (Olmstead, 2002). In summary, to be successful, every organization needs three basic attributes:

1. *Reality Assessment*—the capability to accurately assess the reality of situations facing the organization—the ability of the organization to search out, accu-

rately perceive, and correctly interpret the properties and characteristics of its environments (both external and internal), particularly those properties that have special relevance for the missions and operations of the organization. In short, every organization must have the capability for accurately determining the real conditions within its important environments. "Real" refers to the way conditions are—not how they are supposed to be nor how they are desired to be.

To survive and succeed, every organization must have structures and processes that will enable it to assess the current reality demands of its particular environments.

2. *Adaptability*—The capability for solving problems that arise from changing environmental demands and for acting with flexibility in response to the changing demands.

To survive and succeed, each organization must have structures and processes that will enable it to mobilize the necessary and appropriate resources for adapting to changes in its environments and to act so as to overcome such changes.

3. *Integration*—the maintenance of structure and function under stress and maintenance of a state of relations among sub-units that will ensure that coordination is maintained and the various sub-units do not work at cross purposes.

Integration derives from a sense of identity and, in order to develop and maintain integration, organizational members must possess knowledge, insight, and a reasonable consensus regarding organizational objectives, missions, and the functions necessary for the accomplishment of missions and objectives.

Components of Organizational Competence

In the research, there was also derived from the attributes a set of organizational processes that have been verified as major determinants of effectiveness. Taken together, the set of processes has been subsumed under the rubric *Organizational Competence.*

Organizational competence is analogous to another term *Functional Competence,* which refers to the quality of performance, that is, how well an organism performs the critical, or essential, functions required for the organism to be effective.

The term *function* is the general term for the natural activity of a person or thing that is required in order to accomplish its created or designated purpose. Organizational functions are the activities of an organization that *must be performed* if the organization is to accomplish its purposes.

In open systems approaches to organizations, organizational functions are called *processes*—because they occur over time and their beginnings and ends may sometimes be difficult to identify. The specific nature of a process and the way it must be executed may differ with type, purpose, mission, and objective of the organization. However, it can be concluded with high confidence that the seven basic processes described in the following section apply, in some form, to every organization, regardless of its type.

Organizational Competence refers to the capability of an organization to function as a unified system in order to cope with complex conditions in the present-day world. It is concerned with the quality of system functions (processes) that are critical for the effectiveness of organizations.

Organizational competence is a major operational determinant of organizational effectiveness. Where effectiveness is the ultimate outcome (mission accomplishment, achievement of objectives, productivity, etc.), competence is the capability of the organization to perform those critical functions (processes) that lead to effectiveness.

Competence depends upon the skills of individual personnel in acquiring and interpreting information; making choices concerning to whom acquired information is to be communicated, accurately and completely; making decisions concerning ways to cope with unusual or unanticipated situations; and executing actions deriving from such decisions—all performed at high levels of proficiency and coordination. Although some technological assists may be available, such as data processing equipment and highly sophisticated communication devices, the payoff in competence ultimately reduces to the judgments and actions of operating personnel.

Of equal importance, the performance of organizational processes is a team product, and much of the quality of process performance depends upon teamwork and the coordination of separate responsibilities and activities. Accordingly, equal to the skills of individuals is what is termed here as "the integration of structure and function." This means that the positions, roles, and functions that make up an organizational system must fit together and support each other in their respective activities. Where the integration of structure and function does not occur, the result may be missed signals, aborted decisions, overlooked information, and activities at cross purposes. In the extreme, loss of integration may produce a collapse of essential functions, which can threaten survival of the organization.

In a series of studies conducted in both simulated and operational settings, seven organizational functions, or processes, were found to be critical to organizational competence and, therefore, to effectiveness. The organizational processes found to be critical include most of the functions performed by command and control personnel in any organization. Stated in general terms, the processes are

1. *Sensing*—The acquisition of information concerning the environments, both external and internal to the organization, that are significant for the effective accomplishment of objectives. Examples of significant external environments are the economy, the competition, higher organizational levels, adjacent departments, weather, and so forth. The specific character of sensing activities that may be required can differ according to the type of organization, its mis-

sion, and the particular environments that are significant to it. However, whatever their specific nature, all sensing activities involve seeking, receiving, acquiring, processing, and interpreting information. They are those activities through which an organization obtains as accurate an understanding as possible of all of the environments in which it must function and of the requirements that must be met in order for it to accomplish its mission.

2. *Communicating Information*—those activities whereby information that has been sensed is transmitted within the organization to those individuals who should know about it or act upon it. This process involves both the initial transmission of information by those who have sensed it originally and the dissemination of the information throughout the organization to those individuals who need it for effective performance of their duties. Most important, the process also includes "discussion and interpretation"—those communicative acts through which the members of an organization attempt to clarify information and its meaning and to determine the implications of the information.

3. *Decision Making*—the deliberative acts of one or more persons that lead to a conclusion that some action should be taken by the organization. The decision-making process is not limited to those important decisions made by a manager, but, rather, it includes all decisions, however large or small, made by any member of the organization, if they impact upon activities. Decisions also include conclusions that actions should not be taken.

4. *Stabilizing*—those actions intended to maintain organizational stability or unit integrity or to prevent internal disruptions and negative side effects that might result from on-going actions or changes in such actions; also actions intended to adjust procedures or internal activities so as to accommodate changes in mission-related activities. The purpose is to maintain internal structure and function.

5. *Communicating Implementation*—those activities through which decisions and the requirements resulting from decisions are communicated to those individuals or units who must implement the decisions. In addition to the straightforward transmission of directives, plans, orders, and instructions, the process includes "discussion and interpretation"—those two-way communicative acts through which clarification of requirements is achieved and implications for actions are discussed. Of particular importance in the process are the activities of linking individuals, who relay instructions between the original decision maker and personnel who ultimately implement the decision.

6. *Coping Actions*—those actions through which an organization copes with its environments and with changes therein. Activities involve direct execution of actions against target environments. This process is primarily concerned with the actual execution of actions at points of contact with the target environments and with how such actions are carried out.

7. *Feedback*—those activities of the organization intended to provide it with information about the results and outcomes of actions taken so that the organization can learn from its successes and mistakes and adjust future activities accordingly.

For any particular problem, event, or situation, the seven processes are conceived to occur in the sequence shown above. The sequence is called the "Adaptive-Coping Cycle." Thus, when a problem arises or a change occurs in the environment, the organization first must sense the problem or change, followed by communication of the sensed information, making of decisions concerning how to cope with the problem or change, and so on through the cycle.

Of course, in actual practice, the cycle is not always so clear cut or straightforward. It tends to operate erratically, with much redundancy and backtracking at many points. Nevertheless, there is considerable evidence that processes that occur later in the cycle are dependent upon the quality of those that occur earlier; for example, the quality of decisions depends upon the amount and quality of information available to decision makers—upon the amount and quality of information that has been sensed by various elements of the organization and communicated to decision makers. Similarly, the quality of actions taken to cope with the environment depends upon the character of earlier decisions and the communication used to obtain implementation. This leads to the obvious conclusion that maximum effectiveness requires that all processes be performed equally well. It also means that the correction of dysfunctional processes will result in improvement in overall process performance and, therefore, will contribute to improved effectiveness.

INDICATORS OF QUALITY

Competence is concerned with the quality of process performance within an organization. Although each process must be performed at least to a minimal degree, the frequency with which the processes are performed is not a determinant of effectiveness. The critical requirement is quality, that is, *how well the processes are performed*. The following criteria illustrate the qualitative requirements of each process:

1. *Sensing*
   (a) accurate detection of all available information, including active seeking of information from higher and lower levels as well as all that may be available elsewhere
   (b) correct interpretation of all detected information
   (c) accurate discrimination between relevant and irrelevant information
   (d) relevance to mission, task, or problem of all attempts to obtain information
   (e) accurate and relevant processing of acquired information

2. *Communicating Information*
   (a) accurate transmission of relevant information
   (b) sufficient completeness in transmission to achieve full and adequate understanding by recipient

    (c) timely transmission of information

    (d) correct determination of whether information should be transmitted

    (e) transmission to appropriate recipients

3. *Decision Making*

    (a) timeliness of decisions in view of available information

    (b) correctness of decisions in view of circumstances and of available information

    (c) consideration in the decision process of all contengencies, alternatives, and possibilities

4. *Communicating Implementation*

    (a) accurate transmission of directives, orders, and instructions

    (b) transmission to appropriate recipient

    (c) sufficient completeness to communicate adequate and full understanding of actions required

    (d) timely transmission of directives, orders, and instructions in view of both available information and the action requirements of recipients

5. *Actions: Stabilizing, Coping, and Feedback*

    (a) correctness of action in view of both the operational circumstances and the decision or order from which the action derives

    (b) timeliness of the action in view of both the current circumstances and the decision or order from which the action derives

    (c) correctness of choice of target for the action

    (d) adequacy of execution of the action

The organizational processes that have been discussed constitute a basic framework for analyzing some of the more intangible but exceedingly important aspects of organizational performance. Use of the framework makes it possible to

1. assess the quality of performance of parts or entire organizations;

2. identify processes that are dysfunctional or poorly performed;

3. identify strengths and weaknesses in organization or unit process performance and determine sources of deficiencies;

4. identify individuals, groups, or units in which process performance requires improvement; and

5. in general, assess organizational performance in a manner that produces sound and credible bases for feedback or training.

Similarly, the framework provides a credible basis for clarifying roles and developing teamwork within organizations or unit staff.

IMPROVING ORGANIZATIONAL COMPETENCE

Organizational competence and its integral concepts provide bases for a working framework, or model, which can be used for (1) analyzing the functional competence of an organization and its critical parts; (2) for identifying dysfunctional elements; and (3) for improving an organization's functioning through assessment, development, and training.

The problem for executives and other leaders is to make both managers and operating personnel strongly aware of the importance of organizational functions, highly sensitive to the necessity for effective performance of the processes, and proficient in their execution. In short, *the performance of required organizational functions should be as much a part of a manager's repertoire as any other aspect of his technical performance.*

Although it is not proposed as a panacea, organizational competence plays a major role in the performance of organizations. Accordingly, it warrants major attention in efforts to improve effectiveness.

The conceptual model of organizational competence and operational definitions of the several competence processes offer sound bases for enhancing organizational effectiveness through several ways of improving competence.

The best ways of improving competence are

1. organizational analysis and assessment,
2. organizational design, and
3. development and training.

Organizational Analysis and Assessment

The processes subsumed under organizational competence offer potential for the assessment and diagnosis of organizational functioning and for the correction of dysfunctional elements. For example, it is possible to specify which individuals, positions, or organizational units should perform each process. Such specification will enable the development of operating techniques and training uniquely designed to enhance performance of each process by each individual or unit.

It is possible also to evaluate positions, individuals, and units in terms of how well the processes are performed during daily operations or in training simulations, thus permitting identification of points within the organization that are functional or dysfunctional according to the quality of their process performances. Identification of dysfunctional points can lead to corrective action, retraining, or modification of the duties or roles of a position.

Finally, the elements of competence provide a workable framework for periodic self-assessment by an organization or its sub-units. Training exercises followed by process-centered after-action reviews, critique, and self-assessment by an organization will greatly enhance its competence.

Once a particular process has been identified as dysfunctional, or poorly performed, it will then be possible to analyze specific performances related to the process, where corrective action will be required. For example, if an assessment indicates that coping actions are dysfunctional, it will be necessary to examine the execution of major activities to determine if they are being carried out properly. Or, if assessment indicates that communicating information is faulty, specific communication events may be analyzed to determine where deficiencies occur. Then, corrective action may be taken.

Organizational Design

The way in which an organization is designed can have far-reaching implications for the quality of process performance. Organizational structure—lines of authority, responsibility, and communication—can either enhance or impede process performance. For example, every link in a chain of authority contains potential for both delay and distortion of communication. Therefore, any structure that consists of numerous hierarchical levels has built-in mechanisms for degrading the quality of communication—unless specific techniques or roles for facilitating or confirming communication are designed into the organization.

In a similar vein, an organization that has been specially designed for a specific purpose, or one that makes sense according to the traditional logics of organization, may never function effectively because special process requirements related to particular objectives were not taken into account. Structures that are most conducive to process performance will vary according to the missions, objectives, and anticipated activities of the organizations. Ideally, process requirements should be determined prior to design of the organization and process considerations will be taken into account with the more usual operational aspects. In reality, process considerations are taken into account all too frequently after task organizations have been designed on the basis of operational requirements alone.

Considerations of process requirements in the design of organizations may lead to the establishment of special units or sections that are specifically charged with responsibility for performance of certain processes. One example of such special units is a department that is charged with responsibility for sensing the economic climate and identifying elements that can impact upon the activities of the organization.

Training and Development

Although problems and objectives differ according to types, purposes, and missions of organizations, the processes that constitute competence are universal. Accordingly, the question is not whether the processes occur; they must be performed to some degree in any organization or group that is at all functional. Rather, the question involves how well the processes are executed and how they are coordinated to produce total, integrated group and organizational performance.

Since organizational processes are more or less inevitable, an equally important issue is whether the processes of an organization will be allowed to operate unmonitored and uncontrolled, or whether personnel will be specifically trained, both individually and collectively, to perform and control them properly.

Enhancement of organizational competence can be accomplished best through training and development efforts that include

1. individual cognitive skill training;
2. experiential team training conducted under simulated or field conditions; and
3. internal development efforts based upon analyses of process performance of the organization, continuing assessment of competence performance, and periodic training conducted in tandem with operational training programs.

REQUIREMENTS FOR LEADERSHIP

The problem of developing effectiveness in an organization is one of making a functioning, operational system out of available human and material resources. Viewed as a system, an organization must be capable of performing more or better than all of the resources which it comprises. It must be a genuine whole greater than the sum of its parts, with its performance more than the sum of its individual efforts.

What is needed is a transformation of the resources. This cannot come merely from a directive. It requires large doses of leadership of the highest quality.

Not to recognize these requirements can lead to serious interference with organizational competence and therefore organizational effectiveness, by creating such problems as failures to set performance goals; breakdowns in communication; conflict, strife, and competition between individuals or groups; low morale; and poor work discipline. The sources of such problems are likely to be diffuse and quite complex and may be traced to any or all of an array of factors, including working conditions, superior-subordinate relationships, communication, operational inefficiency, or just about any other condition related to life within an organization. Any such conditions may ultimately be traced to inadequate leadership.

The Essence of Organizational Leadership

Several aspects of organizational leadership are especially important. *First, the work of a dynamic organization involves the continual identification and reformulation of problems.* Although activities may be planned to the smallest detail, this cannot be accomplished with absolute certainty because no one can ever be sure of all the factors that may become involved as an operation proceeds. Therefore, activities often have to be planned on the basis of less than complete information or in anticipation of many possible eventualities, some or all of which may never occur. Even to select the particular facts that are relevant from all the data that may be available is no easy matter. Therefore, much activity involves being alert to and exploring a wide range of data and ongoing events to find possible alternatives that will yield desirable consequences. *One important function of leadership is to guide this exploring process. By providing structure in the form of guidance and problem definition, the leader keeps ambiguity to a minimum.*

A second leadership function involves the provision of appropriate methodological assistance as needed by the organization. The leader must suggest relevant concepts and techniques that will aid in handling operational problems. In addition, he must guide his personnel along lines that will provide a happy compromise between the procedural rigidity and flexibility, which has been touched upon several times in this book. Failure to provide this methodological help may be a serious source of unsuccessful organizational functioning.

A third function of organizational leadership involves the identification and coordination of member resources. Attention must be paid to creating conditions that will enable a person with the ability to fill an identified need to make a contribution. This function requires awareness of the different capabilities that people and units can bring to bear on tasks. It also requires defining members' assignments in each operation in such a way that the most suitable people and units can contribute the most. In this connection, a leader may encounter difficulty if he does not make himself continually aware of the motivations and norms (behavioral standards) of his personnel.

Most people who are concerned with the performance of organizations consider effectiveness to be control over environment. Thus, an effective organization is a unified system equipped with the knowledge, skills, and resources to control its environments, while an ineffective organization, for the lack of such capabilities, remains subject to forces over which it can exert little control.

As stated in various ways throughout this book, for an organization to overcome its operational environments, it requires

1. *Operational proficiency*—the technical competence to successfully execute the tasks arising from the demands of the operational situation;

2. *The capacity to evaluate reality*—the ability to search out, accurately perceive, and correctly interpret the attributes of the operational situation, including conditions both internal and external to the organization; and

3. *Adaptability*—the capacity to solve problems and to react flexibly to changing demands of the operational situation.

To meet the above requirements, an organization must develop the properties of effective groups described in chapter 2.

In a demonstrably effective organization, characteristics such as those discussed above can be frequently observed. For the most part, they either are associated with or derive from the activities of leaders.

In many organizations, leaders' attempts to improve effectiveness most often take the form of modifications of the structural framework—that is, *reorganization*—and of increased emphasis upon the more formalized organizational constraints, such as policies and procedures. Of course, attention to these aspects is important; however, overreliance upon them leads to organizational rigidity. Effectiveness under the complex conditions of today requires flexibility, a quality that has its principal source in the integrated functional processes discussed earlier.

Conditions Conducive to Performance

There are many specific things a leader can do to develop an effective organization. Some are simple, routine functions of administration. Others require rather complex leadership skills. In either case, most of the ways will involve attending to matters that are related to the necessary organizational conditions listed earlier.

1. *Roles of each organizational member should be clear to both role incumbents and all other members.* This refers not just to written job descriptions but, rather, to all expectations, both formal and informal, held by leaders and all other members of the organization. Roles consist of all formal duties and responsibilities and informal expectations and norms that evolve through interaction between personnel. Especially with regard to teamwork, congruity of role perceptions between leaders and incumbents, and among all organization members, is vitally important. When people do not have common understandings about how the various roles should be performed, coordinative behavior is extremely difficult, if not impossible.

   Role clarity is best achieved when (1) a leader makes explicit to personnel precisely what his expectations are with respect to each position and the group as a whole and (2) when members of a group have frequent opportunities to jointly examine performance and to clarify role expectations among the members.

2. *Organization members should be kept aware of objectives.* Through both formal meetings and informal daily activities, the team-minded leader will strive to keep both the objectives of the organization and the objectives for subordinate units constantly before the members of the organization. The problem for the leader and his subordinates is to establish and work toward the accomplishment of concrete objectives whose achievement will result in execution of the basic mission. Objectives are the stepping-stones to mission accomplishment. Effectiveness requires that all members keep these objectives constantly at the forefront of awareness. Accordingly, as he works with subordinates, the team-minded leader must use every opportunity to stress the current objectives and the means for their achievement. Through constant emphasis, the leader will strive to generate individual involvement with the common objectives of the organization.

3. *A cooperative atmosphere must be developed within the organization.* It is extremely important to develop genuinely cooperative relationships between leaders and members of the organization and among all members. It is impossible to impose true cooperation upon people. Therefore, the development of cooperation among members must be truly a matter of leadership by example. The leader must work at and rely upon his own team attitudes to filter gradually through the group until, in time, individual members begin to function more cooperatively, begin to communicate more among themselves, and gradually to exchange dependence upon the leader for interdependence among all members, the leader included.

4. *Adequate communication must be established.* The problem of who should communicate what, to whom, when, and by what means is one of the most important problems in team relationships. It will be recalled that communicating information and communicating implementation are among the most critical processes of organizational competence. Accordingly, team-work will be maximized only when there can be established common terminology; common definitions of objectives, problems, situations and tasks; and common agreements (either explicit or implicit) concerning modes and channels of communication. Most such understandings develop in the course of frequent and free association between organizational members. An important task of the leader is to encourage such contacts and to ensure that overcontrol does not create barriers to communication.

5. *Common understandings must be developed concerning standards of performance.* Agreement on appropriate standards of performance and behavior is intimately related to development of effectiveness because the system of standards in a group serves as a means of quality control. When an individual accepts the norms (standards) of a group, he belongs. When he belongs, he coordinates his actions in accordance with the common needs. A leader can influence the development of common understandings by publicly and officially expressing the standards he deems desirable and, even more important,

by subjecting both his own performance and behavior and that of his subordinates to evaluation against these standards.

6. *Control must be exercised on cooperative efforts within the organization.* Organized groups with strong cohesion have been found to exhibit better teamwork and so disintegrate less rapidly under stress than do unorganized groups. A part of group organization is agreement (implicit or explicit) concerning the amount of control to be exercised by the various levels of authority, the degree of authority to be delegated, areas of assigned responsibility, and the limitations to be placed upon individual freedom to act.

The control exercised on cooperative effort is one of the functions most commonly associated with leadership. Whenever a leader undertakes to define, interpret, or clarify the freedoms extended to individual subordinates or the limitations imposed upon them, he is influencing the performance of the organization and is, at that time, giving leadership to its members.

Probably the most significant aspect of this leadership by control is the degree of discretion to be granted to subordinates, that is, the control of freedom of action or, more simply, the control of alternatives open to subordinates for making decisions. This particular point has long been a bone of contention in analyses of leadership. The positions have ranged from retention of complete and total control of all actions and decisions by a single leader to the other extreme of wide diffusion of responsibility throughout a group of subordinates. However, neither of these extreme approaches has been found to be fully productive. Effective team performance results when subordinates are provided sufficient latitude to exercise responsibility at their own levels, while leaders simultaneously exercise the guidance and control necessary to coordinate those activities that contribute to the mission of the larger unit. This can be achieved through common understandings concerning areas of authority, responsibility, freedom to act, and so forth, and through explicit policies that establish clear-cut criteria as to which decisions should be made at subordinate levels and which should be referred to higher levels.

7. *Rewards must be distributed fairly and equitably within the organization.* The distribution of rewards and other satisfactions can encourage teamwork, or it can splinter a team. Subordinates' perceptions of who gets the credit or their suspicion of exploitation—regardless of whether it actually exists—can be a serious problem. Because of the way function and responsibility are distributed in organizations, it is almost inevitable that some assignments will seem to have more status than others, that some personnel will have jobs more satisfying to them, that the contributions of all personnel will not seem equally valuable and will not be equally rewarded. Such reactions are especially subjective when the issue seems to be reward expressed in status, favor with leaders, and so forth. Disgruntlement and competition arising from such perceptions can be especially destructive for teamwork. A leader must be constantly alert for such problems and must exercise extreme care that misperceptions in this area do not develop in his unit.

8. *Stability is necessary to achieve integration in any organization.* Stability in the relationships among members is essential for effective teamwork. Each mem-

ber must be able to predict with assurance the behavior and actions of all other members. This required assurance results from familiarity and experience among all personnel. When relationships are stable, each member comes to know what is expected of him by others. Furthermore, he learns the roles of other team members as well as their characteristic ways of acting. Accordingly, he knows what to expect from others, where other members are weak, where they are strong, and so forth. He also learns to depend upon other members, to work with them, and to support their efforts. This stability of roles and of performance expectations develops through frequent contacts among the members of a team and from experiences of success in working together. This stability cannot develop if there is constant turnover or other turbulence. It is one function of leadership to ensure that conditions exist within the unit sufficient for such stability to develop.

9. *Teamwork requires an efficient organizational system that will provide the means through which activities of team members can be integrated.* No matter how high the motivation to cooperate, teamwork will not result unless members' efforts can be effectively channeled. The term "organizational system" refers to those procedures and practices used to channel the efforts of personnel through such functions as exercising direction, assigning responsibilities, exchanging information, making decisions, organizing, coordinating, and so forth. The system includes the formal organization and procedures but goes beyond them also to include the various informal means by which the activities of personnel are integrated and coordinated. Those interdependent processes constitute an overall system that channels and guides the activities of the organization. For this reason, it is more appropriate to refer to "the organizational system" rather than merely to "organization" as a critical element in crisis-management organizations.

Effective teamwork within a complex organizational context requires a system that will ensure that, consistent with their objectives, missions, and responsibilities, members are provided with all the information, decisions, guidance, and assistance necessary to perform effectively and to contribute appropriately to overall unit effort. More specifically, the system must function in such a manner that

1. each member of the organization is provided missions and objectives that he will be motivated to achieve and that, when accomplished, will contribute to the superordinate objectives of the organization;

2. the techniques, procedures, and plans developed by leaders are such that members will be motivated to use them to their maximum potentiality;

3. the activities of organizational members fit together and are mutually supporting; and

4. opportunity is provided for contacts between members sufficient for mutual trust and confidence to develop.

IMPLICATIONS

In many organizations the quality of process performance is not very good because, in order to control variability and thus to ensure reliability, many leaders tend toward regulated and formal responses. They tend to prefer the certainty of standardized procedures with their clearly demarcated and logically related stages and, accordingly, they give little systematic attention to process performance. However, overreliance upon standardized responses tends to result in organizational rigidity, whereas, in the fast-changing environments of today, to be effective an organization must maintain a high level of flexibility. This quality is essential in uncertain situations, and it has its source in what has been called here "organizational competence."

Leaders cannot be criticized too severely for overemphasis on standardized responses. Although most people who have given much thought to organizations are aware of certain more or less intangible aspects, which, here, have been called processes, these factors are often viewed as impossible to see and difficult to understand. Accordingly, little is ever done about them in any systematic way.

The conceptual framework presented here under the rubric of organizational competence offers a means for overcoming this problem. The competence components and their processes, together with the methodology for their measurement, provide concrete ways for analyzing internal functioning and for relating such functioning to both antecedent causal factors and ultimate achievement.

In application, competence and its components offer potential for both organizational diagnosis and development. Thus, it is possible to identify individuals, positions, or departments that are functional or dysfunctional in terms of performance of some or all processes. It is possible to determine who, or what departments, should perform each process, how well the processes are performed, and how they could be performed better.

The processes that have been identified provide both a framework for evaluation and bases for training and organizational development. Knowledge of requirements for effective process performance, when coupled with controlled experiences in execution, can be expected to result in decided improvements in the leadership and managerial performance of individuals. However, the greatest benefit is to be found in performance of the organization, considered as a whole. Fundamental to the framework is the view that competence represents capability of the organization and is different from the sum of individual capabilities. Process performance involves organizational responses, and the quality of any single response event is determined by the entire network of antecedent relationships and responses. This suggests that organizational competence can best be improved by efforts that focus upon developing the organization as a system.

In the section entitled "Requirements for Leadership," identifiable characteristics for effective organizations were set forth. Furthermore, some principal conditions needed for effective organizational performance were listed. Both the identifiable characteristics and the list of necessary conditions may serve as bases for checklists to be used in evaluating and developing organizations.

It has become axiomatic that human factors must receive full recognition in any reasonable consideration of organizational effectiveness. However, in attempts to do something about the human element, the most common approach in organizations is to focus upon the characteristics, skills, and deficiencies of individuals. This approach most often leads to emphasis upon selection procedures, performance evaluations and interviews, remedial training, and so forth. These and other activities that focus on individual personnel are important and, indeed, essential for upgrading or maintaining the proficiency of an organization.

On the other hand, it is unreasonable to consider people without recognizing the impact of their environment upon them. People function within situational contexts, and these contexts define and limit behavior. An organization is a very powerful context and, accordingly, produces potent forces that circumscribe and channel the activities, attitudes, and motivations of personnel. For this reason, both individual and group behaviors within an organization are simply not the same as behaviors outside of it. This fact can never be safely ignored. The organizational context is indeed a most potent factor in individual and group effectiveness. This is fortunate, because the organization is one thing that can be greatly influenced and controlled by leaders.

PART 3

Leading Groups at Work

Chapter 7

Developing Effective Groups

In many respects, the hard, practical leadership requirements of a new group are greater than those of an old established one because in a new group so much depends upon the leadership and organizational skills of the top person. The emphasis must be upon building, and a leader must provide his group with the kinds of experiences that will develop the general conditions previously discussed. The developmental process involves more than merely learning this or that rule concerning operational routines and the right way or wrong way of performing duties. Regardless of the skills possessed by members individually, each group must develop capabilities for working together. All members must learn their roles and those of every other member to whom they must relate. Working relationships have to be established, and each member has to develop the confidence and trust, the norms and attitudes that characterize an effective group. In a similar way, all groups must learn to work together (Beckhard, 1972; Bellin, 1998).

DEVELOPING NEW GROUPS

Group development involves the inculcation of new objectives, new concepts, new ways of doing things, and new relationships. For members to accept new goals, to master new techniques, and to develop new relationships takes time. Accordingly, the development of an effective group is, in a very real sense, a time-consuming process.

The development of a new group requires carefully considered leader emphasis. Primary stress must be put on building. Placing emphasis solely upon routine problems, with the hope that positive conditions will develop, is not sufficient.

In developing a new group, the first requirement for a leader is to obtain a clear idea of his mandate. What is expected of him? What are his terms of reference? A mission will have been assigned, probably by higher levels; however, the leader must think it through to the point where the necessary concepts and their implications for action are clearly outlined. The leader can proceed to build the group only when he has his mission thoroughly conceived.

Once the mission is clear, the leader must solve a more difficult problem of setting objectives that will be integrative and meaningful for the members. Both the objectives of the larger group and those of its component parts must be established in such a manner that all are in satisfactory harmony. Objectives that have significance and that carry obvious implications for action take work to establish. The earliest phases of group development require a leader to spend a great deal of time indoctrinating subordinates relative to objectives and to the way that subordinate objectives and corollary activities contribute to the overall mission.

Concurrent with the determination of objectives, the development of a group structure warrants detailed attention. This involves two important problems: the grouping of similar functions and elements in a manner to promote effective coordination, and definition of the proper relationship between functional elements with a view to promoting both coordination and cooperation. Definition of proper relationships is the more difficult problem because relationships have a way of not remaining defined. Since the nature of relationships between organizational elements is often determined by the personnel that the units comprise and since functional relationships change with changes in situations and missions, the definition of appropriate relationships is a continuing task requiring frequent attention.

Groups based on new organizational concepts or with unique missions may have no preestablished structures, and the leader will get the responsibility for developing them. Under such conditions, the development of a structure is usually an evolutionary process with additions and modifications becoming necessary as the work takes on momentum.

In the case of either a preestablished structure or a new concept, the organizational structure may require more of a leader's attention in the early days of development than later. When objectives and a structure have taken shape, the foundation has been laid. Then, numerous other aspects will require the leader's attention.

The development of a new group is a rewarding but sometimes frustrating task. In the early stages, the constant temptation to move forward on all fronts simultaneously must be restrained in favor of a clearly recognized sequence. *Failure to take things in their natural sequence is probably the single greatest mistake in developing a new group.*

This is difficult to avoid because the responsible leader naturally feels that he must make a good showing and produce tangible results in a hurry. If he does not remain deliberate, however, he may find himself hopelessly tangled in a series of uncoordinated moves that merely cause confusion in himself and disruption in his group. This is not to say that he can afford to sit back until intuition makes every move clear. He usually does not have that much time. But there is more danger in failing to make the right moves in their proper order than there is in taking a little more time in the beginning and discovering their natural sequences.

Then, as momentum develops, as circumstances change, as problems come and go, the leader must maintain direction. In the face of the many problems that will arise, he must adhere to his basic objective. Out of all the scores of projects and problems on which the group may be working at a given time, out of all the possible objects of attention and effort to which he might devote himself, which should he select for his personal effort and attention? The decisions he makes in this regard play a large part in determining whether progress will be made or whether time and effort will be frittered away in false starts.

As time goes on, as the group begins to function, the leader will have to shift the emphasis of his activities. Old problems will be solved; new ones will appear. Where formerly it was necessary for him to hold most of the decision-making responsibilities to himself, the leader can now begin more and more to delegate them. He can begin to withdraw from detailed intervention and to restrict himself to broader policy-making activities. There is a problem of timing here, as well as a shift in emphasis.

A leader must maintain a realistic attitude toward the process of development. One of the abiding realities is that the development of an effective group is a time-consuming process. Accordingly, one of the basic problems of the leader is to maintain a sense of proportion. It is a proper sense of perspective—of what is important and what is possible, of what must be done and of what can be done—that will enable him to settle the fundamental questions that come before him.

FACTORS THAT ENHANCE EFFECTIVENESS

The success of any organization requires the collective efforts of numbers of people. Collective behavior is effective only to the extent that all individuals at all levels make useful contributions to the ultimate goal. Such contributions require that all personnel know what actions are required of them, are capable of performing these actions, and are motivated to perform them well. People must also learn habits of working together, and the organization as a whole must develop effective routines of functioning.

It has sometimes been stated that the proper function of an organization is to orchestrate the application of its members' skills and energies to solutions of problems larger than any of them could handle separately. "Orchestrate" suggests many critical activities; however, above all others, the term implies the necessity for an organization to provide conditions conducive to effective performance. The principal conditions necessary for effective performance include

1. Factors that enhance proficiency
   - effective structure and job design
   - efficient procedures and practices
   - excellent training for both leaders and rank and file members
   - communication practices that supply each individual with information and knowledge necessary for intelligent performance of duties
2. Factors that promote a common desire to belong to the group and identify with it
   - good administrative, supervisory, and leadership practices at all levels
   - good working conditions and good equipment
   - opportunity for each individual to perform as a conscious member of a larger whole
   - means of providing occasional, explicit acknowledgment of group progress to all members and of recognition of the shared responsibility for such progress
   - opportunities for members to influence decisions about matters that affect them
3. Factors that enhance motivation
   - a system that makes careful provisions for incentive, reward, and approval of good work
   - procedures that make information about individual and group progress available to members
   - opportunities for individuals and groups to experience success in the performance of tasks
   - opportunities for challenge and growth for each individual
   - opportunities for optimum independence in the performance of work

If one examines these conditions closely, it becomes apparent that all are dependent upon three general factors that control effectiveness in every organization: (1) effective management, (2) effective training, and (3) effective leadership.

EFFECTIVE MANAGEMENT

Management encompasses all of the efforts required to mobilize the energies of an organization toward attainment of its goals. It involves those planning, decision-making, guiding, controlling, and implementing activities necessary to gather, integrate, and coordinate resources. Although certain aspects may be found at all levels, management is most clearly seated at the top.

Regardless of the type and size of an organization, the top executive must make sure that goals are established, plans are made, policies are developed, and personnel are recruited, assigned, and trained. He must establish levels of responsibility, set up mechanisms of coordination, delegate authority, direct subordinates, provide stimulation and inspiration to everyone, exercise control, develop high levels of motivation and morale, and adjust the plans and activities of his organization to broader changes in government, the profession, and the community.

If these activities are not performed well, the group will not function effectively. Any organization is built from the top down. The thinking, ideas, and behavior of the chief executive spread out to include his close subordinates and are translated into a variety of specific actions and patterns of behavior throughout the organization (Adizes, 1974; Anderson and Anderson, 2001). If the original ideas or actions of the (chief executive officer) are unsound, the trends in thinking and actions that permeate the organization are likely to be wrong. If his basic thinking is sound, this will be reflected throughout the organization.

In particular, some broad decisions, or lack of them, concerning the way the organization will be operated have significant effects upon the behavior patterns that will develop at lower levels. The executive who decides to operate the organization along mechanical principles—through stress upon regulations, standardization, and the procedures of operations—will produce communication patterns, administrative attitudes, and supervisory behavior that reflect this attitude. If he places stress upon people and relationships to get the job done, rather than upon the mechanics of operations, this emphasis will be reflected throughout the organization. He will consequently develop in his organization a totally different approach to work, to personnel, and to clients.

Most of this book has stressed the importance of human factors in group performance. Recognition of the importance of human factors leads to the conclusion that the top management has a responsibility for doing certain things that will ensure the effectiveness of the human resources. Many of the specific factors that lead to effectiveness were listed previously. However, above all of these requirements is one overriding premise: what attracts people more strongly to any organization and maintains their feeling of well-being while working in it is their faith in the common purpose, faith in the leadership, and faith in each other.

Faith in the purposes and leadership of an organization depends upon the integrity of decisions managers make about goals, operations, and the internal human affairs of the organization. The human affairs aspect requires that leaders be chosen with due regard for both their ability and their character, particularly from the standpoint of human values. It also requires that the top management, in its policies and practices concerned with personnel matters, make decisions supportive of personnel, thus confirming in this broad way its concern for the welfare of individuals associated with the organization.

It is an advantage to have personnel well motivated and generally satisfied with the organization (Porter, 1971). It is desirable that the experiences of personnel on their jobs and in their work environment be good, not bad. It is only realistic to recognize that neither all experiences nor all aspects of a work environment will always be exactly as every employee would prefer them (Ashkanasy, Hartel, and Zerbb, 2000). However, it is important for employees that their lives at work make sense in terms of their own interests and abilities, because people's attitudes and motivations are largely shaped by the meaning they get from their experiences and those of their friends and acquaintances (Gellerman, 1963; Gellerman, 1998).

This suggests that personnel administration and leadership must be considered integral and important aspects of general management. The successful incorporation of the human factor into management at all points seems to be something that is desired by employees, many managements, and by society at large. It also suggests that managers have a responsibility to handle the human, as well as the operational, aspects of their roles wisely. This realization is becoming more widespread, although there seems to be a continuing confusion in many organizations as to precisely what this means and how to accomplish it.

One far from satisfactory answer must be that there is not any one formula or set of formulas that will provide ready-made solutions to the problem of developing a constructive work context. A constructive work context is usually the result of careful and calculated developmental effects by an enlightened administration over a considerable period. Someone has said that the essential difference between an effective manager and an ineffective one is that the effective manager thinks of today's actions in terms of tomorrow's objectives, whereas the ineffective manager takes each event as it comes without concern for tomorrow. Nowhere is this statement more relevant than with regard to development of a constructive work context.

As one noted writer on administration has put it, *effectiveness is control over environment.* An effective organization is a unified system equipped with the knowledge and skills to control its environment, whereas an ineffective organization, for the lack of such capabilities, remains subject to forces over which it can exert little control. Similarly, an effective leader is one who understands the organization of which he is a part and the forces by which it is moved, whereas the ineffective leader is the plaything of arbitrary and capricious powers acting beyond the range of his limited understanding.

Understanding appears to be one vital key. Managers and supervisors become effective leaders by understanding what is required of them and how, in an organization, human forces such as those discussed in this book may be combined, balanced, and directed toward the ultimate goals.

EFFECTIVE TRAINING

The second factor that contributes to the proficiency of an organization is effective training. The term *staff development* is sometimes used to describe efforts to upgrade the proficiency of personnel. However, for this book, training is preferred over the more polite and more diffuse staff development in order to emphasize a point to be mentioned here and elaborated later. What appears to be needed at all levels are systematically provided experiences specifically designed to develop concrete skills related to actual job requirements—in short, training (Knowles, Holton, and Swanson, 1998).

It is important to distinguish between the concept of *training* and the concept of *education*. Both terms are often wrongly applied to the process of human learning, with little differentiation. Training is any set of more or less formally organized learning experiences designed to prepare an individual to perform certain acts specifiable in advance. If these acts cannot be specified, for whatever reason, a set of similarly organized learning experiences is called "education." In the case of training, for example interviewing training, learning can be sharply focused on later job behaviors. In the case of education, the learning experience must be devoted to providing an individual with a background of general knowledge and attitudes relevant to broad requirements that may be imposed following learning.

What is advocated here is training—the development of concrete skills, conducted within the organization and designed specifically to upgrade proficiency in jobs relevant to the mission of the organization (Nadler and Nadler, 1994). In many organizations, training is not given much attention; in others, it is not very effective. In many small organizations, where it is usually needed most, no training is conducted at all.

Most often, the state of training within an organization will be almost solely determined by the amount of emphasis placed upon it by the chief executive. If the CEO values high-quality training, he will usually find ways of getting it accomplished. If training is regarded as merely another item of overhead, to be conducted in spare time as an added duty for some already overburdened functionary, poor results are likely to be obtained.

Unfortunately, all too often training is viewed as undesirable overhead and is the first activity to be dropped when funds are low. Deemphasis on training as a means of cost reduction is especially short-sighted because it is at precisely the point when funds are short that the productivity of employees needs to be raised. Training is one of the few ways in which this can be accomplished.

Efficient and effective training can contribute to organizational effectiveness in at least the following ways:

- reducing overhead and direct costs by decreasing the time necessary to perform required activities and the time required to bring inexperienced employees to full productivity
- reducing the general cost of administration by creating a climate which orients employees toward high performance
- reducing the costs of personnel administration as reflected in turnover, absenteeism, grievances, and complaints
- reducing costs by improving the flow of work
- decreasing the costs of administration by reducing need for low supervisor-worker ratios through increasing the proficiency of workers
- upgrading the quality of products or services by increasing the proficiency of workers.

To be fully effective, the training program of an organization should be a full-time responsibility for at least one individual and should cover the full spectrum of jobs. In particular, in addition to training of workers, the intensive and continuing training of supervisory personnel is important. Leadership is a particular problem in many organizations. It is clear that leadership training is a high-priority requirement.

Training specifically designed to develop knowledge and skills concerned with supervision and leadership is needed. Many supervisors are professionally educated, but the courses they have taken may not have been noted for their emphasis upon supervision and leadership. What is more, all of the accumulated knowledge about human behavior and social processes is not sufficient to equip an individual to be a good supervisor. He needs excellent training specifically designed to develop hard supervisory and leadership skills that have been scientifically confirmed as relevant for effective performance in real-life situations.

The implications for organizational effectiveness are clear. Personnel need the skills to perform their jobs proficiently, and they also need good leadership. Both of these requirements can be met through training. In company with leadership, excellent training is one of the most important contributors to effectiveness.

Training specifically concerned with leadership will be discussed in chapter 10.

EFFECTIVE LEADERSHIP

Without a doubt the quality of leadership available at all levels determines the character of the work context. Leadership is an influence process, and the influence exerted by leaders may have either constructive or destructive effects upon the environment at work.

An important step for a top executive is recognition that both job satisfaction and motivation depend primarily and almost entirely upon the leadership in the organization. Leaders at all levels control the conditions that make for good or poor motivation and satisfaction. As one example, a key element in a climate of good human affairs is the same degree of integrity in small day-to-day actions concerning any single employee anywhere in the organization as in top-level decisions about large problems that affect many employees. These small actions may be influenced by supervisory employees at any level.

The fact that leaders at all levels control the work context suggests the necessity for a top manager to develop high-quality subordinates and to insist upon good leadership practices at each and every level from the lowest supervisor up to and including the chief executive himself. He must demand the same degree of competence and integrity in lower-level actions as there is in his own behavior.

Directives and training programs that emphasize good leadership are valuable for communicating the importance placed upon it by a chief executive. However, they alone are not sufficient to produce it throughout an organization. If good supervisory practices are to be attained, the reward system in the organization must be geared to that goal. High-quality leadership develops when high-quality leaders are the ones who are rewarded. Building a reward system is a basic step toward establishing a climate conducive to motivation and satisfaction.

Of at least equal importance is what is done by top managers themselves in creating a climate favorable to good leadership practices. There is overwhelming evidence that the kinds of supervisory practices in an organization are likely to follow closely the patterns set by those individuals in higher levels of management (Olmstead, 2000).

Therefore, through his own leadership practices and those he emphasizes throughout his organization, the top executive can influence those low-level leaders who exercise the most potent effects upon satisfaction, motivation, and performance of employees.

At any level, sound leadership is not just a matter of hunch or native skill; its fundamentals can be analyzed, organized systematically, and learned by most individuals with normal abilities. Yet taken alone, no amount of knowledge will improve insight and judgment or increase ability to act wisely under conditions of responsibility. An individual might know every fact in this book and still be a poor leader.

One would hope for a set of rules that would equip an executive or supervisor to cope with the complex leadership problems he faces. Unfortunately, no such rules exist because human behavior occurs in specific situations that have endless variety. Each situation is a new situation, requiring imagination, understanding, and skillful actions.

A leader must be concerned with assessing events and finding appropriate courses of action. What is needed is not a set of rules but good skills both in diagnosing situations and in acting appropriately within them. If a leader has a framework of ideas in mind as a working guide, diagnosis will show him where the limits lie. He can then take the appropriate actions.

Throughout the preceding discussions in this chapter and elsewhere, two elements have been repeatedly stipulated as essential for group effectiveness. They are (1) meaningful goals, or objectives, and (2) efficient and effective communication.

GROUP OBJECTIVES

For this discussion, the term *mission* refers to the overall task assigned to a group. On the other hand, the term *objectives* refers to specific goals to be accomplished. In this sense, objectives specify concrete results to be attained through performance. They designate the actual ends sought through the plans, operating decisions, and policies of a group; they tell specifically what the group is trying to do, regardless of how the mission is stated.

At high levels, the statement of missions is purposely general. Accordingly, they often do not reflect two major factors that may influence effectiveness: the host of decisions that must be made among alternative ways of fulfilling the general mission and the variety of activities that must be pursued. Objectives cover these aspects, not only for high levels but for groups at any level.

Functions of Objectives

The importance of group objectives has been emphasized by many theorists who argue that when there are shared objectives, there is less likelihood of conflicting actions by members, and differences about actions are more likely to be resolved by rational analytic processes. Where objectives are clear, operational, and shared, there is less differential perception of optimal courses of action. However, there is evidence of wide differences in the degree to which organizations rely on objectives and of concomitant variations in the degree to which there is conflict arising from uncertainty about objectives.

Objectives specify concrete results to be attained through performance. They designate the actual ends sought through the operating decisions and policies of the group; they tell specifically what the group is trying to do, regardless of how its purposes may be stated.

Under certain conditions, objectives possess motivational properties. It has become a truism that human behavior is purposive—it is goal-directed. People have certain needs that must be satisfied and behavior is aimed toward obtaining that satisfaction. Whatever will satisfy particular needs are called "goals." One way of describing a goal is to say that it represents a tension within the individual that promises to be relaxed when the satisfying objective is achieved. Thus, a person directs his behavior toward the achievement of objectives that have potential for satisfying his needs—his behavior is goal-directed.

Groups of people also have goals. A goal for a group or organization is a shared tension among the members that promises to be relaxed when the objective is reached. Since behavior is goal-directed, a shared objective has the properties of concentrating the activities of members and of mobilizing their efforts toward its achievement. Thus, under proper conditions, objectives have motivational properties that influence the behavior of people and, therefore, the performance of groups.

The most notable effect of objectives occurs when members of a group internalize them and thus activate behavior beyond the minimum prescribed by specific roles. This occurs when objectives become infused with value, when they in effect become purposes. Under these conditions, the motivation to achieve group objectives stems from the individual's involvement with them, which in turn derives from his identification with the group.

The necessity for careful formulation and assignment of objectives has long been a fundamental aspect of organizational doctrine. Indeed, the necessity for clear and unequivocal objectives is so much accepted that their very real utility as instruments of management may sometimes be overlooked. This can be unfortunate since a leader who fails to use objectives wastes a potent tool for influencing his group.

Experienced group analysts have learned that the roots of many problems rest in the structure of objectives and that they can safely move on to examination of other attributes of groups only after they are satisfied that objectives are not the source of difficulty. For this reason, when asked to evaluate a group, analysts frequently begin their study with examination of its structure of objectives. The kinds of questions to be asked can be subsumed under one or more of the following headings:

- the extent to which a clear objective is present;
- the degree to which the objective mobilizes energies of personnel behind the group's activities;

• the degree to which there is conflict among key members concerning which one of several possible objectives should control activities;

• the degree to which there is conflict concerning the means that the group should employ in reaching its objectives;

• the degree to which the activities of personnel are coordinated in a manner required by the group's objectives.

It is not difficult to illustrate the serious problems that can be traced to the absence or inadequacy of objectives. For example, the absence of controlling aims forces decisions to be made in response to immediate pressures and short-run advantages. In effect, the group drifts, and its greatest potentialities are not realized because the full force of its capabilities can never be brought to bear on any single undertaking. Instead, sub-units and members find themselves striking out in many directions and expending their energies on matters that are not relevant for final outcomes.

The formulation and communication of objectives must be a widely distributed function among administrators and supervisors at all levels. Each should analyze the objective assigned to his group, derive appropriate activities from it, and, frequently, break it down into subordinate objectives for individuals or departments under him. In this fact lies one of the most important requirements in group organization—the necessity for imbuing personnel at all levels with both general purposes and realistic detailed goals so that they remain motivated and able to perform the ultimate activities effectively. A corollary of this is the necessity for those at high levels to constantly understand the concrete conditions and the specific problems of the ultimate workers, from whom leaders are often insulated. Without the up-and-down-the-line coordination of purposeful objectives, broad decisions and general purposes are merely intellectual exercises in an organizational vacuum, insulated from reality by layers of misunderstanding.

Effective Objectives

An essential feature of the concept presented here is that objectives should steer activities so that missions can be accomplished. This raises the question of what determines whether an objective will be capable of guiding activities. The important point is that the particular characteristics of an objective serve as the principal determinants of whether it will be achieved.

The following characteristics have been found to be typical of good objectives: clarity, operationality, realism, and relevance of subordinate objectives. Each of these characteristics will be discussed.

Clarity. The first and probably most significant characteristic of effective objectives is that they are clear. To steer activities and mobilize effort, an objective must be specifically formulated in concrete terms and carefully communicated so that every relevant person understands it. In many groups, a lack of clarity may be due to any or all of the following:

- conflict among leaders as to how the role of the group and the resulting goals should be defined;

- poor communication skills that lead to vague, imprecise statements of objectives;

- an inability to formulate specific, unambiguous objectives because of the newness of the task or mission;

- a tendency to define objectives more ambitiously than is appropriate for the situation or the capabilities of the group;

- a tendency to lose sight of the whole purpose while working on details, unless coordination and leadership are very effective.

Regardless of whether the objective itself is ambiguous or whether there has merely been a failure to communicate it effectively, the resulting lack of clarity will influence both individual and group performance. Working toward a clear goal increases the individual's interest in his work, whereas lack of a clear objective makes his duties less attractive and increases his hostility toward leaders and the organization. A clear objective gives meaning to his group membership, makes him more oriented toward group activities, and increases the ability of leaders to influence him. All of these, in turn, affect the quality of his performance.

The most obvious effect of unclear objectives is poor coordination. Coordinated effort requires that everyone understand objectives in the same way. Lack of clarity leaves room for each member to place his own interpretation upon objectives and upon the kinds of activities to be derived from them. When objectives are ambiguous, there is a greater probability of overlap, duplication, and conflict of activities. The energies of the group may be needlessly expended in such unproductive activities as correcting false starts, holding conferences for purposes of reclarification, and resolving disagreements that arise from divergent understanding of objectives.

Operationality. Objectives are most effective when they are defined in operational terms, that is, when there is some basis for relating them to possible courses of action. If there is some way of determining whether and to what extent an objective will be realized by a particular sequence of actions, it is operational. Thus, the goal of "promoting the general welfare," frequently a part of the definition of objectives in government agencies, is a nonoperational objective because it would be difficult to compare alternative actions in terms of their relative contributions to it.

Such objectives can only be related to specific actions through the derivation of more concrete subsidiary objectives. An operational objective has associated with it a set of activities that must be performed if it is to be accomplished. The actions of personnel will contribute to group achievement only if they are relevant to the requirements of the objectives.

Nonoperational objectives make it difficult to mobilize activities of any kind. One reason that some groups get bogged down and never seem to exhibit much constructive progress is that leaders fail to formulate feasible operational goals. When this happens, activities may be aimlessly executed simply because they are routine or customary. It would indeed be surprising if the group were able to achieve much in the way of improved effectiveness.

Realism. A third characteristic of an effective objective is realism. This means that there must be reasonable congruity between the level of difficulty of the objective and the capabilities of the group to which it is assigned. If objectives are considered to be instruments of motivation, it is unrealistic to assign those that are either too easy or too difficult to achieve.

When a group achieves a reasonably high level of competence, an objective that presents some challenge acquires value. Members, whose attentions are continually directed to the objective by their daily activities, gain an appreciation of its importance, and its attainment comes to have personal appeal for them. However, objectives that present no challenge soon lose their motivating value.

Objectives that are beyond the capabilities of a group present a somewhat more complex problem. It is undoubtedly true that difficult goals are more highly valued, and there is some evidence that occasional failure may have learning benefits. However, attempts to achieve objectives that are obviously beyond the competence of the group can only result in frustration, lowered morale, and internal conflict. Objectives that are far beyond the capabilities of a group will have virtually no motivational value. For a goal to possess motivational properties, it must, though difficult, appear achievable. Stated objectives that are impossible to attain are meaningless.

Relevance of Subordinate Objectives. A final characteristic of good objectives is that subordinate objectives contribute meaningfully to higher level ones. The structure of objectives in a group should be a chain relationship. Each successively smaller unit, with its own goal, should contribute toward the attainment of the larger objective of the organization.

A subordinate goal can serve as a motivational factor only as long as people recognize that it does not seriously diverge from the objectives of the larger group. Objectives that have no apparent relevance for major endeavors also have little motivational value. Demonstration of the relevance of even the most minor objectives and the inculcation of belief in the real existence of a common goal are essential leadership functions.

Some controversy has existed as to whether it is possible to imbue numbers of people with an overriding purpose. There is considerable evidence to show that it is possible (Sheriff and Cantril, 1947). Purpose can and does become a governing force in the lives of many people. The satisfaction an individual obtains from his job can never be complete unless he can participate through his work in some activity that seems worthwhile. Very early, this was shown to be true for civilian workers by Roethlisberger and Dickson (1943) who, after extensive investigation, concluded that workers develop a diminished capacity for work when the social conditions in the work are such as to make it difficult for them to identify themselves or their tasks with any redeeming function. Whether this will occur appears to be largely determined by the extent of compatibility between the objectives of the group and the personal values of the members.

Setting Objectives

Setting objectives for a group includes two related processes. The first involves definition of an effect to be produced (the objective). Here, the group is concerned with defining and formulating the objective in such a way that it can be most effective. In this process, a leader must surely take into account the characteristics of good goals discussed earlier. He must also be aware of other factors that may be important.

The second process involves the transmittal of the desired effect to those who will have to accomplish it. Here, the problems center on communication and obtaining understanding. The two processes will be discussed separately.

Defining objectives involves a kind of decision making. In making a decision, a person must become aware of relevant alternative actions, formulate them, and evaluate them as a basis for choice. A similar process occurs in defining objectives. There are usually several alternatives from which an objective can be selected. However, there may be reasons why a leader is not free to choose from these. In the first place, his superiors may have designated certain alternatives that cannot be considered. Thus, a task force director might be limited to certain fund ceilings within which only he can exercise discretion in establishing priorities between objectives.

Similarly, the capabilities of the group might place constraints on his choice of objectives. The experience, caliber, and training of group members; the amount of funds available; the kinds and quantity of facilities available—all of these factors can restrict choice of objectives.

The definition of objectives also involves a determination of desired results. This is sometimes difficult because a significant property of objectives is that they lie in the future, and therefore their consequences can only be anticipated. Whenever the future is concerned, uncertainty is present because it is impossible to predict with complete accuracy what the situation will be at the time an objective is reached. It is not uncommon for a group to set out on a long trail to achievement of some highly specific goal, only to find that, when the objective is finally reached, the rules of the game have been changed.

Since the future is unknown, a leader can never have complete information on which to base his formulation of objectives. He can only attempt to predict future outcomes, establish priorities on the basis of his predictions, and constantly reassess his objectives so that they may be modified as conditions change.

Not all definitions of objectives are related to the ultimate outcome. Many activities will be guided by a series of intermediate goals, each of which becomes a means for achievement of the ultimate one. This is necessary because the complexity of many long-term goals requires that they be broken down so that they can be made more operational. From a motivational standpoint, this is helpful. In most cases, short-term objectives have stronger motivational value than longer ones.

The preceding discussion has dealt with the definition of objectives in the abstract, as an essentially logical process. To a large extent definition is a logical process. However, in defining goals, leaders are also subject to the influences of many individuals and groups. First, nearly all leaders are subject to the influence of some organizational superiors somewhere. Among other things, this influence can affect, either directly or indirectly, the kinds and levels of objectives chosen by a leader.

Knowledge that a superior desires a good showing might cause a leader to set objectives beyond the capabilities of his group. Or knowledge that board members tend to stress the importance of certain kinds of activities can lead to formulation of goals not completely relevant to the principal purpose of the group.

Second, a leader is subject to the influence of subordinates. In obtaining information needed to formulate objectives, in checking the feasibility of goals with subordinates, in recommendations relative to potential goals, influence can be exerted from below. In both instances, the exertion of influence may be legitimate. Many decisions are not completely logical, and this applies especially to decisions about objectives and their formulation. Objectives are subject to both logical and non-logical processes, some of which may have their sources in the influence exerted by other people.

Objectives have little significance if they exist only in the head of a leader. An equal part of the process of setting goals involves transmitting them downward in the organization. How is this accomplished? The whole organization is geared to carry it out. Beginning at the highest levels, action to achieve a goal normally takes place below the level at which it was formulated. A chain of authority gives rise to a chain of objectives. Starting with a high-level goal, there is a progression down- ward from the general to the specific—the broad goals of the higher levels being steadily refined into an increasing number of ever more limited and specific ones.

Techniques for accomplishing this process should be incorporated into the formal planning system of the group. Taken in its entirety, a formal planning system is a process that satisfies two related requirements: one is to prepare the way for the act of decision by the analysis of a situation, the other is to plan the action called for by the decision. This same system can and should be used for setting goals.

A formal planning system provides an orderly method for analyzing missions, bringing together in logical relationships the information re- quired to determine objectives, formulating goals, and defining appro- priate goals for subordinate units. This orderly progression remains the same for all levels of administration. The broad objectives formulated by a top administrator are broken down into more specific goals for sub- ordinate groups, thus generating supporting action by each functional unit of the organization.

The fundamental requirement for effective functioning of such a sys- tem is mutual understanding among all levels. At any subordinate level, a clear statement of goals, clear directives, and support in accomplishing assigned goals are necessary. At every superior level, there must be in- formation that will permit the formulation of adequate goals and provide the basis for evaluating progress toward them. Satisfaction of the requi- rements at both levels requires communication, not only in the sense of mechanical channels, but in the sense of uniform interpretation and com- prehension of what is being communicated. Each level in the chain of command must adequately service the others in the interest of such un- derstanding.

Purposes are most successful when leaders make calculated efforts to keep them constantly before the eyes of personnel. Regardless of how it is done, the most important point to remember in setting objectives and developing purposes is that they are strategies—ways of leading a group. The setting of goals is perhaps the most obvious way of con- necting purpose and action. Properly formulated goals provide stable guides for the determination of policies, responsibilities, and duties. Goals instill in group members an identity of outlook, a sameness of intentions, a sense of common identification and common values. If the chief function of goals is understood—the creation of unified action—it is apparent that a system of goals provides useful support to the more personal techniques of leadership.

One thing is sure, goals and purposes cannot be imposed solely by directive. All of the available evidence indicates that achievement is closely related to the degree of understanding members have of goals or purposes, of the reasons for them, and of the ways they can be supported by members' activities. The problem for leaders is to provide the necessary understanding.

COMMUNICATION

In any discussion of group effectiveness, two out of three major considerations are goals and communication. The third is leading, to be discussed in later chapters. Here communication within groups will be the topic.

Because it occurs between people, communication within organizations is a complex process involving many dimensions. One dimension is the accurate transmission of material from the sender to the receiver. A second is its accurate reception and comprehension. A third is its acceptance or rejection after it is received. A fourth involves the distortions and inaccuracies that may occur because of the numerous human links through which material must pass in the communication chain.

One especially complicating factor is the diverse nature of the information that must be transmitted in the typical organization. Such varied materials as the following pass through most communication systems:

- Material related to the mission or the work of the group, such as information about the current situation, problems, progress toward objectives, and so forth; ideas, suggestions, and occurrences relevant to the ongoing work; and information with regard to new objectives, changes in policies, and outcomes of actions.
- Material related to the motivational and emotional climate of the group, such as material reflecting morale; attitudes and reactions to events and problems; and expressions of support, appreciation, recognition, or censure.

In view of this variety, it is not surprising that the exchange of information within a group is sometimes difficult. Communication is a complex process requiring constant attention (Reid and Hammersley, 2000).

Barriers to Effective Communication

Communication usually traverses definite channels, either by formal plan or by gradual evolution of informal practices. Information moves from various sources to points of decision; instructions move from points of decision to points of action; information of results moves from points of action to points of decision and control. However, this is not always the simple, direct process that might logically be expected. Inherent in any organization are certain potential barriers to the free flow of information. Depending upon the situation and the people involved, anyone of them could be the most important faced by a group at any particular moment. Except where specified, the barriers operate in both downward and upward communication.

Climate of Distrust. An organizational climate of distrust, punitiveness, hostility, or fear tends not only to reduce the flow of information but also to evoke motives to distort both upward and downward communication. Such a climate can lead personnel to play it close to the vest, to share a minimum of information with others, and to look with suspicion at the information passed on to them.

Like all human behavior, communication involves learning, and the communication practices of each individual are strongly influenced by the kinds of rewards and satisfactions, or punishments and frustrations, that he experiences during his communication efforts. For example, a climate in which the reporting of unfavorable information is greeted by a plague of correspondence implying censure and demanding justification is likely to rapidly stifle all but the most favorable communication. The group climate and general philosophy, as characterized by its policies and their associated practices, provide a variety of rewards and punishments that influence the development of each individual's habitual ways of communicating and of reacting to communication.

Mounting evidence indicates that communication and trust are closely related and that the consequences of a climate of distrust can be serious. When distrust is prevalent, communication channels dry up. Only the most essential information is transmitted. Personnel lose a sense of involvement or commitment. Accordingly, leaders find it more difficult to get information, more and more difficult to get the job done. A climate of distrust presents an almost insurmountable barrier to development of satisfactory communicative relationships.

Malfunctions in the System. Much of communication within an organization must of necessity be through channels, which is a correct and safe procedure. When the system functions properly, each level is informed and there is no danger of some being bypassed. However, in any system consisting of human beings, there is the danger of a certain amount of line loss—the loss or distortion of all or part of the communication while it is in transit through the system. Line loss is due to two principal factors: failure of control centers, and excessive rigidity in the system. These two factors are closely related because both involve human failure, but they arise from somewhat different sources and, for better understanding, will be discussed separately.

Failure of control centers occurs when personnel who occupy sensitive positions within a group do not perform their communication responsibilities properly. Coordination requires that communication be controlled. Here, control does not imply restriction but refers to regulation and the exercise of directing or guiding power. Through the control of communication, the organization ensures that information is channeled to the appropriate points, that all personnel get the information they require, and that inaccurate or irrelevant information is not transmitted.

Each position in the chain of authority is a center for controlling and processing information. In some organizations, certain positions outside the chain of authority also serve as control centers, for example, staff coordinators. These centers perform highly sensitive roles in the communication process because each functions as a gate that controls the passage of information moving up or down its particular channels. Such a control center may be occupied by one individual, or it may consist of several people organized into a department or section for the purpose of processing information. In either case, the person responsible for the center fills a critical role. He is the gatekeeper for all information passing through the center. He can be selective in the information he passes on, he can block communication entirely by failing to initiate or relay information, or he can distort information to the extent that it becomes inaccurate. Each control center, from the highest to the lowest level, has the opportunity to withhold and distort all or part of the information controlled by it.

Problems arising in control centers may take several forms. The first is simple failure to transmit required material. Initiation or relay of relevant information may be indicated, and the individual fails to take the necessary action. But, two other habits are also prevalent among occupants of control centers. One is *selective emphasis*, the other *selective omission*.

Selective emphasis occurs when an individual receives a communication, selects certain parts that he deems important, and stresses these when he passes the information on. The danger is that recipients will attribute more importance to the emphasized parts than was intended by the original source of the communication.

Selective omission occurs when the individual omits to pass on all relevant facts about a situation or all of the information that has been communicated to him. This most frequently happens when people do not wish to transmit to higher levels information unfavorable to themselves but also may occur when superiors pass information down to their subordinates. There can be no question that an individual occupying a control point must evaluate the material that passes through his position. However, he must be constantly alert for the possibility that selective emphasis and selective omission may result in the transmittal of inaccurate or incomplete information.

Another reason for the failure of a control center is that it may become overloaded. In this situation, normally efficient personnel find it impossible to process information with the dispatch and care that should be exercised. A control center may become overloaded either because too much material is passing through the entire channel or because too much is being routed through that particular center.

Whatever the reason for failure of a control center, the consequences can be serious. When control centers fail, the entire communication system is in jeopardy.

The term *rigidity in the system* refers to an excessive degree of restriction on who may communicate with whom in the organization. Rigidity occurs when there is insistence that every communication be through channels, and then the channels fail to process information efficiently. The general result is that the communication system cannot respond appropriately to the information needs because it is inflexible and over-formalized.

Rigidity tends to add more people to the communication chain. Whenever an additional person is inserted, more time is required for information to pass through the chain, and the probabilities of blockage or distortion increase. When restrictions on lateral communication force more material to be processed by more people in the vertical lines, there is greater danger that communication will be delayed, blocked, or distorted.

Informal Channels. Blocked, inaccurate, or incomplete communications are the most obvious consequence of control center failures and excessive rigidity. However, there is a more pervasive and less clear-cut consequence of these malfunctions, which may, in the long run, be more serious. This is the development of informal channels that are inappropriate, unmonitored, and uncontrolled.

People need information to perform their duties, and the motivation to obtain this can be strong. When official communication channels fail, the tendency is to go outside the formal system to obtain the required knowledge. Friends, acquaintances, and other contacts may serve as sources of information. If this occurs often enough, there may develop informal channels that consistently bypass the official system.

Overemphasis upon informal channels sometimes results in the development of cliques—groups that build up an unofficial network of communication and use this as a means of securing influence in the organization. In turn, rivalry among cliques can lead to conflicts that can destroy both morale and cohesion.

Informal channels to some extent occur in all organizations and are sometimes useful, but they are unmonitored and uncontrolled by responsible personnel. They frequently contain false information, rumor, scuttlebutt, and so forth, which can be harmful to group effectiveness. The best prevention for the excessive development of informal channels is to ensure that the formal system operates to provide personnel with all the information that is required.

Group Loyalties. Another potential barrier to communication can develop from the loyalties of people to their particular groups or work units. Any organization is a system of overlapping and interdependent groups. These groups may be the various departments of an organization, each of which demands allegiance and rewards members accordingly. An organization also has different subcultures—as different as those inhabited by clerks, paraprofessionals, experienced professionals, administrators and supervisors, or different age, sex, and ethnic groupings. Each group has its own idealized image and value system, which are guarded carefully because they give members of that group their feelings of identity. Such groups overlap but are far from identical. Each has an important effect upon communication by influencing the views people hold about who should communicate what to whom in what manner.

Barriers arise when loyalties to these groups cause members to restrict or distort communication to other groups or organizational levels. The most common example is reluctance to release unfavorable information about one's work group to a representative of another group. To release unfavorable information about one's group may be regarded as disloyal by other members.

Another significant problem may occur from failure of representatives of different sections to share information. Strong group loyalties are likely to be the basis for competitive feelings toward outside groups, thus producing the need to withhold or distort information in order to more effectively maintain the integrity of one's own group.

In general, it can be said that strong group loyalties may, under certain circumstances, be highly disruptive of communication between work units and between levels. In turn, these disruptions can lead to intergroup conflict, unhealthy competition between units, and further restrictions of communication—all of which are likely to decrease the total effectiveness of the larger group.

Problems in Downward Communication

Although power differences operate most strongly in upward communication, they also exert certain specific effects upon transmittal down the line. For example, as a result of sensitivity to power, efforts to communicate downward may be subject to misinterpretation. Subordinates may try to second guess superiors, asking themselves, "What did he really mean by that?" Or they may expand upon a superior's instructions, carrying their actions further than he intended.

A more serious problem arises when a superior withholds information from a subordinate, either unintentionally or knowing that the exclusive possession of information is one effective means for controlling people. Since subordinates require information to perform effectively, a superior who denies it to them forces them to be dependent upon him, thus restricting their freedom to exercise initiative.

To some extent, the logical need-to-know is smaller than the wish-to-know. However, when the discrepancy becomes too great, problems are likely to follow. Information that is withheld in one direction generates withholding in the other. When a superior withholds information from subordinates, he tends to reduce his own access to information from below. When carried to the extreme, this process either makes accurate decision making impossible or accustoms decision makers to operating on a reduced information basis.

Problems in Upward Communication

A major problem is that much of the information required for decisions at higher levels originates at lower ones and may never reach the level where it is needed unless a leader is extraordinarily alert. Information does not transmit itself; the individual who obtains it must send it somewhere and will naturally be aware of the consequences of transmission for him. Because of subordinates' sensitivity to the power of superiors, there can be considerable suppression of communication up the line (Green and Knippen, 1999).

No one wants to pass bad news upward, especially if it reflects unfavorably on him. Therefore, unfavorable information tends to be communicated upward only if

- its transmission will not have unpleasant consequences for the sender, or
- the superior will hear about it anyway from other sources and it is better to tell him first, or
- it is information the superior needs in dealing with his own superiors and he will be displeased if he is caught without it.

A leader may fall into the trap of thinking that no bad news is good news, whereas it may be a symptom that upward communication is being suppressed.

Complex organizational structures also delay upward communication. Consider the situation where, at the lowest level, an important problem arises that must eventually be settled at the top. The worker tells the supervisor. They talk it over and try to settle it. This takes a day or two. Then it goes to a higher-level manager. He thinks about it a day or two, and then talks it over with an expert consultant who spends some time trying to develop a possible solution. By the time it reaches the chief executive, days or even weeks may have elapsed.

Even though leaders may appreciate the need for effective upward communication, it is not always easy to translate this need into action. All of the barriers described here are persistent and strong. Neither the opportunities nor the rewards for upward communication equal those for communicating downward. Accordingly, it is a much more difficult task to stimulate good upward communication than it is to send information down the chain.

Developing Effective Communication

For many people, language comes to mind as the chief obstacle to communication. Actually, the factors discussed here are the real barriers, and language is only the symbolic form given to the communication and is what is heard or read. The creation of effective communication in groups is mainly a matter of overcoming such barriers or, better still, of preventing their original development.

Two-way communication within a group is not a one-time process. Continual checking and rechecking of communications, both transmitted and received, are essential to ensure accurate understanding and are most fruitful in an open atmosphere characterized by relationships based on mutual confidence. Directives exert their best effects when read by subordinates who have a clear understanding of the leader's intent and have confidence in it. Similarly, the most useful reports are those that are read or heard by an executive who can review the described situations as subordinates see them. When misunderstandings occur, they can be eliminated rapidly because the executive's questions are regarded as bona fide inquiries rather than preludes to criticism. When agreements are entered into freely, they can be redefined, changed, and clarified as actions are taken on the basis of them. Finally, communications originating within a climate of trust help improve a leader's knowledge both of operations and of his subordinates. Such a climate also helps subordinates to perceive the leader as an aid rather than a threat, thus enabling them to communicate more freely with him.

The important part of a climate conducive to communication is a reciprocal appreciation of the desire and need for relevant information by all group members; when both parties understand this, communication should be effective. Here, the key is relevance. Many communication failures occur because the individual with the information does not realize its relevance to the other person. Since communication by one individual is, in most cases, an adjustment to similar efforts by someone else, effective communication must be a reciprocal process in which both parties are equal participants.

There are several principles essential to the effective functioning of an organizational communication system:

- Channels of communication should be formally specified and definitely known to all personnel.

- There should be a definite formal channel of communication to every member of the group. This means everyone must have someone above to report to (upward communication) and be subordinate to someone from whom information can be received (downward communication). In short, everyone must have a definite communicative relationship with the group.

- The complete line of communication should usually be used. A communication from one point to another should pass through every intervening level in the line of authority to avoid conflicting communications (in both directions) that might occur if there is any short-circuiting of the chain of authority. This is also necessary to maintain responsibility.

- Within this limitation, the line of communication should be as direct and short as possible to minimize line loss. Other things being equal, the shorter the line of communication, the greater the speed and the less the probability of error.

- The line of communication should be maintained at all times; otherwise, there is danger that essential information may not reach those who require it in time. This is the reason for the temporary filling of positions by acting officials during the absence of position incumbents. An equally important aspect is that an organization disintegrates rapidly if the formal line of communication is broken. When a control center ceases to function, important segments of the group may become isolated.

- Control centers must be adequate to process all required communication. This principle has critical significance for the effectiveness of a group's communication system. People occupying positions in the communication chain must be competent to evaluate incoming material, to determine what should be retained or what should be passed on, and to accurately transmit outgoing information. This requires mastery of technical subject matter, knowledge of personnel and organizational relationships, and adequate communication skills.

Techniques for developing communication competence in key personnel are the same as for other aspects of leadership and supervision. Good leadership training, official emphasis upon effective communication practices, and high performance standards are the best means of achieving it.

IMPLICATIONS

There are two rather opposed ways of approaching communication within an organization. One approach is to assume that it is the responsibility of leaders to manipulate the flow of communication through the group, to use this manipulation as a tool for controlling activities, to stress administrative responsibility for developing better communications campaigns, and to emphasize the use of communication techniques, particularly with regard to written and oral messages downward.

An alternative approach, advocated here, is to recognize that effective communication is an intrinsic component of efficient work and effective relationships, that communication problems are symptoms of more basic organizational or leader inadequacy, that communication can be improved by more adequate leader actions rather than by programs devised by staffs, and that communication flows more freely because of a conducive climate and positive relationships than because of stimulation by the use of techniques.

The difference in the two approaches is one of focus. The first tends to view communication as a tool by which people can be changed, controlled, guided, or influenced through education, propaganda, or edict. The second approach recognizes that communication derives from the demands of the job, the problem, or the organizational situation. It focuses upon evolving new relationships and more adequate organizations through improved leadership.

When people have trouble understanding each other, they are probably operating from different frames of reference or have been unable to establish secure relationships and a satisfying, effective group. When there are ambiguous objectives, ineffective organizational practices, conflict and distrust between personnel, or poor leadership, communication difficulties occur as symptoms of these more basic problems.

What, then, can a leader do? First, he can establish as a basic premise that communication is a direct leadership responsibility for every level in his group. He can recognize that communication must occur in the process of doing work, solving problems, or getting the job done. He can directly attack the causes, rather than symptoms, of communication difficulties by working with subordinates toward changing organizational practices, restructuring subordinates' perceptions of his attitudes toward communication, and creating more adequate superior-subordinate relationships.

Communication is related to the level of mutual trust and confidence in the organization. People who trust each other tend to communicate more freely and less deviously. A leader can create trust by focusing on the group climate as the principal determinant. He can give all relevant information to subordinates with maximum openness, make efforts to maximize contacts between him and his subordinates, and he can encourage questions, complaints, and any other form of communication that will build a climate of confidence.

Actions are more significant and speak louder than words in communication. A leader who assures a subordinate that he is trusted and then proceeds to make frequent checks on his activities usually is perceived as distrustful. The leader who desires effective communication relies upon his actions to carry the major weight in influencing others. He uses his words more for information than for influencing.

Communication is probably the most underestimated aspect of group effectiveness. Compared with the more concrete problems with which groups must deal, the issue of communication may seem superficial to some, difficult and intangible to others. Nevertheless, it is one of the most important aspects. All of the results that determine effectiveness depend upon it.

Chapter 8

Leading Groups at Work

This discussion of leading groups at work applies to leadership of all of the group types discussed in this book.

In most organizations, leadership is exercised by individuals who occupy positions of authority. However, leadership cannot be equated with everything that is done by people in supervisory positions. Effective leadership may or may not be exercised by those in positions of authority. A supervisor may perform, without exception, every technical duty attached to the position he occupies; however, this is no assurance that he will exert much positive effect on others or that he will be able to enlist much genuine enthusiasm on the part of his personnel. It is helpful to recognize the distinction between the execution of technical responsibilities and the exercise of leadership (Jacobs, 1970).

LEADERSHIP AS AN INFLUENCE PROCESS

Leadership is basically a tool for achieving desired results. Such achievement depends upon the activities of people. Leaders must, in some way, induce their personnel to carry out those activities required to achieve results. Accordingly, leadership involves influencing individuals, both separately and collectively, to act in a desired manner.

Leadership is a relationship between leader and led, because whether a given leader action has its desired effect is in part determined by the followers. Furthermore, the degree to which a particular leader action will influence is partly dependent upon what has occurred between the participants in the past. Therefore, leadership is also a process, occurring over time and developing according to its own unique history. For this discussion, *leadership is defined as the process of influencing the actions of individuals, groups, and organizations to obtain desired results.*

Since leadership is exercised to obtain desired results, the effectiveness of a leader must ultimately be judged in terms of what his group does and its progress toward its objectives. A supervisor may be well liked and personally admired; however, in terms of leadership, if he does not make a difference in his group, he cannot be called effective. On the other hand, he may be personally disliked, but, if his actions produce effects on others that are useful to his group, he could be considered a valuable leader.

The effectiveness of leadership is determined by the amount of influence a leader can exert on the members of his group or organization. His potential for exerting influence, in turn, depends upon how his subordinates perceive him and his actions. Therefore, a leader's actions may have different effects at different times with different individuals. Furthermore, he may be influential for a variety of reasons.

When dealing with a single individual, an influence attempt is most likely to obtain desired results when it appeals to one or more of his personal needs. For example, an individual is more likely to perform well if good performance leads to a desired reward, such as immediate recognition and eventual promotion. Under such conditions, individuals comply with influence attempts because compliance appears to them to have potential for satisfaction of their needs.

The range of personal needs is wide. They may vary from needs for the simplest material comforts to highly complex desires for status or for self-expression, from the need for protection or escape from danger to the desire to avoid punishment. Personal needs may have their source in any aspect of the individual's life, and those that are susceptible to influence may differ with each individual (Gellerman, 1963, 1998; Maslow, 1970).

Leadership can be highly effective when it is possible to appeal to the personal needs of subordinates. However, many situations do not permit consideration of the personal needs of each individual. Accordingly, a notion that effective influence depends solely upon satisfaction of an individual's needs would be incompatible with what is now known about leadership. If individual, highly personalized needs were the sole determining forces in behavior, it would be impossible to satisfactorily account for successful leadership under many conditions.

While it is true that individuals have unique patterns of personal needs that serve as powerful motivators of behavior, it is also true that there are strong group and organizational influences that may materially modify and channel personal needs and may exercise dramatic effects upon each individual's actions. The specific pattern of relationships, attitudes, and values that develop within a group or organization is a major variable affecting each member's behavior, performance, and satisfaction.

When a number of people become identified with a group or organization, group requirements frequently take predominance over personal needs. Under these conditions, group requirements are not necessarily the needs of the individuals making up the group but, rather, are the demands, dictated by the situation, that must be fulfilled if group or organizational objectives are to be accomplished.

Full compliance with influence attempts depends, in part, upon the leader's ability to provide what members believe is needed to overcome the particular situation confronting their group. If subordinates see the leader as possessing the competence to achieve organizational survival, mission accomplishment, and a desirable organizational environment, they will give him the necessary support. This makes it possible for him to ensure that essential operations are performed.

The evidence is clear on this point. Groups want leaders who can help them achieve their objectives. The leader, in whatever situation, must help his group to define its objectives and to move toward achieving them. Therefore, leadership involves the performance of those functions that will help a group accomplish it objectives.

It seems necessary to emphasize that what is done in a practical situation is not dependent solely upon requirements as the members see them but also upon the judgment of the leader as to what he believes the requirements of the group to be. It is conceivable that what members want may conflict with the leader's judgment of the situation. If the leader sees dangers and difficulties that he knows others in his organization do not recognize, his own conception of the situation, his values, and his responsibility to his superiors will play an important, if not essential, part in determining how he must carry out his role.

Leadership Functions

Any group with goals to achieve has two broad classes of functional requirements that must be fulfilled if objectives are to be achieved (Benne and Sheats, 1948). The functions are as follows:

1. *Task Functions*—Those activities devoted to the effective organization of effort related to mission accomplishment or the performance of specific jobs. Task functions are directly related to the work of the group.
2. *Maintenance Functions*—Those activities that contribute to building the group or keeping it in good repair. They perpetuate and strengthen the organization as an operating entity by maintaining high motivation, morale, working relationships, and so forth.

It is the function of leadership to ensure that these two classes of group requirements are met, either by direct action or by supervision of the activities of subordinates. Therefore, most activities of leaders fall into one or both classes of these leadership functions. Where both functions are adequately performed, both individual needs and group requirements will usually be satisfied.

Descriptions of leader actions that serve task functions are as follows: initiates action, sets objectives, develops plans, determines policy, evaluates performance, and trains subordinates. Examples of maintenance functions are as follows: arbitrates disputes, provides encouragement, rewards performance, stimulates morale, and improves working conditions.

When the functional requirements of a group are met, accomplishment usually results. However, if both types of leadership functions are not performed, the group may falter because of lack of either operational direction (task requirement) or internal strength (maintenance requirement). If it remains indefinitely on dead center, neither moving toward its objectives nor improving its internal resources, it may be concluded that virtually no leadership functions are being performed.

Task and maintenance functions do not always support each other. For example, the soundest changes in an administrative procedure can result in increased suspicion and distrust among personnel. The changes might be fully justified from the standpoint of efficiency (task function); however, if they are introduced without adequate attention to their effect upon morale (maintenance function), their long-run benefits may never be realized. Similarly, a leader who puts all his efforts into creating a happy department (maintenance function) may jeopardize work activities (task function). Both types of functions must be adequately considered and balanced in leader judgments and actions. Leaders sometimes find it difficult to strike a proper balance between the two types of functions. It is not uncommon for a supervisor to make maintenance his major concern to the detriment of work to be done or to stress operational matters while giving insufficient attention to maintenance.

In a large organization, one person could never perform all the activities necessary to meet the functional requirements. Therefore, distinct activities may be combined into separate positions, and the occupants of these positions assume the duties of providing their unique activities and sometimes no others. However, a supervisor is ultimately responsible for ensuring that all functions are performed, even though he may not always perform them personally. Through his position, the various activities must be coordinated and channeled so as to satisfy the requirements for mission accomplishment.

Leader Actions

The concept of leadership functions contains two important ideas. The first, discussed above, is that there are certain functional requirements, that is, task and maintenance, which must be met if a group is to perform effectively. The second idea is that a given function may be served by many different actions, according to the circumstances. It is the responsibility of the leader to determine what specific action will most appropriately serve the needed function at a particular time.

Under specific circumstances, any given activity may or may not serve a needed function. As one example, the nature of a group's assignment will determine the kinds of activities required to fill a leadership function. The actions of a supervisor of an assembly line are not the same as those required for a manager of a computer center. Although both task and maintenance functions are required in each instance, the specific needs of the department demand that the leader provide certain actions in order to serve the appropriate functions. If the mission changes, different actions may be required.

A given leader action may serve both task and maintenance functions simultaneously. Thus, a manager who effectively coordinates the work of his staff in solving a difficult operational problem may also have helped it to develop internal solidarity.

On the other hand, an action may serve one function at the expense of another. For example, initiating action might always be expected to help a group reach its objectives (task function). However, in a highly capable group where each subordinate knows his job and performs it well, a supervisor who puts out a constant stream of excessively detailed orders may, in fact, stultify motivation to the extent that effectiveness is impaired. Or, an eager supervisor may spur his unit toward objectives in such a way that pressure causes friction to develop between groups or individuals. Even though the short-term objectives are achieved, the long-term effectiveness of the group may be damaged.

Changing situations generate different functional requirements. A major problem for leaders is to determine which function is required and which action will serve that function most appropriately.

Determinants of Leader Actions

Which action will most effectively serve a leadership function is determined by the nature of the particular situation as it is evaluated by the leader (Barnard, 1948). In most leadership situations, three broad elements require consideration. These are personal factors within the leader, personal factors within subordinates, and nonpersonal factors in the general situation.

Factors Within the Leader. A leader's behavior will be influenced greatly by the many factors operating within his own personal makeup. He will perceive his relationship problems on the basis of his background, knowledge, experiences, and personal characteristics. Among these factors having special relevance will be the following:

1. *Leadership Inclinations.* Some leaders function more comfortably and naturally in a team role where they work closely with subordinates. Others operate better as highly directive leaders, maintaining somewhat distant relationships with subordinates.

2. *Confidence in Subordinates.* Leaders will differ in the amount of confidence they feel in other people's ability to perform effectively. A lack of confidence in others is likely to result in a leader's giving more attention to detail and attempting to do the job himself. On the other hand, confidence in subordinates can result in more delegation, less direct supervision, and so forth.

3. *Feelings of Insecurity in Uncertain Situations.* Some people have a greater need than others for predictability and stability in their environment. Low tolerance for ambiguity may result in efforts to obtain tighter control over the situation and over subordinates. Personal need for high predictability of outcomes can result in rigidity of action, which makes it difficult to react rapidly to unanticipated occurrences. Tolerance for uncertainty permits flexibility in coping with a variety of events.

4. *Value System.* What is the relative importance he attaches to organizational efficiency, development of subordinates, and such factors as motivation, morale, and so forth? How strongly does he feel that subordinates' ideas and opinions should be invited and considered in making decisions? How convinced is he that the leader should carry most of the burden of decision making and problem solving?

Awareness that these and other personal variables may be operating will enable a leader to better judge the appropriateness of a contemplated action and to predict its potential effect (Green and Butkus, 1999).

Factors Within Subordinates. Whether a leader's action will have the desired effect is partly determined by personal factors operating within each subordinate. In addition to such personal variables as attitudes, needs, and values, subordinates will be influenced by their expectations of how the leader should act in relation to them. The leader may not agree with such expectations, but awareness that they exist makes him better able to predict which of his actions will enable subordinates to perform more effectively. Such factors as the following may require consideration:

1. *Needs to Work Independently.* People differ in the amount of control under which they can work most effectively. Do subordinates possess relatively high

needs for independence, or do they seem more comfortable under close control?

2. *Tolerance for Ambiguity.* Can subordinates tolerate ambiguous situations? Some people function best only under clear-cut directives; others can also perform well when problems are hazy and requirements are not clearly defined.

3. *Identification with Mission.* Do subordinates understand and closely identify with the mission and objectives of the group or organization?

4. *Knowledge and Experience.* Do subordinates have the necessary knowledge and experience to carry out their duties without strong guidance?

The abilities, experience, and general attitudes of close subordinates are likely to be major determinants in any situation. Whether a leader understands his subordinates relative to these factors will partly determine the nature of his actions.

Factors in the Situation. In addition to personal factors within the leader and his subordinates, certain characteristics of the general situation also require consideration:

1. *Type of Organization.* Like individuals, organizations differ considerably in terms of the kind of leadership that will be most productive. In each case, the type of organization and the way it is structured are of major importance in determining the pattern of leadership required. Similarly, such variables as the size of the organization, its geographical dispersion, and so forth, also need to be considered.

2. *Experience and Proficiency of the Group.* Generally, groups that have experience in working together can be expected to cope with new tasks or problems more readily than inexperienced ones. However, this is not always true. Some organizations develop consistent histories of failure. In either case, past performance is also a factor for consideration.

3. *Nature of the Mission.* Is the mission one in which the group has experience? How difficult is it? What are the knowledge and skills required? Does the supervisor have knowledge about the mission that is not available to other members of the group?

4. *The Time Perspective.* Here, the question involves the amount of pressure felt by the leader with respect to time for getting things done. When time pressures become intense, less carefully considered leadership actions may result.

5. *General Conditions in the Environment.* The way in which environmental conditions dictate the appropriateness of leader behavior can be illustrated by distinguishing between two extremes of what Barnard called "the conditions of leadership." The first extreme involves stable conditions. Such conditions are relatively free from violent changes, uncertainties of unusual character, and important hazards. Under stable conditions, the behavior of leaders can be calm, reflective, deliberate, and anticipatory of future contingencies. Their actions usually lack the dramatic characteristics often observed at the other extreme. Stable conditions may create difficulties because leadership must be

exercised without the support of strong emotion or obvious necessity and must combat the indifference that frequently accompanies lack of stress and excitement. Stable conditions call for self-restraint and deliberation. The other extreme involves great instability, uncertainty, speed of decision and action, great risks, important stakes, and important issues. Here, leaders must exhibit physical and moral courage, decisiveness, inventiveness, and initiative.

A number of elements require consideration in determining which actions will most likely achieve maximum influence. The kinds of actions that may be effective will differ widely depending upon the situation.

The Leadership Process

Leadership problems change continually. No two problems are exactly alike and each is, in part, affected by the larger organizational and interpersonal situation within which it occurs. Therefore, the individual who would be effective as a leader must be able to recognize and control a variety of constantly shifting problems and situations.

Recognition of the uniqueness and shifting nature of leadership problems leads to several conclusions that have profound significance for effective leadership:

1. *There does not appear to be a single pattern of leadership that can be practiced so as to consistently yield the best organizational performance.*

   Most students of leadership have concluded that it is unproductive to attempt to specify leader behaviors supposed to be effective in all situations (Bennis, 1959; Likert, 1961; McGregor, 1960; Olmstead, 1997; Vecchio, 1998; Vroom, 1969).

2. *It is more useful to view leadership as a process of adaptation to changing conditions, requiring the ability to assess situations and then to furnish appropriate actions based on the prediction of consequences.*

   This view of leadership as an adaptive process has an important implication. Adaptation to changing conditions requires a wide repertoire of behaviors.

3. *Accordingly, leadership cannot be put in terms of any one predetermined, correct way to behave guaranteed to get results under all conditions.*

A leader is most effective when he can address the concrete needs of the situation in front of him. Therefore, leaders must guide themselves according to the reality of the situation. This means that, in any situation, there are certain facts that must be taken into account and that cannot be ignored. There is a set of real, existing conditions within which one must operate. When a leader tries to act as if these conditions do not exist or as if they were different than they are, his actions are going to do nothing more than aggravate the problem, rather than solve it. Usually, it just makes bigger problems out of little ones.

Leadership based on reality is not a predetermined set of best ways to influence people. The only predisposition that is needed is that the leader must first diagnose what is reality and then use the appropriate action (Argyris, 1957). This requires the ability to make an accurate evaluation of the specific events that are taking place, to recognize symptoms of what is happening, and then to move from symptoms to causes. Also required is the ability to supply skillful actions intended to alleviate the causes.

Therefore, the leader is concerned with assessing events and providing appropriate courses of action.

SKILLS OF LEADERSHIP

Skills required of a leader fall logically into two general classes (Benne, 1961).

1. *Diagnostic Skills.* These are skills involved with observation, listening, analysis, and assessment of situations, together with prediction of potentialities, trends, and valid directions that situations are likely to take.

2. *Action Skills.* This class involves the skills of acting, or intervening, in situations as they are diagnosed. They involve such skills as planning, leadership strategies, manipulation of organizational conditions, and behaving effectively in interpersonal situations.

Diagnostic Skills

The essential prerequisite to appropriate action is accurate diagnosis of the problem. Accurate diagnosis depends upon an ability to identify critical elements in a situation, while stripping away and disregarding the many factors that may be present but not essential to the major issue.

Recognition of the realities of situations reaches its highest importance at the point of diagnosis. Accurate diagnosis is most likely to be accomplished when approached from an attitude intended to understand problems as they actually exist rather than as the leader thinks they should be or as he wishes they were.

A number of specific aspects of realistic attitude can be cited (Schoen, 1957):

1. A realistic attitude requires an approach that is free from unsubstantiated assumptions about the nature of people, groups, organizations, and the causes of observed events.

2. A realistic attitude requires a high degree of acceptance of people as they are. This does not suggest that it is necessary to condone irresponsible actions, sloppy performance, or laziness. However, it is difficult to respond realistically

to concrete situations if the leader cannot distinguish between people as they are and people as they should be.

3. A realistic attitude requires a leader to be aware of possible differences between his viewpoint and that of other people. The leader who cannot concede, even to himself, that others may have different values, aspirations, and reactions is not likely to predict the consequences of his actions with much accuracy. Corollary with this point, however, is the necessity for a leader to maintain an independent point of view in the face of such differences.

4. A realistic attitude includes the leader's understanding of himself and of the impact of his actions on other people. Complete self-understanding is impossible, but the leader who can predict with some degree of accuracy the probable effects of his actions on subordinates is better able to assess situations that may have been partly created by those actions.

5. A realistic attitude requires recognition of the chain of authority and the resulting differences in responsibility, status, and position in the organization. Also required is a realistic understanding of the way these differences affect people's behavior, the leader's included. It is realistic to recognize that such differences do exist, that rank has its privileges, and that people do not ordinarily act with their superiors the way they act with their peers or their subordinates.

6. Finally, a realistic attitude requires an awareness of both formal organizational procedures and such informal practices as traditions and customs, communication grapevines, and attitudes of personnel relative to the organization and to its leaders. This awareness permits the leader to predict (within limits) how his group may respond to his actions.

Thus, diagnostic skills require a realistic approach to life, people, and organizations. The essential element is an attitude that asks, If I do this, what *will* happen? rather than, Since I believe that such and such *should* happen, other people surely see it the same way and will respond accordingly.

Action Skills

It is one thing to know what should be done, and another to get it done. Accurate diagnosis is essential, but influence can only be exerted through action. Skillful leadership involves both diagnosis and action.

For any situation, a leader has available a repertoire of actions that, singly or in combination, he may bring into use in his efforts to exert influence. Since each leadership problem will be somewhat unique, skill is required in selecting and executing that action that is most appropriate for the specific situation. Therefore, effective performance as a leader requires flexibility of action, a capacity for choosing among a range of alternatives without undue commitment to any one way of handling all problems.

Action flexibility is related to the leader's personal resources, his experience, his competence, and his grasp of the situation. Personal rigidities, lack of experience and training, and similar impediments may restrict the leader's capacities for behaving and thus his flexibility in leading. Consider, for example, a manager who is successful in conducting informal staff conferences, in bringing opinions out into the open, and in obtaining full information for decision-making purposes. However, he is not especially effective in direct action. Consider, on the other hand, a supervisor who is a driver, lacking a sense of organization but effective in anything he personally undertakes. Because of his hard-hitting, direct methods, he is not inclined to carry others along with him, and he is likely to ruffle egos of subordinates. Both supervisors are restricted in their available repertoire of actions, and, accordingly, their potential for maximal effectiveness is impaired.

The ability to shift behavior according to the demands of the situation is an essential requisite for effective leadership. Through flexibility of action, the leader performs his functions as they are dictated by changing organizational requirements.

IMPLICATIONS

Leadership is an influence process requiring abilities to diagnose the functional (task and maintenance) requirements of a group and to furnish actions that will fill these requirements. Through such actions, the leader influences his group members to perform so as to accomplish objectives.

The definition and the discussion appearing in this chapter stress leadership as a group function rather than leadership as a personal quality. This is a useful distinction, which requires emphasis.

1. The idea of leadership as a group function stresses the requirements of organizations and of leadership situations. It leads one to look at the kinds of actions that will fill these requirements.

2. On the other hand, leadership as a personal quality refers to a special combination of personal characteristics. It leads one to look at the qualities and abilities of individuals.

The problem with leadership as a personal quality is that, except for a high level of motivation, successful leaders seem to differ widely in their characteristics. There has not been found a single set of abilities and inborn traits characteristic of all successful leaders.

Although the particular characteristics of a leader seem to influence his success, those that are essential vary considerably depending upon the circumstances. On the other hand, leaders who differ widely in abilities and traits are sometimes equally successful in the same or similar situations.

Although the personal characteristics of individual leaders are certainly important, it is not fruitful to consider leadership as a universal pattern of characteristics possessed by certain people. It is more useful to recognize the importance of skills, attitudes, and actions that can be acquired by individuals who differ widely in their inborn traits and abilities.

Chapter 9

Supervision and Leadership

The substance of the preceding discussion is that supervision and leadership are not the same. Supervision becomes effective only when good leadership practices are superimposed upon the managerial techniques dictated by the kinds of jobs, the caliber of group members, and the work methods characteristic of the mission or task.

DIFFERENCES BETWEEN SUPERVISION AND LEADERSHIP

Since leadership is the process of influencing individuals and groups in order to achieve desired results, each leadership act, each leadership decision, and each deliberation of leadership problems must have as its first consideration the effect upon human performance. The ultimate criterion of effective leadership can only be the quality of performance demonstrated by the members. Performance remains of necessity both the proof and the aim of leadership (Olmstead, 2000).

This takes nothing away from a leader's role as manager or supervisor. He must still provide guidance, make decisions, and see that plans are made, that programs are formulated, that activities are properly coordinated, that results are evaluated, that subordinates perform effectively, and so on. However, he is responsible for seeing that work gets done, rather than doing it himself, and he will be most effective if he facilitates the work of subordinates by creating conditions in which their capabilities and motivations can be fully realized.

This process of facilitation cannot be performed passively. It is the active pursuit of effective relationships between superior and subordinates, without which there will be poor linkage between positions, faulty communication, and operating difficulties. It is also likely that subordinates' morale will be affected because inadequate relationships tend to produce tension, anxiety, and frustration.

It is important to note that the need for facilitation is postulated not upon the idea of making subordinates happy (however important this may be) but upon the accomplishment of work. Undoubtedly, facilitation takes time, energy, and patience, but the costs of more restrictive, unilateral, approaches to leadership are much higher.

What emerges from this discussion is a broadened concept of the roles of managers and supervisors. The manager or supervisor, instead of seeing himself solely as the boss—one who plans, organizes, controls, and decides by himself—or as a trainer, or both, must also think of himself as a resource to his group, an expert in communication, and a catalyst to his subordinates. A major function will be facilitating as well as directing, maintaining a healthy flow of clear communication, and relating effectively to subordinates as well as to his operational duties.

Given such a concept, the particular style of leadership will vary with the individual, the problem, and the situation. Not every supervisor can polish his leadership skills to a high gloss, but this will not matter too much if his attitude is facilitative. If his attitude is wrong, high skills will probably not help very much. Fortunately, skills can be learned, and the required attitude can be cultivated, if only the supervisor sees the need for them.

Skills in diagnosing situations and in acting within them help a leader to cope with the multiplicity of elements that he constantly faces in his daily work. The first thing of which a leader or potential leader should become aware is the fact that behavior in organizations is usually the result of many determinants. In approaching a leadership situation, many people see only the leader, or the problem, or the subordinates. Yet, in reality, one is rarely confronted with the simple relation of a supervisor to a subordinate or a group of subordinates. Instead a great many relations are frequently joined in a network. To seize upon one or two factors as a basis for action and neglect the rest is usually a gross oversimplification. It can only cause the leader to misunderstand the problem and take the wrong action toward its resolution. The good leader understands that individual facts or actions cannot be interpreted except as components of a larger picture.

This means looking at the event or action in relation to groups of people, their attitudes, and their standards of behavior. It means looking at the total group situation, including goals, motivation, and attitudes, to see, for example, whether the organizational climate is influencing the behavior of individuals or of groups. It means looking at the work situation to determine whether successes or failures, efficiencies or ineptitudes, are exerting an influence upon behavior. It means taking into account previous experience and background of group members.

A leader cannot avoid the fact that his own attitudes have fundamental significance in any leadership situation. They are a critical element because they are bound to affect his interpretation of events and his thinking about them. They influence the reactions of subordinates to him. The leader is a highly important determinant of the behavior of his subordinates and his work group. What he says, what he does, or what he does not say or does not do all have an effect that is often far-reaching.

One point remains to be made. It has been quite conclusively determined that leadership is, in large part, situationally controlled. That is, factors within the work and organizational context strongly influence the effectiveness of leadership and leadership behavior (Deal and Kennedy, 1982).

SITUATIONAL DETERMINANTS

The significance of situational determinants for effective leadership has been demonstrated clearly. For example, it has been shown that a leader's effectiveness is influenced not only by his relation to his subordinates but also by his relation to his superiors. The total pattern of authority within an organization may prevent a leader from being successful, however much he may try to use principles of integration, participation, interdependence, and supportiveness. For example, it has been shown that training in human relations does not improve a supervisor's performance as a leader when he has to work in an organization that encourages or emphasizes contrary principles of leader-worker relationships.

Other studies have shown that task variables, that is, type of work, contribute to group performance and morale. Where task variables are determinants, effectiveness would require a leader to initiate changes in the organization of tasks rather than in his interpersonal relationships. However, under some conditions, task variables may require a leader to change his behavior toward employees if he would be effective. Thus, it was found that task characteristics in one company were related to different kinds of supervisory behavior. People who were engaged in tasks requiring a large amount of group cooperation preferred employee-centered supervision, whereas people whose tasks did not require group cooperation preferred directive, production-centered supervision.

The amount of cooperation required appears to be one of the critical situational determinants of the appropriateness of leadership styles. For example, participation (power equalization) is most appropriate for tasks that require a great deal of cooperation. High differentials in power are unlikely to lead to high productivity in creative, planning, or problem-solving tasks.

Another factor, somewhat related to requirements for cooperation, is the extent to which commitment of personnel is necessary for success of the organization. It appears that two factors determine the amount of commitment required by an organization. The first is the extent to which negative work attitudes can adversely affect the output of the organization. In general, the more each employee can control the quality and quantity of the organization's product and the more work is done in groups rather than individually, the more commitment is required. The second factor is the relation of the organization to its environment. If an organization is in a struggle for survival, commitment is critical, and failure by personnel to maintain a high commitment can mean the difference between survival and failure.

There may be strong relationships between the requirements for worker commitment and styles of leadership characterized as *instrumental* and *expressive*. The instrumental orientation to leadership is task-centered. Its primary concern is with productivity, quality of product, the efficiency of work groups, and meeting the demands of the environmental situation. Employee satisfaction is considered to be an inevitable by-product of efficient organizations rather than the direct product of leader behavior.

On the other hand, an expressive orientation involves concern with the fair and equitable distribution of the work load, opposition to authoritarian leadership practices, and the avoidance of excessive pressure, suspicion, fear, and hostility. Emphasis is upon internal cohesion and the integration of roles.

Some studies have found a pronounced instrumental orientation in top management and an expressive orientation in lower supervisors in organizations requiring a high worker commitment. In organizations requiring a low worker commitment, the pattern was just the reverse. It appears that the more that commitment is required, the more leadership tends to make a difference and the more first line supervisors tend to use expressive leadership (Hare, 1976).

Factors completely beyond the control of the supervisor may complicate and interfere with the effectiveness of his leadership. When organizational survival is endangered, top managers become increasingly instrumental in their orientation, less inclined to delegate authority, and more inclined to set specific, practical objectives for subordinates and to institute means for checking to see that these objectives are carried out. Demands are relayed to lower supervisors in terms of more and more specific requirements and objectives. When this occurs, the lower supervisor faces a conflict; although he may be oriented to expressive leadership, he is under increased pressure to engage in instrumental leadership—closer supervision, more stringent performance requirements, less tolerance of deviation from standards, and a more punitive orientation to personnel.

The conflict between these demands and the supervisor's own personal inclinations usually causes stress and impairs his effectiveness. His leadership practices oscillate between the poles of instrumental and expressive leadership so that to his subordinates he seems inconsistent and arbitrary. This behavior is frequently accompanied by a decline in the commitment of workers as well as in their productivity, which causes more pressure from above and the repetition of this cycle.

IMPORTANCE OF THE WORK CONTEXT

The importance of the work context to group effectiveness cannot be exaggerated (Deal and Kennedy, 1982). The environment within which people work has come to be recognized as probably the single most critical determinant of performance. Although the abilities and personal characteristics of individuals contribute significantly to their performance, more and more evidence indicates that the conditions surrounding these individuals frequently make the difference. It is universally acknowledged that elements that compose the work context warrant the critical attention of responsible administrators, whatever the nature of their organizations.

Attention to structural aspects of the work context is necessary for at least two reasons. First, an effective structure, including policies, procedures, and concomitant processes of authority, communication, and control, is essential for operational efficiency. When circumstances or inclinations dictate a disregard for structural considerations, chaos is the usual result (Hite, 1999). Second, a poorly designed system tends to create frustration and conflict among personnel. Excessive interference with work activities because of breakdowns in the system can be devastating to motivation. This is important because of its multiplying effects upon attitudes. People get frustrated and angry with one another when they have difficulties doing their jobs.

The necessity for attention to climate is even more obvious. Climate is the atmosphere within an organization that results from customary ways of working. It pervades every aspect of an organization and exerts some astounding effects upon the motivations, satisfactions, and performance of personnel. Stated very generally, climate is the motivational aspect of organization. Because motivation is critical, the elements that contribute to climate can be disregarded only at severe risk.

In many organizations, the most common attempts to improve effectiveness take the form of modifications to the structural framework, that is reorganizations, and of increased emphasis upon the more formalized organizational constraints, such as policies and procedures. Attention to these aspects is imperative; however, overreliance upon them leads to organizational rigidity. Effectiveness under the complex conditions of today requires flexibility, a quality that has its principal source in the relationships, motivations, commitments, and loyalties of personnel. These aspects are mainly determined by the climate within the organization (Deal and Kennedy, 1982).

EFFECTS OF ORGANIZATIONAL LEVEL

In one sense, the skills of leadership do not differ radically between the lower and higher levels of an organization. Both the first-line supervisor and the chief executive are concerned with diagnosis and action. In another sense, the requirements are vastly different. The nature and complexity of the problems encountered and the variety of available actions change dramatically as one moves upward in the chain of authority. Because of this fact, the basic process underlying leadership—adaptation to changing situations through the use of diagnosis and action—is modified by the role of the leader and the nature of the responsibilities assigned to him.

Katz and Kahn (1966) have proposed three categories of levels of leadership acts, differentiated in terms of their effects upon the formal aspects of organization: *the origination of structure*, or the initiation of change and policy formation; *the interpretation of structure*, or the piecing out and implementing of policies to meet immediate problems; and *the use of structure*, or the routine application of prescribed remedies for predicted problems. It appears that these categories are characteristically encountered at high, middle, and low organization levels, respectively, and each requires for successful use a different cognitive style, different kinds of knowledge, and different characteristics. They concluded that no pattern of leadership is appropriate for all phases of organizational life.

Barnard (1938), in his classic book on the organizational executive, classified management activities into three areas: maintenance of organizational communication, securing of essential services from individuals, and formulation of purposes and objectives. He distinguished between organizational levels only in terms of the third category and concluded that purposes and objectives become more and more specific as they filter down through the organization and each lower level translates higher-level policy and objectives into more and more operational forms. Other writers have also made the point that lower-level managers sharpen and implement the broader goals and objectives developed by executives at high levels. They also noted a shortening of time perspective as one moves down the chain of authority.

It also appears that technical skills become less important and administrative skills become more important as one moves up in the hierarchy. This conclusion is in part supported by Argyris (1962), who suggested that the effectiveness of first-line supervisors is significantly influenced by the nature of the work and by imposed controls, whereas goals and interpersonal factors become more important to the effectiveness of executives at higher levels. While the first-line supervisor is seen as dealing with the technical aspects of the job and the day-to-day supervision of employees, each successively higher level is viewed as demanding broader perspectives and the ability to translate policy into action through the coordination of different work units.

In the sections that follow, two extremes will be discussed: leadership at senior levels and leadership in first-line supervision. These extremes point up the principal differences in leadership requirements that can be attributed to differences in level. In the comparison, it should be noted that organizational size and complexity may also determine leadership requirements. The head of a small organization with only two or three levels obviously faces problems different from those of a large, complex organization. Likewise, supervisors in tall organizations with narrow spans of control face problems different from those of supervisors in flat organizations with broad spans of control. Also, it appears that there is a greater difference between the leadership requirement for middle and first-line managers than between those for middle and senior levels.

Leadership at Senior Levels

Leadership becomes increasingly complex as one moves up the chain of authority, not simply because the problems are larger but because a new orientation is necessary. As one example, the use of personal influence applies most clearly to lower-level supervisors. Individuals at lower supervisory levels usually have more strictly defined responsibilities and more limited discretion in the execution of their duties. More effective use can be made of day-to-day direction of subordinates and the development of close working relationships.

Such an orientation begins to lose force, however, as the top of the organization is approached. The higher up the chain of authority an individual goes, the more access he has to information and other resources of the organization, the more power he has over other people, and the more importance or status he gains. The high-level leader has more latitude in directing his organization and must deal with more current issues, not for themselves alone, but for their long-run implications for the performance of the organization. Leadership at high levels is more than steering an organization by the routine solution of everyday problems. Leaders must be concerned with developing, maintaining, and directing an organization so that personnel and departments are both competent and motivated to perform their necessary activities. They must be concerned with coordinating these interdependent activities so that all fit together and contribute effectively to accomplishment of the overall task of the organization. It is in this realm of building and directing a complex organization that the distinctive quality of high-level leadership is found.

It is the function of leadership at senior levels to define the goals and to make them operational as the purposes of organizational existence, to create a viable system distinctively adapted to these objectives, and to ensure that the organization's energies are channeled in the required directions. The leadership role of higher-level administrators involves four broad activities: formulating goals, purposes, and roles for the organization; developing and maintaining the organization as a viable system; promoting organizational performance; and representing the organization to its external environments.

Formulating Goals, Purposes, and Roles. Here, the principal concern is with the leadership role in formulating goals and purposes for the organization, translating them into an operational plan, and initiating practices that will convert these abstract ideas into effective actions. An essential part of the leadership role consists of interpreting these aims to everybody in such a way as to win support for them and to build them into the internal life of the organization. The character of the organization must be shaped and sensitized to ways of thinking and responding so that goals serve as concrete operational targets toward which all efforts may be directed. The mandate given the head of an organization is often very broad, and this presents him with one of his most important tasks. From a general mission, he must formulate specific goals that are meaningful and realistic for all levels of activities.

When a new organization is activated, the necessity for formulating goals is usually given some degree of recognition. However, it is equally important to periodically examine the goals of long established organizations. Once an organization becomes established, with many forces working to keep it functioning, it is likely to neglect the task of occasionally evaluating the continuing relevance of its goals. This default may stem from the tendency to become immersed in daily operations; but, just as often, it may stem from a reluctance to change existing conditions and disturb a smoothly functioning operation that might be threatened by sharp changes in goals, with their attendant claims and responsibilities. Nevertheless, because of changes in needs and conditions, it is important that goals be periodically examined.

Beyond the definition of goals lies responsibility for building purpose into the organization, for giving objectives meaning. This serves to give long-run significance to day-to-day behavior and to otherwise inconsequential duties. Successful purposes are never merely artificial or manipulative, even though they may be put forward deliberately with the intent to further success or survival. A purpose will never be effective if it is merely an empty verbal statement. The executive must have the insight to recognize the necessity for it, to discover a successful formulation, and most important, to find ways of building it into the fundamental attitudes and motivations of the personnel.

Goals and purposes are statements of intent and usually say little about their mode of achievement. Following from his goal-defining responsibilities is the obligation of a high-level leader to identify and make operational the role of his organization as indicated by these goals and purposes.

The necessity for careful formulation of objectives and a role for an organization has long been a fundamental concern of managers. Indeed, the necessity for clear and unequivocal objectives is so much accepted these days that their very real utility as an instrument of leadership may sometimes be overlooked. This can be unfortunate because a manager who fails to use objectives effectively wastes a potent tool for influencing his organization.

Objectives serve the important functions of providing an organization with direction and of mobilizing efforts around common aims. It is impossible to effectively organize the activities of numbers of people unless they have a common target or set of targets toward which they can strive, around which they can focus their efforts, and against which they can evaluate their accomplishments. Furthermore, whenever members of an organization become attached to an objective because of its significance to them, the result is a prizing of that objective for its own sake. Therefore, it changes from an impersonal target to a valued source of satisfaction. In these ways, objectives serve both cognitive and motivational functions.

Objectives represent the specific things that an organization is trying to accomplish. They are usually fairly long-term and provide members with incentives for accomplishment. Since objectives give direction to the efforts of the organization, a manager must play a vital role in their formulation or, if they are assigned to him, in making them meaningful for his subordinates by interpreting these aims to everybody in such a way as to win support for them. Thus, the character of the organization is shaped and sensitized to ways of thinking and responding so that objectives become concrete operational targets toward which all efforts may be directed.

Role definition for organizations is, in effect, a decision by an organization or its leaders regarding how it ought to function. This involves estimates of its relationships with other organizations (including the demands to which it should respond), of the means to be used for achieving its objectives, and of its capabilities, potentialities, and limitations.

As conditions change, roles may shift. This necessitates periodic reevaluation by a manager. If reassessment is not accomplished, changed conditions can result in the performance of activities that are no longer relevant or that, in the new situation, conflict with those of other organizations.

Insofar as possible, roles should be prescribed when an organization is activated. When this can be done, the only problem remaining is to ensure that frequent reassessment occurs to adapt to changing conditions. When, however, organizations that are based on new concepts are activated, roles must often be worked out on the basis of evolving experience, and leadership of a high quality is required.

Developing and Maintaining an Organization. Probably the single most significant function of leadership at high levels is to develop and maintain an organization as an integrated, viable system of activities and relationships. Few aspects of leadership are so important yet so badly misunderstood as the problem of organizational development. When the question of developing an organization arises, there is a tendency to think only in terms of clearly enunciated policies and procedures, well-delineated responsibilities for individuals and units, and smoothly functioning channels of authority and communication. These are elements of the machinery of efficiency rather than the dynamics of effectiveness. Leadership has the job of transforming an engineered, technical arrangement of individuals and units into a functioning entity.

The development and maintenance of an organization call for developing a core of key personnel, formulating ground rules for working, building an effective communication system, and promoting a high level of motivation. It is important to recognize the critical significance of these activities and that, in performing them, the leader establishes those organizational conditions that will best sustain effective performance.

- *Developing Core Personnel.* An important activity in managing an organization as a system is the development of a core of personnel, homogeneous as to outlook, attitudes, and motivation, who will occupy the key positions. This core group may include staff personnel, subordinate managers, and the occupants of critical positions at many levels. When developed properly, it serves as the nucleus around which the organization can be built. These individuals reflect the basic outlook of the organization and ensure that the development of derivative policies and practices will be guided by a shared perspective.

  The development of a core group may involve recruitment and will certainly necessitate the selection of personnel who appear to meet both the technical and personal requirements of the particular organization. Of even more importance, however, is indoctrination of key people and definitions of the responsibilities, roles, and relationships that are supposed to exist between both individuals and units. This may be accomplished by formal statements, but it is more effective when developed by the sharing of experiences, during which expectations can be communicated more clearly and less formally.

An important activity in both the development of core personnel and in the general promotion of organizational performance is training. The development of a high level of proficiency within an organization is ultimately a training process.

• *Formulating Ground Rules for Working.* Organizational practices and ways of working are matters of legitimate concern for managers. The practices and the attitudes associated with them shape the character of the organization and thus contribute to performance. A part of the management function involves ensuring that each individual knows what the organization is supposed to accomplish, how his duties relate to the organization's objectives, and what constitutes the ground rules for performing his activities.

Ground rules are basic understandings that are supposed to be adhered to by all concerned. Many organizations are less than effective because basic ground rules have not been clearly set forth. If ways of working are not fully understood and agreed upon, departments spend their time competing against each other, line and staff personnel get into each other's hair, managers waste their energies fighting over cloudy jurisdictions, and it all ends by everyone losing confidence in the organization.

Under certain conditions, such as the activation of a new organization or department, formal statements are useful for communicating policies about ways of working. However, the manager's greatest opportunities for leadership in this area arise in the course of daily work. It is here that he is best able to communicate desires and attitudes relative to ways the organization should function.

• *Developing an Effective Communication System.* Viewed as a system, an organization is an elaborate network for gathering, evaluating, recombining, and disseminating information. For this reason, communication is the essence of organized activity and is the basic process out of which all other activities derive. The capacity of the organization to respond to changing situations and pressures, the motivation of personnel to contribute consistently and eagerly to the welfare of the organization, and the ability of managers to mobilize the vital human resources for accomplishment of objectives—these depend in large part upon the effectiveness of communication.

The effectiveness of organizational communication rests upon fulfillment of several requirements. The first is that the formal communication system, which operates through the chain of authority, must function efficiently and according to its design. Therefore, much attention must be given to ensuring that everyone receives the information he needs and that blockages do not develop within the system.

A second requirement involves obtaining uniform understanding and compliance with formal communications. This is a problem because each of the units within an organization has its own particular mission and certain unique objectives. Therefore, when a communication is sent to a number of subordinate units, each unit may extract a different meaning from the message, depending upon its significance for that unit's mission and the things it is striving to accomplish.

Accordingly, one task for a manager involves interpreting the purposes, intentions, and reasons for everything to everybody, especially reasons for changes that may exert drastic effects upon missions, roles, values, and the relationships among subordinate units. Interpretation means more than merely issuing a formal statement. The manager has to construe meanings to different units and individuals in such a manner as to obtain both understanding and support.

A third requirement involves regulation of the relationships that may affect the communication process. In organizations, personnel are structured into certain systems of relationships, for example, those based on authority structures, functional (work) structures, or friendship structures. These systems of relationships both stimulate and inhibit effective communication. They facilitate communication because they provide stable expectations about who should communicate with whom about what and in what manner. However, uncertainty in these relationships can also inhibit communication. Personnel losses, transfers, promotions, replacements, and new policies and procedures can modify the relationships between people. When this occurs, communication can become less effective.

More than any other individual, a manager can govern these relationships and, by so doing, affect communication within his organization. By controlling and regulating relationships, he can stabilize the communication system, thus contributing to organizational performance.

- *Promoting a High Level of Motivation.* The power of organized activity depends upon the willingness of individuals to cooperate and to contribute their efforts to the work of the organization. In short, outstanding organizational performance requires that personnel be motivated.

It is characteristic of many organizations that motivational problems may be viewed as administrative ones. Thus, when such problems are identified, a manager may attempt to handle them through administrative fiat—through the issuance of new directives, the changing of policies, the correction of bad physical conditions, and so forth. However, there is a significant distinction between these kinds of actions, which merely reduce already existing problems, and those aimed at developing and maintaining a positive state of attitude that can serve as an active force for achievement.

High motivational conditions require conscious and calculated efforts by leaders to develop and sustain them. A manager must use both his leadership skills and his organization's resources in order to create motivational conditions that are conducive to effective performance. The problem is that just about everything in an organization has effects upon motivation. This suggests that every decision and every action by a manager must be considered in the light of its possible consequences for motivation, as well as for its effect upon operations. This is not to say that decisions and actions that favor operations over motivation will likely suffer as a result. Such awareness permits a manager also to undertake appropriate measures to counter the anticipated drop in motivation. It is another matter, however, to make such a decision with total disregard for its effects upon motivation.

Promoting Organizational Performance. A third aspect of leadership at high levels is to promote the performance of the organization. This function is to be distinguished from those decision-making activities involved in technical operations. A decision is merely a potential action. Adhering to the definition of leadership as an influence process, the function of promoting organizational performance is concerned with those activities intended to influence individuals and groups toward effective accomplishment.

- *Keeping Organization Moving toward Goals.* A leader must activate all those measures necessary to keep the organization moving toward its goals, arrange for changes when and where they are needed, and initiate policies that serve to keep the organization pointed in the right direction. Even where he does not originate action himself, he must provide general guidance to subordinates so that all activities contribute most appropriately to the overall goals. He can see the whole of the organization and each part of it and the relationship between parts and between the parts and the whole. He must have ideas to offer, suggestions to make, and substantial help to give wherever he deems it necessary.
- *Emphasizing Training.* Another aspect of the promotion of organizational performance is training. An organization functions as an integrated unit only when members are able to perform their duties at a high level of proficiency. Staff development is ultimately a training process in two areas. The first is the inculcation and perfection of technical skills, mainly accomplished through formal courses, on-the-job training, and so forth. This is usually well understood and emphasized. However, a competent, unified organization requires more than proficiency alone. Effective performance depends to a considerable extent on the attitudes and ways of thinking of personnel, particularly those who occupy key positions. The second area of staff development is the shaping of these attitudes in directions favorable to the organization. The greatest opportunities for influence available to a high-level leader can be found in his daily interactions with his subordinates. At such times, he can interpret goals and purposes, transmit his views of appropriate actions and ways of functioning, and inculcate both specific and general perspectives relative to the proper role and character of the organization. In this sense, staff development is a constant activity, which requires recognition of the development opportunities that may be available and careful attention to the potential effects of day-to-day experiences upon long-term proficiency.
- *Quality Control Standards.* A third aspect of the promotion of organization performance is quality control through the development and communication of standards of excellence and the introduction of such standards into daily activities. Formal quality control is an essential tool of managerial direction. An executive attempts to influence individuals or groups by developing expectations of performance that give his subordinates clear standards against which to judge accomplishment. The quality control of performance becomes a fundamental aspect of leadership and plays a major role in determining overall organizational achievement.

A major activity involves controlling the quality of performance through the development and communication of standards of excellence and through inculcation of such standards into daily activities within the organization. Formal control devices are essential. However, control is most effective when a manager develops explicit expectations relative to the quality and quantity of performance and communicates these expectations so that all personnel have clear standards against which to gauge accomplishments.

Explicit standards of performance are not always easy to develop. However, everyone who directs the activities of other people uses some frame of reference for judging whether the work of his organization and his subordinates is satisfactory. In certain instances, these standards are highly explicit; in other cases, the person making the judgments cannot himself enunciate clearly the basis for his evaluations. But, regardless of whether his ideas are hazy or clear, every manager uses some guidelines for judging performance, and these standards should be a matter of record within the organization.

Representing the Organization. A final requirement of leadership at high levels may be to represent the organization to higher levels, supervising authorities, other organizations, and the community. This is usually considered to fall within the realm of administration but is also critical to leadership, because the extent to which a manager protects the interests of the organization, represents its views to critical publics, and obtains the necessary resources exerts some extremely powerful influences upon the performance and motivation of all subordinates.

Ultimately, a high-level leader is responsible for the overall performance of a sizable number of people functioning in an integrated system of activities. In his leadership role, he must strive to create those conditions most conducive to maximum effectiveness of each subordinate group and individual. Performance of the activities described in this section may place some especially complex demands upon him. He may be faced with such problems as building a smoothly functioning system of duties and work activities; creating a closely knit network of functional relationships between subordinate units; developing solidarity and organizational identification within the organization; and coping with motivation, morale, and performance limitations of the entire organization or of individual subordinates. Such problems require high degrees of skill in diagnosing organizational behavior and providing actions appropriate to the specific situations encountered.

Effectiveness in handling such problems rests on the ability of the leader to sense the constantly changing currents in his organization, to recognize particularly sensitive areas, and, most important, to direct his organization in such a manner that serious problems do not arise. This calls for constant awareness of the human factors in day-to-day operations and skill in successfully adapting to a variety of situations arising from these factors (Cohen, Fink, Gordon, and Willits, 1980; Murdock and Scott, 1997).

Leadership in First-Line Supervision

High-level leaders are limited in the extent to which they can directly influence the actions of most of their subordinates. First-line supervisors, on the other hand, are in a position to translate the larger objectives, intents, and purposes into action, and through their daily contacts they can directly influence the attitudes, motivations and performance of even the lowest-ranking group members.

There are four basic elements involved in supervisory leadership: (1) behavior that enhances someone else's feeling of personal worth and importance (support); (2) behavior that encourages members of the group to develop close, mutually satisfying relationships (interaction facilitation); (3) behavior that stimulates an enthusiasm for meeting the group's goal or achieving excellent performance (goal emphasis); and (4) behavior that helps achieve goal attainment through such activities as scheduling, coordinating, and planning, and by providing resources such as tools, materials, and technical knowledge (work facilitation). These four classes of activities encompass most of the leadership behavior of supervisors.

Providing Support. In general, anything that contributes to insecurity or feelings of being threatened will tend to reduce the effectiveness of subordinates. If, in contacts with group members, the supervisor communicates attitudes of distrust, hostility, or lack of confidence, influence attempts will not be effective because the members will be too busy protecting themselves. Similarly, people who, because of insecurity, are forced into yes-man roles with supervisors cannot contribute with maximum effectiveness.

A sense of personal worth rests on a base of personal security. In responsible and capable individuals, it also requires the opportunity for them to participate in the solution of meaningful and worthwhile problems, to discuss decisions that may affect them, to assume responsibility when they are ready for it, and the right to appeal. Opportunities to contribute, to be heard, to be active members of an important organization are what most people like. Supervisors who provide such opportunities will have subordinates who display greater motivation, higher morale, and greater involvement with the work and with the organization.

Interaction Facilitation. It is probably true that the greatest barriers to effective performance in groups are interpersonal—emotional relationships between people who feel threatened in some way by the presence of other people whom they dislike or whom they do not understand. Pleasant relationships reduce threat and permit members to shift their attention from interpersonal problems to work goals.

When a work group is so led that some of its members are communically peripheral to others, these individuals are likely to become disheartened, frustrated, and unproductive. A group that is organized or led so that contacts between all members are restricted is not likely to become very cohesive. The effective leader organizes the work so that the fact of a common task to accomplish gives personnel valid reasons for interacting. He coordinates activities in such a way that his personnel have adequate opportunities to consult on problems, and he ensures participation in a wide range of assignments so that all members get a chance to know each other closely.

Goal Emphasis. One of the most consistent findings in leadership research is that the effective leader emphasizes goals and goal accomplishment rather than becoming immersed in the details of minute tasks. This is probably the most difficult point for a supervisor to accept. He is responsible for making sure that his group accomplishes its tasks and frequently feels compelled to become deeply involved in the details of the work. Instead of becoming deeply involved in the details of task accomplishment, a more constructive approach for him is to continually provide subordinates with performance goals to which they will be committed and performance standards that clearly specify his expectations. Most people will strive hard to reach performance goals to which they are committed and will exercise self-discipline and self-control to the extent of this commitment. The best results can be obtained by actively promoting excellence through continual stress upon high performance. In this way, a supervisor can add new dimensions to his subordinates' views of their roles. He can stimulate new avenues for achievement, new opportunities for development, and new endeavors for reaching all sorts of goals that can stir even the most settled of workers into renewed activity. Any action that excites enthusiasm for meeting both group and individual goals and for achieving excellent performance is part of this behavior.

Work Facilitation. There can be little doubt that employees value a supervisor who helps them accomplish work objectives. In addition to directing activities, the supervisor must also contribute to the efficiency of the group (e.g., through planning and good management) and minimize inefficiency (e.g., by eliminating problems and disrupting influences within the work situation).

Much of the time of effective supervisors is spent in planning, coordinating, scheduling, and mobilizing resources. They work on activities that assist their personnel to move toward the group's objectives without lost motion and wasted effort. This implies that a supervisor must think ahead, anticipate difficulties, and take whatever actions are necessary to forestall problems. The important conclusion is that an effective supervisor takes a slightly larger perspective than his subordinates and adjusts his activities to that perspective.

Performance of these four classes of leader activities contribute to all of the conditions for effectiveness discussed earlier. In general, it can be concluded that the supervisor who provides support to subordinates but still permits autonomy, who encourages interaction among subordinates and works at developing group solidarity, who emphasizes goal accomplishment and high performance standards rather than detailed task execution, and who provides whatever actions are necessary to help workers do their jobs, including planning, scheduling, coordinating, and so forth, will be the more effective supervisor in terms of both worker satisfaction and worker performance.

Chapter 10

Training for Leadership

Although many factors may influence the performance of an organization, there can be little doubt that the quality of leadership that is available will be one of the most critical determinants of ultimate success (Bennis, 1959; Olmstead, 2000). In recognition of this fact, training intended to help leaders and potential leaders to perform their jobs more effectively has commanded considerable attention in business, government, and the armed forces for many years. Tremendous effort and resources have been expended, with varying degrees of success, to develop personnel who will occupy the positions of leadership needed to meet present and future organizational requirements.

Current and future conditions make the effective training of leaders and potential leaders more critical than ever before. Requirements for leadership have their bases in the kinds of performance demanded of organizations. The kinds of performance required of many of our organizations appear to be changing and, with these shifting demands, the problems of leadership and the process of leading are becoming more complex and more difficult. Indeed, changes in technology, society, and organizations are presenting numerous new challenges that will require more sophisticated and more skillful leaders for the future (Olmstead, 2000).

These changes are placing new demands upon leaders in business and governmental organizations (Anderson and Anderson, 2001). In addition to increasingly complex technology, changed social values and increased economic expectations make traditional organizational constraints less effective in obtaining needed performance from their personnel. High-quality leadership is becoming increasingly important as a means for stimulating effective performance (Peters, 1982).

The armed services in particular are faced with requirements that will place new demands upon leaders. For example, the necessity for continuous readiness and quick reaction in the turbulent and unpredictable environments of the present and future places a premium upon the capability of a military organization to respond flexibly to a more or less continuous flow of uncertain situations. Yet, the responsiveness must be accomplished in the face of technological advances in equipment, communications, and logistics that complicate both decision processes and the execution of required operations.

These requirements raise significant questions about the most effective methods of training leaders to help their personnel perform effectively under conditions of rapid change and complex technology (Kanter, 1983; Olmstead, 1980). Leader training has indeed become both more difficult and more challenging (Kirkpatrick, 2001; Peters and Waterman, 1982).

LEADING IN ORGANIZATIONS

In a broad sense, it can be argued that the principal purpose of organizational activities is to make favorable conditions for the achievement of certain goals. Efforts are made to increase, as much as conditions will permit, the probabilities of success in accomplishing an organization's objectives, mission, or purpose. The making of decisions, the improvement of procedures and the specification of methods, the designation of responsibilities and the assignment of duties, the direction of work, and the execution of tasks—all these processes have one organizationally legitimate purpose: to increase the chances of successfully accomplishing an organization's objectives. Upon this point rest all of the criteria by which the effectiveness of organizational activities are evaluated.

Probabilities of success are increased only by taking relevant and appropriate actions. For organizations, whose very survival may depend upon the successful accomplishment of goals, the actions require high levels of competence by numbers of people working together. The effectiveness of such an action system requires the coordinated efforts of individuals and groups performing parts of a total task so that the activities of each person and each group contribute, in some fashion, to accomplishment of the overall goal. Under these conditions, group performance becomes a paramount issue.

Effective groups demonstrate the characteristics that have direct relevance for goal achievement, which were set out in chapter 2 (Likert, 1961). It is not surprising, in these terms, that the effectiveness of a group with respect to the achievement of goals should be so closely related to the effectiveness of its leaders. Regardless of the type or size of a unit, group, department, or organization, the individuals who occupy positions of leadership must make sure that objectives are established and communicated, plans are made, policies are developed, and personnel are obtained, assigned, and trained. They must establish levels of responsibility, set up mechanisms of coordination, delegate authority, direct subordinates, provide stimulation and inspiration to everyone, exercise control, develop high levels of motivation and morale, and adjust the plans and activities to broader changes in the larger organization. If these activities are not performed well, the group will not function effectively.

Activities such as these have important bearing upon leader effectiveness. Leaders become effective by understanding what is required of them and how, in their organizations, the human forces may be combined, balanced, and directed toward ultimate goals.

When the changing and increasingly complex conditions discussed in chapter 1 are superimposed upon these requirements for leadership in any organization, it becomes apparent that leadership, in either civilian or military organizations, can no longer be a matter of hunch or native ability, backed by a few elementary concepts and reinforced through the trial and error of experience. Instead, it must rest upon systematic knowledge and a rational and conscious application of sound principles and practices (Statt, 2000). The needed knowledge and associated skills of application can be acquired best through training (Eitington, 1996). For this reason, the provision of high-quality leadership training is a critical task for any organization.

FOCUS OF THIS CHAPTER

The purpose of this chapter is to present a brief assessment of the present state of the art of leadership training. Such an assessment is warranted because the current and future requirements placed on leaders make high-quality training increasingly important. Yet, despite an enormous expenditure of resources, the field of leadership training is in considerable disarray, and there is not available any organized knowledge base concerning the pedagogy of leadership instruction. Accordingly, an assessment of the present state of the art should be useful to trainers, training designers, and training managers, as well as individuals charged with program evaluation or research responsibilities.

A number of books and publications that have addressed leadership and managerial development have included brief reviews of the training literature. However, few have focused directly on the issues involved in leadership training, and, certainly, none has provided much guidance to trainers. Therefore, the individual required to design a program intended to develop leaders is forced to resort to tradition, hunch, and perhaps a few educated guesses. The difficulty is compounded when, as is frequently the case, the trainer may be almost completely naive concerning both learning principles and leadership training methodology.

Because leader behavior has its source in the values and attitudes of the leader, as well as some fairly complex interpersonal skills, serious training for leadership is probably one of the most difficult educational processes there is. Indeed, the individual charged with responsibility for designing a leadership training program finds himself faced squarely with the necessity for solving some exceedingly difficult problems. As he makes decisions about the proper training methods to use, he encounters the question of the objectives toward which training should be directed. As he goes about selecting objectives, he must resolve the deeper problems of his concept of leadership and, more specifically, his notion of the kinds of behavior necessary in order for an individual to perform effectively as a leader. The concept embraced by the program designer has important implications for the decisions he must make relative to program content, methods, and so forth. Yet, in attempting to select a concept, he must become familiar with and evaluate the many competing theories of leadership that are currently in vogue.

One attractive way of avoiding the necessity for choosing from among the many theories of leadership is to develop program objectives based upon empirical analysis of the specific behaviors and roles of leaders, for example, through use of Instructional System Development procedures. Even here, however, the program designer cannot escape some very difficult decisions.

The kinds of assumptions made about both leadership and the learning process at various decision points in the course of program development determine the path training will take. However, program designers frequently have formulated their concepts of the leadership learning process rather casually, or they have uncritically adopted ideas that prevail in their particular organization or culture (Rothwell and Kazanas, 1999).

Although a few publications have provided some guidance on the use of specific training methods, the central issues to be considered in the development of leadership training have rarely been systematically analyzed and discussed. Nowhere does there exist comparative analysis and guidance concerning the potentials and limitations of the instructional methods commonly used for developing leaders.

The plain fact is that, despite the large amount of resources, effort, and time that is devoted to activities that fall under the rubric of leadership training, astonishingly little attention has been paid to the pedagogy of such training. It is hoped that this chapter will contribute toward alleviation of that condition by bringing the field into perspective, providing some guidance to trainers, and, most important, highlighting issues that have important relevance for both program design and research to improve leadership instruction.

Training for leadership may occur in many different contexts and for a number of diverse purposes. In some instances, the term *leadership* is used quite loosely, and programs or courses whose titles include the term may actually consist of content that purists would contend is only remotely related to the exercise of leadership, for example, technical decision making and problem solving. In other cases, especially within business and government, one can find programs in which leadership is never mentioned but that contain much content that is directed toward improving the ability of trainees to influence the activities of their personnel. Thus, training for leadership can include a wide spectrum of programs, which may carry a variety of labels.

For this discussion, it is neither desirable nor necessary to be concerned with the many competing theories of leadership, with their sometimes subtle implications for training. Furthermore, training for leadership of informal groups is deemed not relevant.

Most leadership training occurs within and for formal organizations. Trainees are individuals who either occupy or will be promoted to positions that require them to influence the actions of other people in order to obtain results desired by their organizations. The broad purpose of most such training is to enhance, in some way, the abilities of trainees to exercise such influence.

Accordingly, for discussion in this book, *leadership* is the process of influencing the actions of individuals, groups, and organizations in order to obtain desired results, and leadership training includes all courses and programs designed to enhance the abilities of participants to exercise such influence. This definition of leadership training encompasses instruction in all people-related aspects of work and performance. Thus, programs concerned with military leadership, as traditionally defined, are included, but instruction devoted to military tactical or technical decision making and problem solving, as well as other tactical or technical activities, is not considered to be leadership training.

In a similar vein, programs in business and government concerned with human relations, supervision, and people-related aspects of management are deemed to be training for leadership; however, training for supervisors and managers that addresses the technical or administrative aspects of work is not considered to be instruction in leadership. Most Organizational Development (OD) activities are not here considered to be leadership training, because they are devoted to analysis of the particular organizations to which participants belong and to improvement of the functioning of these organizations. However, where organizational diagnosis leads to provision of instruction in any aspects discussed here, this instruction is judged to be leadership training.

THE STATE OF THE ART

There is little disagreement about the desirability of leadership training. A few writers have argued that attempts to train leaders is a waste of time, for example, McNair (1957), who, years ago, damned the whole idea of human relations training as a ritualistic shibboleth; and Fiedler (1965, 1970), who contended that it is easier to change the job situation than to change a person's behavior or leadership style through training. With a few exceptions, however, most people who have been involved in the field concur that training leaders is a critical activity for sound organizational improvement (Murdock and Scott, 1997; McCall and Lombard, 1967; and Palmer, 1998).

A Field in Disarray

Despite this near-consensus on the value of leadership training, the field seems to be in considerable disarray. Among the many programs, one can find a number that are well designed and excellently administered. All too many, however, show no discernible concern for sound training principles, they evidence few common assumptions and hypotheses regarding learning, and they vary widely in theoretical and methodological approaches. Even more tragic, many programs devoted to training managers, supervisors, and military leaders are astonishingly superficial. It is not unfair to say that many leadership training programs have distinguished themselves more by the number of students graduated than by demonstrated effectiveness.

There may be many reasons for this situation, however; two, in particular, appear to be major contributors. The first derives from some widely diverse orientations to leadership and, therefore, to leadership training. The second involves the misuse of training methods. They are closely related, and both are important determinants of the present confused state in the field of leadership training.

Diverse Approaches to Leadership

In a literature survey conducted earlier (Olmstead, 1980), one factor was revealed that has apparently had a significant impact upon the state of leadership training. This factor is the wide diversity of approaches to leadership exemplified by the training programs covered in the survey. When descriptions of these programs were carefully examined, it was possible to identify a number of different concepts of leadership, all of which have critical implications for training. Following a more recent review, it was concluded that the situation has not changed significantly (Olmstead, 1997).

Within these different orientations, leadership appears to be variously conceived as concerned with (1) the influence of human-social factors on work, (2) superior-subordinate relationships, (3) an ethic of leadership, or (4) all of the phenomena of human interaction within organizational contexts.

The Human Relations Approach. In business and industry, the rubric human relations has traditionally been applied to a movement devoted to sensitizing managers to the necessity for being aware of the human element in organizational life. Based on the pioneering work of Mayo (1933) and his collaborators, Roethlisberger and Dickson (1939), the movement emphasizes the social system that evolves when a group of people work together and the effects of that system on performance and attitudes. Under this approach, leadership is a matter of working effectively with others and building cooperative efforts into the organization. It requires taking the human elements into account and integrating them with technical aspects.

The result of this movement has been a multitude of training efforts ranging from the early Training Within Industry programs of World War II to many of the elaborate in-company programs that exist today. Although they vary in content, these programs have one thing in common. Most are appreciation courses, designed to help managers appreciate the human element in work by indoctrinating them to the importance of good human relations. They most often use directed conference methods, although some case study is also used.

Most programs of this type are intended to make participants more conscious of human relations. They are designed on the assumption that a manager who is more consciously aware of the human element in work will perform his duties more effectively. The process by which this is supposed to occur appears to involve a cognitive reorientation. The free discussion of various facts and points of view is supposed to result in heightened awareness of human affairs, which will then be reflected in improved on-the-job performance.

Although making people more appreciative of the importance of human relationships at work has to be a commendable goal, the rationale for this approach raises some problems. For example, it is questionable whether awareness alone is sufficient to effect a change in behavior. When one considers that even extensive experience with physical facts does not necessarily lead to the correct perception of physical phenomena, it is not surprising that being told of the importance of human relations will not necessarily result in improved interpersonal behavior. Furthermore, even if the cognitive structure involving human relations can be modified by appreciation courses, there remains the need for skills in performing effectively within the new orientation. Normally, such courses make no attempt to develop skills.

A final, but most important, problem involves the level at which interpersonal relationships are treated in the typical human relations program. No less a person than Roethlisberger, one of the fathers of the human relations movement, frequently expressed concern over the superficial way many courses dealt with human relationships (1951).

The Superior-Subordinate Approach. Human problems in organizations are most likely to be felt by people occupying leadership positions. The image of effective operations held by many leaders is characterized by numbers of hard-working subordinates, each performing efficiently at a high level of motivation, with eye on the goal and shoulder to the wheel. In reality, of course, very few subordinates fit the stereotype. Problems of handling subordinates, therefore, become a major preoccupation of many supervisors and managers.

Consequently, leadership is often viewed solely as a matter of superior-subordinate relationships. In this view, the goal of training is to educate leaders in ways of directing subordinates, motivating them, controlling their actions, and modifying their behavior to fit the needs of the organization.

Training programs based upon these requirements usually concentrate on equipping leaders with skills for coping with fairly specific problem areas, such as those noted above. Because this approach is highly pragmatic, training has tended to take the form of rules of conduct and specific techniques designed for application in prototype situations. Its goals stand in contrast to the goal of developing cognitive awareness, exemplified by the human relations approach. Specific techniques for coping with common situations also leave much to be desired, however. Human behavior is too complex to be susceptible to solution by formula. The leader who is armed with a set of techniques is apt to find himself ill equipped to handle the infinitely changing patterns of relationships with subordinates.

The Ethical Approach. A contrasting approach, with a somewhat different orientation, has arisen in recent years. It views the field as concerned with the democratic ethic, and it is characterized by a definite philosophy and a set of more or less specific methods for practicing leadership.

Democracy as it applies to human relations and leadership has little to do with democracy as a political system. In this ethical view, human relations involves the processes of working together, with the sharing of power, interests, and accomplishments. Accordingly, leaders should aim toward development of the individual and his realization of his constructive potential. Development and growth are fostered by giving every individual an opportunity to fully exercise his competencies and achieve mature self-direction (Murdock and Scott, 1997).

From this standpoint, a democratic leader is one who stimulates or enables every individual to contribute whatever he can to the total group effort (Halman, 1950). Democratic leading, therefore, involves coordination rather than compulsion. It is concerned with creating the conditions under which subordinates are able to realize their full potential (Gordon, 1955). In most organizations, when used, the emphasis usually takes the form of greater participation in decision making, goal setting, assigning tasks, and so forth.

Training to develop more democratic leaders usually requires more complex methods than either of the previously discussed approaches. Because values and attitudes give direction to interpersonal behavior, training in the democratic ethic is deemed to require a major reconstruction of the personality. In this orientation, the problem for leadership training is one of "rebuilding the personality by breaking down the barriers to change, introducing new ideas, values, and assumptions into the trainee's personality, and thus altering the motivations that guide his activity as a leader" (Seashore, 1957).

This process can be exceedingly complex as well as difficult. Accordingly, a variety of training methods is usually brought to bear, ranging from group discussion, to role playing, to workshops on group-centered leadership, to T-Group and laboratory training. In each case, the objective is a basic change in attitude with, in some instances, concomitant development of action skills. Clear-cut evidence of permanent personality change resulting from these or any other training methods has yet to be produced.

Few people would oppose the democratic ethic as a desirable orientation to life. One can seriously question, however, the feasibility of attempting to indoctrinate leaders with the full democratic ethic if they are expected to function in essentially authoritarian organizations, such as those that prevail in industry, government, and the military services.

The necessity to reconstruct the value and attitude systems of trainees can also be questioned. Although total commitment to the democratic ethic might require some basic changes in value systems, it seems reasonable that a person could be skillful as a leader for pragmatic reasons, without espousing ethical democracy as a way of life.

The Reality-Based Approach. A way of thinking about organizations that has undeniable importance for leadership training has recently come to the fore (Statt, 2000). This approach has received its greatest emphasis from certain organizational psychologists and Organizational Development (OD) practitioners who embrace open systems theory, group dynamics concepts, and theories of social motivation. In this approach, leadership is conceived to be concerned with all the phenomena of human organizations. This means that leadership cannot be limited to one or a few highly specific areas such as the superior-subordinate relationship or the influence of social factors on work. Furthermore, leadership is not restricted to person-to-person interaction or even leader-group relationships. An organization, in this approach, is viewed as an interactive system, a network of social-psychological relationships in which all the phenomena that arise from human intercourse may be encountered. Therefore, leaders must be concerned not only with two-person, face-to-face relationships but also within-group interaction, inter-group relations, and the hierarchical systems that go to make up large organizations. Leaders must be concerned with controlling and manipulating these various relationships in such a manner as to maximize the effectiveness of their organizations and their subordinates.

Therefore, a leader must be more than merely adept at influencing individual subordinates. In addition, he should have a knowledge of group and organizational characteristics and, more important, must be able to use this knowledge to achieve group or organizational objectives.

When the field is seen as involving all the phenomena of interaction, leadership is concerned with coping with the realities of human relationships however and wherever they may occur. A leader is viewed as one of the actively participating parties in a reciprocal interaction situation. Seen in this light, the nature of leadership problems changes continually, and to be effective, the individual must be able to recognize and cope with a wide variety of constantly shifting interpersonal situations as a participant in them. Thus, leadership cannot be put in terms of any one predetermined, correct way to behave. To maintain contact with things as they are requires adaptability, change, and flexibility of operation.

In this approach, the basic guiding concept of leaders is the *reality principle*. According to Thelen (1954), this principle states

There are facts which need to be taken into account: there is a prior reality—a set of existing conditions independent of the will of a person or group—within which one must operate. When a person tries to act as if these conditions do not exist, or as if they were different than they are, his action is aggravating to the problem-situation rather than constructive; it jeopardizes immediate goal achievement; and, through thwarting the potential for individual and group growth, it may curtail long range possibilities.

Argyris considered effective leadership to be "reality-centered." According to Argyris (1957), "Reality-centered leadership is not a predetermined set of 'best ways to influence people.' The only predisposition that is prescribed is that the leader ought to first diagnose what is reality and then use the appropriate pattern."

Argyris concluded that effective leadership requires effective diagnostic skills. Following this position, one would expect a leader to be most effective when he can address the concrete needs of the situation confronting him. This would require the ability to evaluate realistically the specific events that are taking place and also to recognize symptoms of what is happening and move from symptoms to causes and then to skillful actions intended to alleviate the causes. Therefore, a leader faces a variety of situations that demand a broad repertoire of behaviors if he is to be successful. Leaders must be concerned primarily with assessing events and devising actions appropriate to them.

Training that evolves from such a definite view of leadership would be expected to rest upon a fairly clear-cut rationale. Such is the case. The view that leadership does not involve any special set of specific actions suggests that a person cannot be taught what it takes to be a good leader or how to lead people. Under this approach, training should (1) teach a student about things to look for (phenomena of interaction), (2) train him how to look for them (diagnostic skills), and (3) help him to react appropriately to them (action skills).

Some similarity between this and the ethical approach may be apparent. Admittedly, similarities do exist at certain points. For example, some proponents of the democratic ethic also stress the importance of diagnostic and action skills and use high-involvement methods in training. However, despite similarities, several distinct differences have important implications.

The principal differences involve the concept of leadership and the processes involved in learning. The ethical approach views leadership as concerned with the democratic ethic and the distribution of power. Effective training is to be achieved through changing attitudes, revamping the personality, and developing diagnostic and action skills needed for implementing the ethical orientation. On the other hand, the reality-based approach considers leadership as dealing on a pragmatic basis with all of the phenomena of interaction. No value orientation is involved. Effective training is achieved through the conscious and systematic development of diagnostic and action skills. Revamping the personality is not required.

Consequences of Diverse Approaches. Approaches to the nature of leadership are of more than academic interest; they count heavily in both the design and the conduct of training programs. If the several approaches described above are scrutinized closely, it should become apparent that they, in fact, make either tacit or explicit assumptions about the kinds of behavior necessary for effective leader performance. These assumptions are reflected, in turn, in the goals and methods selected for training leaders.

A trainer who believes that leadership involves considering the human-social factors at work and that effective behavior requires taking these factors into account in decisions and actions (human relations approach) will probably attempt to teach students to be more aware of the human element in work. On the other hand, a trainer who is convinced that leadership is a problem of superior-subordinate relationships (superior-subordinate approach) will view leader behavior as capable handling of subordinates; and training will involve teaching leaders techniques of manipulating subordinates toward better performance.

Commitment to the democratic ethic (ethical approach) leads to the conviction that the fundamental problem involves the equal distribution of power and the growth of individuals. Effective leader behavior, therefore, will require actions that may equally distribute power and thereby create conditions conducive to individual and group growth. With this orientation, a trainer will aim to inculcate the democratic ethic and will teach methods of participative leadership.

However, if a trainer embraces the proposition that leaders must deal with all of the phenomena that arise from the interaction of people within organized systems (reality-based approach), he is likely to view effective behavior as coping successfully with the realities of organizational life in all its forms. Training will be directed to developing the ability to actively understand and control a wide variety of constantly changing situations.

The kinds of assumptions made about the nature of leadership and the behavior through which it is manifested clearly determine in large degree the path a training program will take, with respect not only to content but also to methods. However, trainers frequently have formulated their concepts of leadership in relatively casual ad hoc ways; or they have uncritically adopted the ideas that prevail in their organizations or cultures and attempted to fit whatever training methods are currently in vogue to the ideas.

Misuse of Training Methods

A second important contributor to the present state of leadership training is the misuse of instructional methods. Traditionally, most leadership training has been approached from one of two directions. The first approach uses conventional teaching methods carried over from the field of education. This approach generally involves an instructor who delivers classroom presentation of concepts, theory, and recommended ways of handling a job or problems related to it. In recent years, however, it has become apparent that such methods are not very effective for training people for positions of leadership. Genuine improvement in leadership practices requires some fairly fundamental changes in the behavior of the individuals involved. People do not seem to learn leadership skills merely by studying theory or being told how they should behave.

The second traditional approach to training is of somewhat more recent vintage. It appears to be based on the proposition that improved leader performance can be achieved by exhortation or a few gimmicks designed to involve the students. Although most such programs appear to be harmless, they are also inadequate. Token programs simply are not very effective in generating behavioral change.

Even when some of the more sophisticated and effective methods are used, trainers are tempted to accept one method as correct for all purposes. This identification with one method is likely to obscure the fact that selecting a training device is ideally influenced by the character of the changes sought. Any worthwhile training program will ordinarily require different activities at different times for different purposes, and choices should be determined by evaluating a method against the specific objectives, conditions, and situations under which it will be used.

It would be easy to stop at this point and lay all the blame at the feet of inadequately qualified trainers. In fact, some trainers are inadequate. Because of the requirement to achieve fundamental changes in the behavior of trainees, serious training for leadership is one of the most difficult educational processes there is (Jaques, 1992; Thelen, 1954). Yet, in few other fields can there be found so many instructors who are expert neither (1) in their subject matter nor (2) in teaching.

Program designers and trainers need to know with some assurance how to relate variations in the training process to specifically desired outcomes. Ideally, a trainer should be able to stipulate the kinds of behavior he wants students to exhibit at the end of a program and then select the methods most likely to produce the desired behaviors.

In training for hard (i.e., technical) skills, the procedure is fairly straightforward and can be accomplished for most jobs with minimum difficulty. The program designer simply identifies the tasks performed on the job, decides how best to demonstrate the task activities, and develops sessions that permit practice until task mastery is achieved.

Training in soft skills, such as leadership, however, presents any conscientious trainer with some extremely slippery problems. As he sets out to select methods, he encounters the question of the objectives toward which training should be directed. Indeed, as he goes about selecting objectives, he must resolve the deeper problem of the kinds of changes trainees must undergo if the objectives are to be achieved. Is the result of training to be a cognitive change based on the acquisition of information, an attitudinal change brought about by the additional information and experience gained through the program, a behavioral change—an improvement in certain specific skills accomplished through practice—or all of these? His answer should dictate the training methods he selects because each of the above alternatives may require use of a different method.

The currently accepted solution, of course, is to develop training by analyzing the specific jobs or roles of the persons to be trained. This performance-based, objectives-based approach to training development offers the greatest potential yet for producing training that is job-relevant and efficient. However, when it is applied to leadership training, achievement of effectiveness remains a very difficult problem.

In performance-based training, terminal objectives are supposed to reflect the skills required to perform a job effectively. Assuming that a valid set of leadership skills has been identified, the difficult question for training is, How are these skills to be developed?

Suppose that job or role analysis turns up the fact that an important leader function is to develop and maintain high levels of motivation in subordinates. Suppose further that a set of skills related to developing and maintaining motivation has been identified. If one ignores the exceedingly relevant problem of the nature of such motivation, a number of questions remain. Is it sufficient that trainees be made aware of and sensitive to the fact that other people have motives and needs that should be taken into account at work? Instead, should they be drilled in techniques of motivating subordinates? Or should they be taught the ethics of power distribution and techniques of participative leadership so they can involve subordinates and, thus, increase motivation to perform? Maybe they should be trained in diagnostic and action skills?

It is clear that, to answer questions like these, a trainer must know precisely what he is trying to do, that is, what kinds of changes he is attempting to achieve within trainees. This requires an explicitly clear concept of leadership and of effective leader behavior under that concept.

Despite the existence of many superficial or ineffective programs, there is strong evidence that leadership skills can be effectively taught, when training is truly considered important by organizational managements and when it is thoughtfully designed and carefully implemented. Although it is difficult when conducted properly, training leaders is feasible. The key rests with the systematic design of programs, careful matching of training methods with specific program objectives, and use of trainers who know precisely what they are supposed to do and how to do it. Under these conditions, successful leadership training can be accomplished.

A RATIONALE FOR LEADERSHIP TRAINING

Regardless of whose leadership theory one embraces or which approach to leadership is most attractive to a trainer, one fact applies universally. This fact is that, *in any formal organization, a leader faces a variety of situations that demand a wide repertoire of behaviors if he is to be successful.*

Fundamental Concepts of Leadership

A leader must be able to assess the needs of constantly shifting situations and adapt his behavior so as to produce desired results. This view of leadership as an adaptive process has been proposed by numerous writers (Argyris, 1956; Bennis, 1959; Jaques, 1992; Knowles, Holton, and Swanson, 1998), all of whom recognize that a leader is most effective when he addresses the concrete needs of the immediate situation. To do this, a leader must be able to make realistic evaluations of specific events that are taking place and the relationships between his behavior and those events (Murdock and Scott, 1997). The leader must be concerned with assessing events and finding appropriate courses of action; he must be able to recognize symptoms of what is happening and move from symptoms to causes and then to skillful actions intended to alleviate them. The effective individual can accurately identify the essential elements in a situation and, moreover, can address them in such a way as to control them (Murdock and Scott, 1997). In effect, this is skill in behaving—in seeing and acting.

This is an important distinction for training. As opposed to his having solely intellectual understanding, the successful leader is effective in seeing and acting. Training designed in accordance with this proposition would require a participant to examine deeply the validity of the underlying assumptions on which he acts and would result in an individual who is consciously aware of the implications of his behavior for others and of their activities for him. The problem for trainers, then, is to determine the best way to help students modify their behavior—to become more proficient at seeing and acting, and to become more aware of the implications of their behavior for other people and of others' actions for them.

Practical Learning

Fundamental to this rationale is the premise that genuine learning involves a change in behavior (Cantor, 1958). In short, if a trainee does not behave differently after training than he did before, learning has not occurred. Following this pragmatic approach, the targets of training must be growth within the individual and change in his behavior. These are deeper and broader goals than mere transmission of knowledge.

The acquisition of knowledge through solely cognitive processes is one important aspect of individual growth. However, knowledge that remains merely cognitive cannot much influence an individual's ability to function effectively (Bradford, 1961; Knowles, Holton, and Swanson, 1998). This knowledge must be translated so it becomes genuinely significant in the learner's experience.

For this discussion, knowledge is important to the learner only as it contributes to modification of attitudes or skills (Gibb, Platts, and Miller, 1951). According to this view, effective learning is insightful and meaningful; and isolated information and principles not tied to problems perceived by the learner as related to his life and needs contribute little to this insight. Such information and principles are not really understood. If retained at all, they are pigeonholed or converted to abstractions that possess no real significance for performance.

Useful learning is not a matter of simply filling a void with information. It is a process of reorganizing complex thought patterns, perceptions, assumptions, attitudes, feelings, and skills and relating these reorganized concepts to the external world and the problems faced in it (Statt, 2000). Thus, the learning process is effective only when something dynamic takes place within the learner (Gragg, 1960).

Such learning must be active, participative, and involving (Eitington, 1996). It is best accomplished by experimenting, continually attempting to adjust concepts and skills, and continually checking one's ideas, interpretations, and learned behavior against reality.

Motivation to Learn

Most theories of instruction accept the premise that there must be a readiness for learning before it can occur. In practice, this means that the individual must perceive some need for change, must be capable of changing, and must perceive the learning situation as one that can facilitate such change in a direction acceptable to him. In short, learning will not occur unless the individual is motivated and ready to learn.

Fundamental to this rationale for leadership training is the concept that the motivation to learn new leadership behavior is a matter of attitudes and, accordingly, successful instruction must not only stimulate positive attitudes toward learning but, more important, must overcome attitudes that make the potential learner resistant to change (Bradford, 1961; Cantor, 1958; Gibb, Platts, and Miller, 1951; Schein, 1962).

Attitudes are generally organized and integrated around the person's image of himself, and they result in stabilized, characteristic ways of viewing the world, one's work, and other people (Schein, 1962). This subtle way of viewing the world is comfortable for the individual, and people sometimes go to great lengths to preserve stability even in the face of facts and information that appear to warrant a change in viewpoint. To suggest the need for change not only implies some criticism of the person but also threatens the stability of their relationships with their world.

Such threats are especially common in leadership training situations. Because leadership involves an individual's characteristic ways of behaving and relating to other people, to suggest the need for learning implies the existence of deficiencies in some very personal areas. The suggestion of a deficiency, or need for change, is likely to be perceived as a threat to the individual's sense of identity and status position in relation to other people (Schein, 1962). Therefore, information too threatening for him to accept, because it attacks his self-image, is blocked out or interpreted in such a way as to pose less threat. The result is that learning does not really occur; that is, behavior is never changed.

Furthermore, learning raises images of potential discomfort or even failure. Learning new things means leaving the tried, sure, and comfortable ways of thinking and behaving, unsatisfactory as they may be. It means setting out along unknown paths and possibly encountering unanticipated obstacles, which may prove difficult or impossible to overcome. Accordingly, each trainee inevitably enters a potential change situation with at least some apprehension, either conscious or subconscious, and, at most, some severe anxiety.

In this view, both learning and the maintenance of change once it has occurred have emotional as well as cognitive aspects (Bradford, 1961). Stimulating a motivation to change thoughts, attitudes, and behavior and to maintain these changes is mainly a matter of overcoming both resistance within the trainee and forces in his environment that push against change. Much of leadership training methodology must be devoted to creating conditions that minimize resistance and stimulate motivation to learn.

Conditions for Learning

Lasting changes in behavior do not come easily, either for trainees or for instructors. On the other hand, instruction which is not genuinely intended to achieve change is a waste of time, effort, and money. Accordingly, one of the most critical tasks facing every leadership instructor is to create conditions that are conducive to change.

Since learning to improve leader performance is not solely an intellectual process, the development of conditions conducive to maximum learning should take into account both cognitive and emotional aspects. To achieve learning, training must minimize resistance, expose trainees to new ideas, and develop an active functional frame of reference that encompasses both an awareness of the need to change and recognition of the real-life benefits to be derived from new ways of thinking and acting. Instructional methodology that will accomplish these purposes must meet several requirements (Bradford, 1961; Goetz and Bennis, 1962). The requirements are (1) supportive climate, (2) opportunity to acquire a workable frame of reference, (3) opportunity for realistic and varied experience, and (4) opportunity for objective analysis of own performance.

A Supportive Climate. Probably the most critical requirement is a supportive climate that reduces resistance to learning (Bradford, 1961). Changing one's patterns of thought and action is difficult, and a climate that reduces individual defensiveness and anxiety about exposure of inadequacy is paramount to overcoming resistance to learning.

The purpose of a supportive climate is not to protect trainees from exposure of inadequacies but, rather, to create an atmosphere that will encourage them to undertake the tasks of learning to cope with anxieties and concerns and to experiment with new ways of thinking and behaving. Development of a supportive climate requires at least two essential conditions within the learning situation (Bradford, 1961). First, threat must be minimized. The climate must reduce defensiveness and provide emotional support while the learner is undergoing changes in thinking and actions. Second, the learning situation must provide reinforcement for new ways of thinking and behaving. As the trainee tries and tests different ideas and skills, correct responses must be reinforced positively, and incorrect responses must be reinforced negatively so that they will disappear.

Opportunity to Acquire a Workable Frame of Reference. Most of the problems of leadership are complex. Yet, effectiveness as a leader depends upon control over such problems, and control requires understanding. An effective leader is one who understands his organization, his personnel, and the forces by which they are moved; the ineffective leader is subject to arbitrary and capricious powers that act beyond the range of his limited understanding.

Understanding is one vital key to leader effectiveness, and anyone who attempts to cope with the complex problems of leadership without bringing to bear an organized way of thinking about them runs considerable risk of failure. Similarly, training can be quite threatening to students who do not possess a workable framework for approaching and understanding the problems and challenges to which they are exposed.

For this discussion, the specific content of the framework is irrelevant. What is important is that, in order for learning to occur, trainees must be provided with some systematic way of thinking about the problems of leadership and the factors that contribute to them. Moreover, the concepts with which they are provided must be practical and relevant to the after-training context within which they will be used.

Therefore, a second requirement for learning is the opportunity for trainees to acquire a workable frame of reference for thinking about and coping with leadership problems.

Opportunity for Realistic and Varied Experiences. The extent to which a trainee becomes ego-involved in the learning process is a major determinant of its effectiveness (Eitington, 1996). Involvement is greatest when the learning situation can be structured so that trainees actively participate rather than remain passive. Although students may be taught *about* effective leadership, the skills of leading can become a part of their repertoires of behavior only when they live through and learn from a stream of events called experience (Argyris, 1956). Accordingly, a fourth requirement for learning is the opportunity for trainees to actually experience themselves performing in situations that are as challenging, as realistic, and as job-relevant as possible (Goetz and Bennis, 1962).

The effective leader possesses the ability to identify the essential elements in a situation while stripping away and disregarding the many irrelevant factors that are usually present. Furthermore, in real life, conditions are constantly changing, and the effective leader must be able to identify the unique characteristics of each situation encountered. Skill in coping effectively with unique situations is best developed by exposing trainees to numerous problems that are sufficiently different to require a wide variety of responses. Accordingly, this fourth requirement includes the opportunity for trainees to experience not only realistic and relevant situations but a variety of them.

Opportunity for Experimentation. Observing the performance of others does not, by itself, lead to individual growth, even when good conditions for controlled observation in realistic and relevant situations are provided. Such observations help trainees develop an analytical attitude but do not require them to examine their own orientations to leadership or enable them to see themselves in action.

Learning new ways of thinking and acting is difficult. Improved learning in these areas usually comes in a series of small steps in which the learner tries out a variety of ideas or actions, discarding those that are inappropriate and reinforcing those that are successful. This can occur only when there is freedom to make mistakes. Accordingly, a fifth requirement is the opportunity to experiment with new concepts, new approaches to problems, and new ways of behaving under conditions where mistakes will not have serious consequences for the learner (Goetz and Bennis, 1962).

Opportunity for Objective Analysis of Own Performance. Although the opportunity to experience new and varied situations is critical for learning, experience alone rarely benefits anyone. The critical factor is the use an individual makes of personal experience (Argyris, 1956). Thus, while the opportunity to experiment is essential, it should be provided under conditions that give the trainee accurate information about the effectiveness of his attempts at new behavior.

Learning is best when trainees can consciously test their ideas and new skills in action, obtain knowledge of the results, and analyze the information in terms of consequences for future behavior in actual work situations (Nadler and Nadler, 1984). Accordingly, a sixth requirement is the opportunity for trainees to obtain feedback on the quality of their learned concepts and skills and to analyze their learning in terms of consequences for the future (Goetz and Bennis, 1962).

IMPLICATIONS FOR TRAINING

The rationale above stresses cognitive reorientation, conditions conducive to change, and controlled experience and practice as the essential requirements for learning effective leadership. Several general implications for training follow from the rationale.

Systematic Formal Instruction

The first implication is that extensive formal instruction in leadership concepts is needed for constructive change to occur. Knowledge of leadership and the human and organizational factors associated with it has advanced to the stage where its fundamentals can be analyzed, can be organized systematically, and can be learned by most individuals with normal abilities. Since trainees need explicit frames of reference from which to approach the complex problems of leadership, it is important to provide intensive instruction in some coherent, integrated set of concepts that are directly applicable to anticipated work contexts.

The needed frames of reference are best acquired through direct analysis of the concepts and problems involved in real-life leadership. Training should therefore provide extensive, in-depth instruction aimed directly at inculcating understanding of both leadership and the human and organizational factors that affect it.

Realistic Leadership Laboratories

A second implication is that effective training requires realistic leadership laboratories. Trainees must be given opportunities to experience themselves actually functioning in leadership situations, to try out new skills, and to obtain feedback on the effectiveness of their experimental behaviors (Nadler and Nadler, 1994). Such opportunities can best be provided in carefully designed laboratory situations that are intentionally structured to focus on leadership problems. These laboratory situations enable trainees to observe and try new behaviors under controlled conditions where mistakes do not have serious consequences.

Experiential training methods are the vehicles of choice for use in leadership laboratories. Ideally, training should progress from concentrated practice in mini-simulations, such as role playing, which focus upon specific leadership skills, to performance in full man-ascendant simulations, which provide experience in handling complex human problems that require integration of skills. Finally, experience should be provided in simulations designed to generate problems that are predominantly technical (e.g., financial decision-making, military tactical operations, etc.). Technical simulations permit trainees to exercise learned leadership skills under conditions similar to those in the real world.

Although opportunities to practice leadership while conducting everyday technical activities are important, such practice should be preceded by participation in the less complex laboratory exercises described above. In this way, it is possible to provide trainees with progressively complex experiences.

One recent development that shows considerable promise for providing controlled, progressive experiential training is interactive computer training. This method offers opportunity for revolutionizing soft-skill training. On the other hand, interacting with programmed computer outputs can never fully substitute for the variability to be experienced from interaction with real human participants. Interactive computer training can be used to save training time and expense before exposure to human participants.

Intensive Training Programs

To be genuinely effective, leadership training must be a process of reorientation and acquisition of new concepts, attitudes, and skills. Trainees must be given the opportunity to discard old ideas and acquire new ones, to discard old prejudices and develop new, more constructive attitudes about their roles as leaders, and to learn and practice the kinds of skills they will need to implement their new understanding. Changes such as these can be accomplished only when students become deeply involved in the training process.

To achieve genuine and lasting change, training should provide experiences that will demand, and result in, total commitment of trainees to the development of leadership skills. Accordingly, training for leadership should be highly intensive. Training will be most effective when conducted in concentrated programs, under conditions where trainees are free from distracting influences, and of sufficient duration to permit trainees to become totally immersed in program activities. Furthermore,

periodic reinforcement sessions, also conducted intensively, are warranted.

Perspective on Leadership Training

Knowledge about leadership has advanced to the stage where it can
be organized systematically and its fundamentals can be identified. Furthermore, this knowledge can be transmitted to individuals who need to
use it to perform their duties.

The fundamental problems in leadership training are not the organization and transmittal of knowledge. Rather, the difficult problems are
to assist trainees to translate that knowledge so that it becomes meaningful in their conscious experience, to make the knowledge an integral
part of the frames of reference used to approach leadership problems,
and to equip trainees with skills for coping effectively with such problems. All of these requirements involve the production of changes—cognitive, attitudinal, and behavioral—in trainees, and the fundamental
problems are all concerned with ways to accomplish such changes.

Many leadership training programs do not seriously attempt to cope
with these problems. Accordingly, the products of such programs are
individuals who either reject the concepts presented during training or
who emerge only partially equipped to handle the problems they will
face in the real world.

Inept trainers may be part of the problem. As stated earlier, leadership
training is one of the most difficult instructional processes there is. Yet,
in no other field do we find so many trainers who are neither (1) experts
in the subject taught nor (2) expert trainers.

However, a far greater villain than inept trainers appears to be poor
training design. All too often in program design, the wrong training
methods are selected, a single method is expected to serve too many
purposes, the methods chosen are expected to accomplish too much, or
the correct methods are chosen but used improperly.

These inadequacies in training design appear to be due to (1) unclear
concepts about what the program is supposed to accomplish, (2) poor
understanding of the capabilities and weaknesses of the various training
methods, and (3), in some cases, submission to the urge to make a program appealing to trainees, regardless of the amount of learning it produces. The first and second inadequacies can be overcome through
careful identification of training requirements and considerable thought
about objectives and the methods that will accomplish them. The third
can be overcome simply by a reordering of priorities and recognition
that learning in the field of leadership may be difficult and even painful.
To be sure, programs should be stimulating and appealing to trainees,
because such attributes enhance the motivation to learn. However, gen-

uine learning about leadership and changes in leader behavior do not come easily. To expect otherwise is a mistake that can only lead to superficial and ineffective programs.

Finally, many of the inadequacies in leadership training programs can be traced to attitudes that organization managements have about training in general and leadership training in particular. In short, when managements do not support and insist upon high-quality programs, inadequate programs are likely to be produced.

If asked, most managements would contend that they desire high-quality, effective programs. However, it appears that many do not have serious commitments to such programs to the extent that they are willing to allocate the money and trainee time necessary to achieve genuinely productive results. In part, this reluctance is due to a lack of understanding by most managements of what is required to produce genuinely effective leadership training. It is also due in part to the low priority given to leadership training in relation to other activities.

In closing this discussion of the state of leadership-instruction, it should be reiterated that, although training programs for leaders are widespread, many are ineffectual. This is particularly unfortunate, because the considerable potential of leadership training is not being realized at a time of increasing concern over the quality of leadership exhibited in many organizations.

Chapter 11

Summary and Conclusion

In this book, an analysis of groups in organizations and elements that influence group effectiveness was presented. In addition, some ways for leading groups at work were suggested.

Among all of the elements that can impact upon performance, probably the most compelling influences are the groups that organizations comprise and to which members belong. An organization does not consist of an undifferentiated mass of people, all of whom have identical motives, attitudes, and loyalties. The very fact of organization means a network of smaller groups, each of which possesses its own values and standards of behavior. Through such values and standards, groups exert powerful influences upon their members and play an important role in the performance and satisfactions of all members.

The book is organized around detailed discussions of three broad types of groups:

1. work groups (work units, sections, departments),
2. teams (work teams, crisis-management teams, project teams), and
3. operating groups (task forces, operational staffs, and high-level decision-making groups).

WORK GROUPS

When people work together toward mutual goals and undergo meaningful common experiences, the resulting interaction produces changes in their perceptions, emotions, thinking, attitudes, and actions. The distinguishing feature of these changes is that the individual comes more and more to identify his feelings, thinking, attitudes, and actions with the work group, and motivationally significant ties evolve.

Although work group cohesiveness is a major determinant of job performance and employee satisfaction, an additional factor involves the group's norms concerning work performance. Therefore, two conditions are necessary for effective performance by a work group: (1) a group situation that is attractive to the members and that generates pride and solidarity and (2) strong group norms that value high performance. In addition, technical proficiency of all personnel is a requirement for work group effectiveness.

Characteristics of effective work groups were discussed. Among the properties of the ideal work group that were analyzed are knowledge and skills, attitudes of members, motivation of group members, working relationships, and atmosphere within the group. These properties constitute a model that can be used for assessing the state of work groups.

A number of general factors that may influence cohesiveness and group effectiveness were reviewed. The following determinants of effectiveness were discussed: (1) tasks and task organization, (2) superordinate goals, (3) similarity of personnel, (4) common experiences, (5) success experiences, (6) organizational stability, (7) communication, (8) interpersonal conflict, (9) cooperation and competition, (10) reward systems, and (11) administrative practices. In addition, the effects of work group size were discussed, and the optimal size of a work group was discussed in relation to the number of personnel one supervisor can direct (span of control).

Some problems in leading work groups were analyzed, and a number of specific ways a supervisor can develop or improve work group effectiveness was discussed.

TEAMS

At this point, the discussion turned to an analysis of teams. In the consideration of groups in organizations, teams are a special case. Here, the term *team* refers to a group that is specifically designed to require the integrated and highly coordinated activities of several people. Within this requirement, teams may be as varied as working teams, which are task-defined and frequently machine-dominant groups; crisis-management teams, such as police swat teams, fire department companies, medical emergency teams, military combat teams; and project teams.

Because teams, teamwork, and the components of team performance constitute a complex topic that can be subject to much misunderstanding, a conceptual model for teams was first proposed. According to the proposed model, a team is a role system that is driven and controlled by operational (task) demands and maintained by shared values and norms. The roles in the system are the official positions occupied by members of the team. Integration is the force that melds the activities of members, and it derives from norms and shared values held in common by members of the team. The strength or degree of integration that exists in the team is dependent upon the level and nature of cohesion within the team and the parent organization and is manifested by the integration of team structure and function, that is, teamwork. It was concluded that, to be effective, a team must perform as a unified role system that executes competently all of the activities and group functions needed to enable the team to accomplish its tasks and achieve its goals.

Cohesion and its effects upon teams were discussed, and some conditions necessary for cohesion to develop were listed. The necessary conditions are (1) common objectives conducive to cooperation; (2) shared experiences, especially success experiences; (3) a stable and efficient organization; and (4) shared norms of performance and behavior. Each condition was discussed at length.

Teamwork depends upon team integration, which, in turn, depends upon cohesion. However, even though high cohesion is a major necessary ingredient, it is not the only one. Many factors operate to encourage the development of team relationships. A number of these factors were listed.

In addition, the development of a closely knit team requires each member to possess a frame of reference that embraces cooperation and coordination as operational requirements. Cooperation and competition within teams were analyzed and their effects were discussed. It was concluded that the principal determinants of teamwork are

1. superordinate objectives that are meaningful, clear, and desired by all,
2. a system of potential rewards for contributing to team effort, and
3. an organizational system that provides effective operating procedures and efficient patterns of communication among team members.

Clear superordinate objectives and a meaningful system of rewards focus efforts upon common aims and motivate members to cooperate and coordinate. The organizational system channels the motivation to cooperate into effective actions. Each of the above determinants of teamwork was analyzed in detail.

Following this discussion, team types and skill requirements for differing types of teams were analyzed. A method for classifying team situations was described. The method permits classification of task situations, based upon the nature of the team's task and the context in which it is performed.

Two types of situations were discussed. An *established situation* is one in which (1) all external conditions are specifiable and predictable, (2) all actions of the system are specifiable and predictable, and (3) the probable consequences of alternative team actions can be predicted. In brief, the ultimate established situation is one in which all input and action aspects are controllable and outcomes are fully predictable. The ultimate established situation involves a machine-dominant task in which inputs to and outputs from a machine, computer, weapons system, and so forth fully control the activities of team members.

In contrast, an *emergent situation* is one in which (1) all external conditions cannot be anticipated in advance, (2) the state of the system does not correspond to relied-upon predictions, and (3) the consequences of possible team actions cannot be fully predicted. Emergent situations may vary widely; however, the ultimate may be emergency or crisis-management situations such as military operations, civil disasters, police activities, and fire department operations. In business affairs, certain decision-making teams may function under emergent conditions.

When an emergent situation arises, the coordination demands placed upon a team increase and may influence performance. These coordination requirements tend to complicate team performance. They also tend to degrade performance unless countermeasures are taken. Functioning in such situations becomes highly complex, requiring a greater variety of skills and other more complex attributes related to teamwork and coordinative behavior. Because these task situations are more complex, *team training becomes more valuable.*

The effective functioning of teams in the modern world requires at least the following: (1) role-specific individual skills, (2) team performance skills, and (3) team integration. Each requirement was discussed in detail.

A discussion of team types followed. Teams may have innumerable purposes, goals, and activities. However, despite its particular purpose or configuration, every true team is a role system driven and controlled by operational (task) demands and maintained by shared values and norms. These similarities in generic attributes make it possible to identify points of access that will permit assessment and training of most teams. Three widely different types of teams were discussed as examples:

1. *Working teams*—teams that are most often task-controlled and machine-dominant. The most predominant required skills are role-specific individual skills. In addition, some degree of Team Performance Skills are required. Examples are certain operations in auto and aircraft assembly plants, military gun crews, and certain ship handling activities.

2. *Crisis-management teams*—a wide variety of teams that must make prompt and usually vigorous responses to situations that may threaten life, property, or even survival of an organization. This type of team includes police teams of various types, fire department companies, medical emergency teams, and military teams ranging from small independent action forces or infantry fire teams to air defense tracking and fire control centers. These teams are most often involved in highly emergent situations.

Although team performance in emergent situations depends upon the practiced skills of individuals who function in coordination, task activities and sequences cannot always be specified or predicted. Similarly, the probable consequence of some actions cannot be predicted. Accordingly, effective team performance requires a variety of skills with special emphasis upon team performance (coordinative) skills.

3. *Project teams*—a group that is formed to accomplish a specific purpose. Because many project teams consist of personnel selected to provide a variety of qualifications, members of such teams may be quite diverse, which can create difficulty in achieving a desirable level of team integration.

Although project teams should have clear goals and concrete guidance, they must cope with emergent situations, because tasks and activities can be specified only in general terms, all information is not available, and both information and actions depend upon preceding activities. Thus, intervening activities and final outcomes cannot be predicted. Both individual role skills and team performance skills are requirements for team effectiveness.

The section on teams was completed with a discussion of team training. A set of premises to be used in planning training was presented. Also included were eight recommendations for planning and conducting team training.

A number of skills essential for leading teams were identified. They are (1) team management skills, (2) communication skills, (3) problem-solving skills, and (4) goal-setting (tactical) skills.

TASK FORCES, OPERATIONAL STAFFS, AND DECISION-MAKING GROUPS

Work groups and teams are most often small, compact groups, whose members have clearly delineated roles and perform highly specific duties and functions. Usually, the boundaries of such groups are so tightly circumscribed that a work group or team will take on an identity that sets it apart from all similar groups. In addition, most such groups have very simple structures, with a supervisor or team leader and subordinate members.

In contrast, *operating groups* (task forces, operational staffs, and high-level decision-making groups) may have complex organizations, with numerous levels. Furthermore, their missions may be quite broad, the roles of members may vary widely, and the groups may consist of many more personnel than do work groups or teams.

Despite these differences, task forces, operational staffs, and high-level decision-making groups all possess the fundamental group attributes discussed earlier. Accordingly, they can be managed and led by addressing these same properties.

Definitions and distinguishing characteristics of task forces, operational staffs, and high-level decision-making groups were presented and discussed. Both similarities and differences were discussed. It was concluded that the fact that such groups have broadly defined missions, high-level personnel, and divided responsibilities can result in considerable difficulties for leaders.

Requirements for operating group effectiveness were discussed. Effectiveness in accomplishing missions depends upon a group's ability to cope with and control its operational environment. For a group to be successful, it requires (1) the capacity to evaluate reality, (2) adaptability, and (3) operational proficiency. To meet these requirements, operating groups must develop properties that are essential for full effectiveness. The properties are classified as (1) group properties, (2) leader resources, and (3) personnel resources. A total of 12 essential properties were listed and discussed.

Demonstrably effective groups usually display the listed properties. The discussion turned to an analysis of bases of group effectiveness. Effective performance by an operating group is a matter not only of technical and organizational proficiency but also of such factors as the nature of its objectives, its level of morale, the state of motivation and discipline, and the degree of functional integration among the various personnel and units that compose it. The group most likely to be effective is a tightly knit, efficiently functioning system of people and activities. This system is composed of interlocking units effectively linked by capable managers and served by an efficient communication system. Performance standards are high and dissatisfaction may occur whenever achievement falls short of objectives.

This highly constructive orientation toward the group and its objectives is achieved by mobilizing all the major motivational forces that can exercise influence in a group setting. These forces, with bases in both the formal and informal areas of organizations, are exceptionally potent sources of leader effectiveness.

This discussion was followed by an analysis of the rationale and principles of formal organization. Emphasis upon the formal structure and principles is important for two reasons. First, proper observance of organizational channels and principles is essential for operational efficiency. Second, an inefficient system tends to create frustration and conflict among personnel, which, in turn, affect performance.

The considerations just discussed force recognition of the special di-
lemma faced in leading operating groups. Some special difficulties derive
from the numbers of highly competent people whose activities must be
influenced and coordinated. The necessity for obtaining smoothly functioning, well-integrated performance from them can create some critical
strains in the operating group.

One deep source of strain occurs because the mission necessitates organizational complexity and formalization, which are the most common
causes of group rigidity. A second strain centers on the continuous effort
to maintain a high level of motivation while also exercising control.

A manager operating within exacting requirements for coordination
and control must rely upon formal structures and organizational principles to obtain much of his results. However, he must also strive simultaneously to combat negative motivational forces that are, in part,
created by the very system that is intended to make performance more
effective.

This contradictory interplay of procedures required for coordination
and control and of practices designed to stimulate performance creates
a conflict that constitutes one of the central problems of group leadership. The fundamental problem is How can the leader of a high performance group consisting of a diverse membership with varied
responsibilities develop his group into the integrated system described
earlier?

The general conditions essential for the formation and functioning of
an effective group were reviewed and examined in detail from the special standpoint of high-level operating groups. Some of the practical aspects of developing a new operating group were discussed.

Included was an analysis of ten factors that require a leader's attention.
The factors are classified as (1) factors that enhance proficiency, (2) factors that promote a common desire to belong to the group and to identify
with it, and (3) factors that enhance motivation. Each of the ten factors
is capable of being assessed and developed, where improvement is indicated. It was concluded that the development of an effective group is
a time-consuming process and a basic problem for a leader is to maintain
a proper sense of perspective. Five principles for leading operating
groups were presented.

Internal group functioning was discussed. For many groups, problem-
solving and decision-making are primary endeavors; yet problem-
solving and decision-making in groups are much more complex
processes than when performed by individuals alone. The discussion
included analyses of a number of factors that influence coordinated
decision-making and the group problem-solving process. Prominent
among such influential factors are (1) objectives and (2) communication.

Group Objectives

Goals are specific objectives to be accomplished by a group and, under certain conditions, they possess motivational properties for personnel. When held in common by most members and valued by them, an objective has the properties of concentrating the activities of members and of mobilizing their efforts toward its achievement.

The absence of controlling objectives causes a group to drift, and the full force of its capabilities can never be brought to bear on any single undertaking. For this reason, good goals are essential to a group's effectiveness and should be made a part of the perceptions and motivations of personnel at all levels.

Good goals are those that are effective in mobilizing the energies of all personnel behind them. Some of their characteristics are clarity, operationality, realism, and relevance of subordinate to major goals. Each characteristic was discussed.

A common problem in many groups is the displacement of goals, which occurs when major goals are neglected in favor of activities associated with maintaining the group. Displacement is a potential dysfunction in most groups. An example that is especially relevant is overemphasis upon compliance with rules and procedures at the expense of goal attainment. Although rules and procedures are essential for effectiveness, some individuals may become so consumed with them that these overshadow the goals of the group.

One important way of preventing goal displacement is to instill purpose into the group so that goals become infused with value and so important to personnel that they receive first priority in thoughts and actions. Purposes are broader than goals and state a reason for achieving the objectives.

Setting objectives for a group involves two related processes: (1) definition of an effect to be produced (the goal), and (2) transmittal of this objective in such a way that it can be most effective. In defining goals, leaders are subject to influence from both higher organizational levels and subordinates. This forces recognition that goal setting has some nonlogical aspects of which a leader should be aware. Transmittal of goals down an organization requires mutual understanding, together with uniform interpretation and comprehension of both goals and goal-attaining requirements at all levels.

Setting goals and developing purposes are strategies—ways of leading groups. Their function is to create unified action among numbers of people, and as strategies they provide useful support to more personal techniques of leadership.

Communication

Communication within groups is a second major factor. The structure of any organization is an elaborate system for gathering, evaluating, combining, and distributing information. Since organizational effectiveness hinges upon necessary information being at the appropriate place at the proper time, the free flow of communication both downward and upward is a major requirement.

Inherent in any group are a number of potential barriers to the free flow of communication. These are a climate of distrust; malfunctions in the system, including failure of control centers (positions in the chain of authority) and rigidity arising from over-formalization; the development of informal channels that are inappropriate, unmonitored, and uncontrolled; loyalties to special groups within the organization; social distance between levels; and differences in power between levels. Each of these potential barriers and their consequences were discussed.

Problems in downward communication may occur either because subordinates try to second-guess their superiors or because superiors withhold information in order to keep subordinates dependent upon them. Problems in stimulating upward communication may occur either because subordinates are reluctant to transmit anything but favorable information or because complexity in organizational structure restricts the timely transmission of information upward.

A number of implications were drawn. Those factors discussed as barriers constitute the real problems of communication within operating groups. Effective communication can occur only in an open atmosphere characterized by mutual confidence and appreciation of the information needs of all personnel. It was recommended that managers establish as a basic premise that communication is a direct administrative responsibility for every level in the organization, recognize that the most effective communication occurs in the course of doing work or solving problems, not as the result of formal campaigns to improve communications; attack causes rather than symptoms of communication failures by working with subordinates to change their practices and restructure their views toward communication; and create more effective superior-subordinate relationships—which constitute the true basis of effective communication.

Communication is one of the most important aspects of group effectiveness, yet probably the most underestimated (Peters and Waterman, 1982; Statt, 2000). All of the results that determine effectiveness depend upon it.

The section on operating groups was completed with a discussion about leading such groups. In addition to the technical and procedural aspects of group work, the effective leader must be aware of the less tangible, but equally important, social and interpersonal aspects that affect group performance (Deal and Kennedy, 1982; Hogg and Abrams, 2001).

Several relevant aspects of leadership were discussed. First, group work usually involves the continual exploration and reformulation of problems. One important function of group leadership is to guide this exploring process. A second leadership function is the provision of methodological assistance that can aid the problem solution. A third function involves the discovery and coordination of member resources. Five principles for leading operating groups were discussed (Olmstead, 2000).

Part II was concluded with a chapter (6) devoted to an analysis of crisis-management teams and organizations in order to illustrate some of the more important aspects of group performance as applied in real-life situations.

Organizational competence was proposed as a meaningful conceptual basis for a working framework, or model, which can be used for (1) analyzing the functional competence of an organization or group; (2) identifying dysfunctional elements; and (3) for improving group or organizational functioning through assessment, development, and training.

LEADING GROUPS IN ORGANIZATIONS

The book was concluded in part III with a general discussion of groups in organizations and of leadership of such groups. It can be asked legitimately, What distinguishes between a mere collectivity of people and a group? The answer is that a collectivity becomes a group when its members develop (1) common goals, (2) shared norms, (3) differentiated roles, and (4) some degree of cohesion. The leadership, or management, of groups must be devoted, at least minimally, to development of these attributes—if any level of effectiveness is to be achieved.

Development of the above group attributes would be exceedingly haphazard and difficult except for the fact that the groups discussed here all occur in organizations. Whatever their specific nature, all organizations possess certain common properties that can be exploited, and, when a problem arises, identification of the problem in relation to basic organizational and group properties makes possible more insightful and lasting solutions.

Seven common organizational properties were identified and discussed. Differences between organizations occur because of variations in the form and degree of the above properties and the specific configurations that evolve because of particular goals, tasks, and circumstances. However, every organization possesses the properties in some form and to some degree. Taken together, they constitute a foundation upon which assessment and developmental efforts can be based.

IMPLICATIONS

A main theme of this discussion has been that supervision and leadership are not the same (Stogdill, 1974) and that supervision becomes effective only when good leadership practices are superimposed upon the managerial techniques dictated by the kinds of jobs, the caliber of personnel, and the work methods characteristic of the mission or task.

Leadership is the process of influencing individuals and groups in order to achieve desired results. Each leadership act, each leadership decision, and each deliberation of leadership problems must have as its first consideration the effect upon performance. The ultimate criterion of effective leadership can only be the quality of performance demonstrated by the people who are supervised. Performance remains, of necessity, both the proof and the aim of leadership.

What emerges from this discussion is a broadened concept of the role of managers and supervisors. The manager or supervisor, instead of seeing himself solely as the boss—one who plans, organizes, controls, and decides by himself—or as a trainer, or both, must also think of himself as a resource to his group, an expert in communication, and a catalyst to his subordinates. A major function will be facilitating as well as directing, maintaining a healthy flow of clear communication, and relating effectively to subordinates as well as to his operational duties. Given such a concept, the particular style of leadership will vary somewhat with the individual, the problem, and the situation. Not every supervisor can polish his leadership skills to a high gloss, but this will not matter too much if his attitude is facilitative. If his attitude is wrong, high skills will probably not help very much. Fortunately, skills can be learned, and the required attitude can be cultivated, if only the supervisor sees the need for them.

Skills in diagnosing situations and in acting within them help a leader to cope with the multiplicity of elements he constantly faces in his daily work. The first thing of which a student of leadership must become aware is the fact that behavior in organizations is usually the resultant of many determinants. In approaching a leadership situation, some people see only the leader, or the problem, or the subordinates. Yet, in reality, one is rarely confronted with the simple relation of a supervisor to a subordinate or a group of subordinates. Instead, a great many relations are frequently joined in a network. To seize upon one or two elements as a basis for action and neglect the rest is usually a gross oversimplification. It can only cause the leader to misunderstand the problem and take the wrong action toward its resolution. The good leader understands that individual facts or actions cannot be interpreted except as components of a larger picture.

This means looking at the event or action in relation to groups of people, their attitudes, and their standards of behavior. It means looking at the total organizational situation, including goals, motivation, and attitudes, to see, for example, whether the organizational climate is influencing the behavior of individuals or of groups. It means looking at the work situation to determine whether success or failures, efficiencies or ineptitudes, are exerting an influence upon behavior. It means taking into account previous experience and background of group members.

A leader cannot avoid the fact that his own attitudes have fundamental significance in any leadership situation. They are a critical element because they are bound to affect his interpretation of events and his thinking about them. They influence the reactions of subordinates to him. The leader is a highly important determinant of the behavior of his subordinates and his group. What he says, what he does, or what he does not say or does not do, all have an effect that is often far-reaching.

One point remains to be made. It has been conclusively determined that leadership is, in large part, situationally controlled. That is, factors within the work and organizational context strongly influence the effectiveness of leadership and leadership behavior.

It is probably inevitable that the future will place even greater demands upon organizational leaders than does the present. Leadership requirements are based on the kinds of performance demanded of organizations. The kinds of performance required of most organizations appear to be changing, and with these shifting demands, leadership will become both more complex and more important.

Leadership of the responsive organizations required for the future will embody a major responsibility for creative action. For such organizations to be effective, leading cannot be just passive reaction to problems as they occur; it must go beyond merely fighting fires that may arise. Instead, it will be necessary for leaders to actively strive to shape their organizations and constantly push back the limitations that both human fallibility and system rigidity tend to place upon an organization's capabilities for performing responsively.

Effectiveness under such conditions will require well-trained individuals who are knowledgeable about the fundamentals of leadership, thoroughly schooled concerning human factors that influence organizational performance, and skilled in applying this knowledge to the problems involved in guiding complex and, in some cases, highly ambiguous activities. Leadership can no longer be a matter of hunch or native ability, backed by a few elementary concepts and reinforced through the trial and error of experience. Instead, it must rest upon systematic knowledge and a rational and conscious application of sound principles and practice.

Without a doubt, the quality of available leadership at all levels determines the character of an organization and the effectiveness with which it accomplishes its objectives. Accordingly, the development of individuals who occupy leadership positions is one of the most critical functions in any organization.

Although difficult when conducted properly, effective training for leadership is feasible. Despite the fact that some programs are not very effective, there is sufficient evidence to conclude that leadership can be taught when training is sincerely deemed important by managements and when it is thoughtfully designed and carefully implemented.

References

Adizes, I. *How to Solve the Mismanagement Crisis*. Homewood, IL: Irwin, 1979.

Albert, R. S. "Comments on the Scientific Function of the Concept of Cohesiveness." *American Journal of Psychology*, 59, 1953, 231–34.

Alexander, L. T., and A. S. Cooperband. *System Training and Research in Team Behavior*. Santa Monica, CA: System Development Corp., TM 2581, 1965.

Altman, I. "The Small Group Field: Implications for Research on Behavior in Organizations," in R. V. Bowers (Ed.), *Studies on Behavior and Organizations: A Research Symposium*. Athens: University of Georgia Press, 1966.

Anderson, D., and L. A. Anderson. *Beyond Change Management: Advanced Strategies for Today's Transformational Leaders*. San Francisco, CA: Pfeiffer, 2001.

Argyle, M., G. Gardner, and I. Cioffi. "Supervisory Methods Related to Productivity, Absenteeism, and Turnover." *Human Relations*, 11, 1958, 23–40.

Argyris, C. "Some Unresolved Problems of Executive Development Programs." *Journal of Educational Sociology*, 30, 1956, 20–30.

Argyris, C. *Personality and Organization: The Conflict between System and the Individual*. New York: Harper & Brothers, 1957.

Argyris, C. *Interpersonal Competence and Organizational Effectiveness*. Homewood, IL: Irwin–Dorsey Press, 1962.

Ashkanasy, N. M., C.E.J. Hartel, and W. J. Zerbb (Eds.). *Emotions in the Workplace*. Westport, CT: Quorum Books, 2000.

Barnard, C. I. *The Functions of the Executive*. Cambridge: Harvard University Press, 1938.

Barnard, C. I. "The Nature of Leadership," in C. I. Barnard (Ed.), *Organization Management*. Cambridge, MA: Harvard University Press, 1948.

Beckhard, R. "Optimizing Team Building Efforts." *Journal of Contemporary Business*, Summer 1972.

Bellin, R. M. *Management Teams: Why They Succeed or Fail*. Oxford, UK: Butterworth-Heinemann, 1996.

Bellin, R. M. *How to Build Successful Teams*. Oxford, UK: Butterworth-Heinemann, 1998.

Benne, K. D. "Case Methods in the Training of Administrators," in W. G. Bennis, K. D. Benne, and R. Chin (Eds.), *The Planning of Change: Readings in the Applied Behavioral Sciences*. New York: Holt, Rinehart & Winston, 1961.

Benne, K. D., and P. D. Sheats. "Functional Roles of Group Members." *Journal of Social Issues*, 4(2), 1948, 41–49.

Bennis, W. G. "Leadership Theory and Administrative Behavior: The Problem of Authority." *Administrative Science Quarterly*, 4, 1959, 259–301.

Bennis, W. G. *Changing Organizations: Essays on the Development and Evolution of Human Organizations*. New York: McGraw-Hill Book Co., 1966.

Berkowitz, L., and B. I. Levy. "Pride in Group Performance and Group-Task Motivation." *Journal of Abnormal and Social Psychology*, 53, 1956, 300–306.

Boguslaw, R., and E. H. Porter. "Team Functions and Training," in R. H. Gagne (Ed.), *Psychological Principles in Systems Development*. New York: Holt, Rinehart & Winston, 1962, 387–416.

Bowers, D. G. *Work Organizations as Dynamic Systems*. Technical Report. Ann Arbor: Institute for Social Research, University of Michigan, 1969.

Bradford, L. P. "The Teaching-Learning Transaction," in L. P. Bradford (Ed.), *Human Forces in Teaching and Learning*. Washington, DC: National Training Laboratories, National Education Association, 1961, 5–15.

Brannick, M. T., E. Salas, and C. Prince. *Team Performance Assessment and Measurement: Theory, Methods and Application*. Mahwah, NJ: Lawrence Erlbaum Associates, 1997.

Briggs, G. E., and W. A. Johnson. *Team Training*. Technical Report NAVTRAD-EVCEN 13274-4. Columbus: Ohio State University, Human Performance Center, 1967.

Cantor, N. *The Learning Process for Managers*. New York: Harper & Row, 1958.

Cartwright, D., and A. Zander (Eds.). *Group Dynamics: Research and Theory* (2nd ed.). Evanston, IL: Row, Peterson & Co., 1960.

Coch, L., and J.P.R. French, Jr. "Overcoming Resistance to Change." *Human Relations*, 1, 1948, 512–32.

Cohen, A. R., S. Fink, H. Gadon, and R. Willits. *Effective Behavior in Organizations*. Homewood, IL: Irwin, 1980.

Collins, J. J. *A Study of Potential Contributions of Small Group Behavior Research to Team Training Technology Development*. Alexandria, VA: Essex Corporation, 1977.

Deal, T. E., and A. A. Kennedy. *Corporate Cultures*. Reading, MA: Addison-Wesley, 1982.

Deutsch, M. "Some Factors Affecting Membership Motivation and Achievement Motivation in a Group." *Human Relations*, 12, 1959, 81–95.

Dyer, J. L. *Annotated Bibliography and State-of-the-Art Review of the Field of Team Training as It Relates to Military Teams*. Alexandria, VA: U.S. Army Research Institute for the Behavioral Sciences, 1985.

Eitington, J. E. *The Winning Trainer: Winning Ways to Involve People in Learning* (3rd ed.). Oxford, UK: Butterworth-Heinemann, 1996.

Fiedler, F. E. "Engineering the Job to Fit the Manager." *Harvard Business Review*, 43, 1965, 115–22.

Fiedler, F. E. *On the Death and Transfiguration of Leadership Training*. Technical Report 70–16. Seattle: Dept. of Psychology, University of Washington, 1970.

Forgas, J. P., and K. D. Williams. *Social Influence: Direct and Indirect Processes*. Philadelphia: Psychology Press, 2001.

Forsyth, D. R. (Ed.). "100 Years of Group Research." *Group Dynamics: Theory, Research, and Practice*, 4(1), March 2000.

Gellerman, S. W. *Motivation and Productivity*. New York: American Management Association, 1963.

Gellerman, S. W. *How People Work: Psychological Approaches to Management Problems*. Westport, CT: Quorum Books, 1998.

George, C. E., G. R. Hoak, and J. Boutwell. *Pilot Studies of Team Effectiveness*. Research Memorandum No. 28, Alexandria, VA: Human Resources Research Office, 1963.

Gibb, J. R., G. N. Platts, and L. F. Miller. *Dynamics of Participative Groups*. St. Louis: John S. Swift Co., 1951.

Gill, D. L. "Cohesiveness and Performance in Sport Groups," in R. S. Yeeton (Ed.), *Exercise and Sports Sciences Review* (Vol. 5). Santa Barbara, CA: Journal Publishing Affiliates, 1977.

Goetz, B. F., and W. G. Bennis. "What We Know About Learning and Training." *Personnel Administration*, 25, 1962, 20–29.

Gordon, T. *Group-Centered Leadership*. Boston: Houghton Mifflin, 1955.

Gragg, C. I. "Because Wisdom Can't Be Told," in K. R. Andrews (Ed.), *The Case Method of Teaching Human Relations and Administration*. Cambridge, MA: Harvard University Press, 1960, 3–12.

Green, T. B., and R. T. Butkus. *Motivation, Belief, and Organizational Transformation*. Westport, CT: Quorum Books, 1999.

Green, T. B., and J. T. Knippen. *Breaking the Barrier to Upward Communication*. Westport, CT: Quorum Books, 1999.

Greenbaum, C. W. "The Small Group Under the Gun: Uses of Small Groups in Battle Conditions." *Journal of Applied Psychology*, 15, 1979, 392–405.

Gross, E. "Primary Functions of the Small Group." *American Journal of Sociology*, 60, 1954, 24–29.

Haiman, F. S. *Group Leadership and Democratic Action*. Boston: Houghton Mifflin, 1950.

Hall, E. R., and W. A. Rizzo. *An Assessment of U.S. Navy Tactical Team Training*. Orlando, FL: Training and Evaluation Group, 1975.

Hare, A. P. *Handbook of Small Group Research* (2nd ed.). New York: The Free Press, 1976.

Herbst, P. G. "Measurement of Behavior Structure by Means of Input-Output Data." *Human Relations*, 10, 1957, 335–46.

Hinton, B. L., and H. J. Reitz (Eds.). *Groups and Organizations: Integrated Readings in the Analysis of Social Behavior*. Belmont, CA: Wadsworth, 1971.

Hite, J. *Learning in Chaos: Improving Performance in Today's Fast Changing, Volatile Organizations*. Houston: Gulf Publishing Co., 1999.

Hogg, M. A., and D. A. Abrams. *Intergroup Relations: Essential Readings*. Philadelphia: Psychology Press, 2001

Indik, B. P., and S. E. Seashore. *Effects of Organization Size on Member Attitudes and Behavior*. Ann Arbor: Survey Research Center, Institute of Social Research, University of Michigan, 1961.

Jacobs, T. O. *Leadership and Exchange in Formal Organizations*. Alexandria, VA: Human Resources Research Organization, 1970.

Jaques, D. *Learning in Groups* (2nd ed.). Houston: Gulf Publishing Co., 1992.

Kahn, R. L., and D. Katz. "Leadership Practices in Relation to Productivity and Morale," in D. Cartwright and A. Zander (Eds.), *Group Dynamics: Research and Theory*. Evanston, IL: Row, Peterson & Co., 1953, 612–28.

Kanter, R. M. "Power Failures in Management Circuits." *Harvard Business Review*, 57(4), 1979, 65–75.

Kanter, R. M. *The Change Masters: How People and Companies Succeed Through Innovation in the New Corporate Era*. New York: Simon and Schuster, 1983.

Katz, D., and R. L. Kahn. *The Social Psychology of Organizations*. New York: John Wiley & Sons, 1966.

Katzell, R. A., R. S. Barrett, and T. C. Parker. "Job Satisfaction, Job Performance, and Situational Characteristics." *Journal of Applied Psychology*, 45, 1961, 65–72.

Kerr, W. A., G. J. Koppelmeier, and J. J. Sullivan. "Absenteeism, Turnover, and Morale in a Metals Fabrication Factory." *Occupational Psychology*, 25, 1951, 50–55.

Kirkpatrick, D. L. *Managing Change Effectively*. Oxford, UK: Butterworth-Heinemann, 2001.

Knerr, C. M., D. C. Berger, and B. A. Popelka. *Sustaining Team Performance*. Interim Report. Springfield, VA: Litton Mellonics, 1979.

Knerr, C. M., L. B. Nadler, and L. E. Berger. *Toward a Naval Team Taxonomy*. Interim Report. Springfield, VA: Litton Mellonics, 1980.

Knowles, M. S., E. Holton, and R. Swanson. *Adult Learner* (5th ed.). Oxford, UK: Butterworth-Heinemann, 1998.

Leonard, H. W. (Ed.). "Consulting to Team-Based Organizations." *Consulting Psychology Journal: Practice and Research*, 52(1), Winter 2000.

Likert, R. "A Motivational Approach to a Modified Theory of Organization and Management," in M. Haire (Ed.), *Modern Organization Theory*. New York: John Wiley & Sons, 1959.

Likert, R. *New Patterns of Management*. New York: McGraw-Hill Book Co., 1961.

Likert, R. *The Human Organization: Its Management and Value*. New York: McGraw-Hill Book Co., 1967.

McCall, M., and M. Lombard (Eds.). *Leadership: Where Else Can We Go?* Durham, NC: Duke University Press, 1976.

McCurdy, H. G., and W. E. Lambert. "The Efficiency of Small Human Groups in the Solution of Problems Requiring Genuine Co-Operation." *Journal of Personality*, 20, 1952, 478–95.

McDavid, J. W., and H. Harari. *Social Psychology: Individuals, Groups, Societies*. New York: Harper & Row, 1968.

McGregor, D. *The Human Side of Enterprise*. New York: McGraw-Hill Book Co., 1960.

McNair, M. P. "Thinking Ahead: What Price Human Relations." *Harvard Business Review*, 35(2), 1957, 15–39.

Maslow, A. H. *Motivation and Personality* (2nd ed.). New York: Harper & Row, 1970.

Mayo, E. *The Human Problems of an Industrial Civilization*. New York: The Macmillan Company, 1933.

Meister, D. *Behavioral Foundations of System Development*. New York: John Wiley & Sons, 1976.

Merton, R. K., and A. S. Kitt. "Contributions to the Theory of Reference Group Behavior," in R. K. Merton and P. F. Lazarsfeld (Eds.), *Continuities in Social Research: Studies in the Scope and Method of "The American Soldier."* Glencoe, IL: The Free Press, 1950.

Mills, T. M. *The Sociology of Small Groups*. Englewood Cliffs, NJ: Prentice-Hall, 1967.

Murdock, A., and C. N. Scott. *Personal Effectiveness*. Oxford, UK: Butterworth-Heinemann, 1997.

Nadler, L., and Z. Nadler. *Designing Training Programs: The Critical Events Model* (2nd ed.). Oxford, UK: Butterworth-Heinemann, 1994.

Nieva, V. F., E. A. Fleischman, and A. Rieck. *Team Dimensions: Their Identity, Their Measurement, and Their Relationships*. Washington, DC: Advanced Research Resources Organization, 1978.

Olmstead, J. A. *Small-Group Instruction: Theory and Practice*. Alexandria, VA: Human Resources Research Organization, 1974.

Olmstead, J. A. *Leadership Training: The State of the Art*. Technical Report 80–1. Alexandria, VA: Human Resources Research Organization, 1980.

Olmstead, J. A. *Battle Staff Integration*. IDA Paper P-2560. Alexandria, VA: Institute for Defense Analyses, 1992.

Olmstead, J. A. *Leadership in Organizations*. Professional Paper 97–1. West Columbia, SC: The Vanguard Research Group, 1997.

Olmstead, J. A. *Work Units, Teams, and Task Forces: Groups at Work*. Professional Paper 98–1. West Columbia, SC: The Vanguard Research Group, 1998.

Olmstead, J. A. *Executive Leadership: Building World-Class Organizations*. Houston, TX: Gulf Publishing Co., 2000.

Olmstead, J. A. *Creating Functionally Competent Organizations: An Open Systems Approach*. Westport, CT: Quorum Books, 2002.

Olmstead, J. A., H. E. Christensen, and L. L. Lackey. *Components of Organizational Competence: Test of a Conceptual Framework*. Technical Report 73–19. Alexandria, VA: Human Resources Research Organization, 1973.

Olmstead, J. A., B. L. Elder, and J. M. Forsyth. *Organizational Process and Combat Readiness: Feasibility of Training Organizational Effectiveness Staff Officers to Assess Command Group Performance*. Interim Report IR-ED-78-3. Alexandria, VA: Human Resources Research Organization, 1978.

Olson, E. F., and G. H. Eoyang. *Facilitating Organizational Change: Lessons from Complexity Science*. San Francisco, CA: Pfeiffer, 2001.

Palmer, S. *People and Self Management*. Oxford, UK: Butterworth-Heinemann, 1998.

Parsons, H. M. *Man-Machine System Experiments*. Baltimore, MD: The Johns Hopkins Press, 1972.

Pepitone, A., and R. Kleiner. "The Effects of Threat and Frustration on Group Cohesiveness." *Journal of Abnormal and Social Psychology*, 54, 1957, 192–200.

Peters, T. J., and R. H. Waterman. *In Search of Excellence*. New York: Harper & Row, 1982.

Porter, L. W. "Role of the Organization in Motivation: Structuring Rewarding Environments." Technical Report No. 7. Irvine: University of California Graduate School of Administration, 1971.

Porter, L. W., and E. E. Lawler. "Properties of Organizational Structure in Relation to Job Attitudes and Job Behavior." *Psychological Bulletin*, 64, 1965, 23–51.

Reid, M., and R. Hammersley. *Communicating Successfully in Groups: A Practical Guide for the Workplace*. Philadelphia: Psychology Press, 2000.

Richards, C. B., and H. F. Dobryns. "Topography and Culture: The Case of the Changing Cage." *Human Organization*, 16, 1957, 16–20.

Roby, T. B. *Small Group Performance*. Chicago: Rand McNally, 1968.

Roethlisberger, F. J. "Training Supervisors in Human Relations." *Harvard Business Review*, 29(5), 1951, 47–57.

Roethlisberger, F. J., and W. J. Dickson. *Management and the Worker*. Cambridge, MA: Harvard University Press, 1939.

Roethlisberger, F. J., and W. J. Dickson. *Management and the Worker* (2nd ed.). Cambridge, MA: Harvard University Press, 1943.

Rothwell, W. J., and H. C. Kazanas. *Building In-House Leadership and Management Development Programs*. Westport, CT: Quorum Books, 1999.

Savell, J. M., R. E. Teague, and T. R. Tremble, Jr. "Job Involvement Contagion Between Army Squad Leaders and Their Squad Members." *Military Psychology*, 7, 1995, 193–206.

Schein, E. H. "Management Development, Human Relations Training and the Process of Influence," in I. R. Weschler and E. H. Schein (Eds.), *Issues in Human Relations Training*. Washington, DC: National Training Laboratories, National Education Association, 1962, 47–60.

Schein, E. H. *Organizational Psychology* (2nd ed.). Englewood Cliffs, NJ: Prentice-Hall, 1970.

Schoen, D. R. "Human Relations: Boon or Bogle?" *Harvard Business Review* 35(6), 1957, 41–47.

Seashore, S. E. *Group Cohesiveness in the Industrial Work Group*. Ann Arbor, MI: Institute for Social Research, 1954.

Seashore, S. E. *The Training of Leaders for Effective Human Relations*. Basle: UNESCO, 1957.

Sherif, M., and H. Cantril. *The Psychology of Ego-Involvements: Social Attitudes and Identifications*. New York: John Wiley & Sons, 1947.

Sherif, M., and C. W. Sherif. *Groups in Harmony and Tension*. New York: Harper & Brothers, 1953.

Sherif, M., and C. W. Sherif. *An Outline of Social Psychology* (rev. ed.). New York: Harper & Brothers, 1956.

Smith, C. G., and A. J. Tannenbaum. "Organizational Control Structure: A Comparative Analysis," in B. L. Hinton and H. J. Reitz (Eds.), *Groups and Organizations: Integrated Readings in the Analysis of Social Behavior*. Belmont, CA: Wadsworth, 1971.

Statt, D. A. *Using Psychology in Management Training: The Psychological Foundations of Management Skills*. Philadelphia: Psychology Press, 2000.

Stogdill, R. M. *Handbook of Leadership: A Survey of Theory and Research*. New York: The Free Press, 1974.

Thelen, H. A. *Dynamics of Groups at Work*. Chicago: University of Chicago Press, 1954.

Thorndyke, P. W., and M. G. Weiner. *Improving Training and Performance of Navy Teams: A Design for a Research Program*. Rand Report R-2607-ONR. Santa Monica, CA: Rand Corporation, 1980.

Tyler, T. R., and S. Blader. *Cooperation in Groups in Procedural Justice, Social Identity, and Behavioral Engagement*. Philadelphia: Psychology Press, 2000.

Vaill, P. B. "Toward a Behavioral Description of High Performing Systems," in M. McCall and M. Lombard (Eds.), *Leadership: Where Else Can We Go?* Durham, NC: Duke University Press, 1976.

Van Zelst, R. H. "Sociometrically Selected Work Teams Increase Production." *Personnel Psychology*, 5, 1951, 175–85.

Vecchio, R. P. *Leadership*. Notre Dame, IN: University of Notre Dame Press, 1998.

Vroom, V. H. "Industrial Social Psychology," in G. I. Lindzey and E. Aronson (Eds.), *The Handbook of Social Psychology* (2nd ed.), Vol. V, *Applied Social Psychology*. Reading, MA: Addison-Wesley Publishing Co., 1969.

Wagner, H., N. Hibbits, R. D. Rosenblatt, and R. Schultz. *Team Training and Evaluation Strategies: State of the Art*. Alexandria, VA: Human Resources Research Organization, 1977.

Zaleznik, A., C. R. Christensen, and F. L. Roethlisberger. *The Motivation, Productivity, and Satisfaction of Workers: A Prediction Study*. Boston: Graduate School of Business Administration, Harvard University, 1958.

Annotated Bibliography

Adizes, I. *How to Solve the Mismanagement Crisis*. Homewood, IL: Irwin, 1979. This book has a number of cogent comments about management, mismanagement, and the consequences of both.

Albert, R. S. "Comments on the Scientific Function of the Concept of Cohesiveness." *American Journal of Psychology*, 59, 1953, 231–34. A brief report of a study in which only a small correlation was found between a measure of group cohesiveness and judged group effectiveness.

Alexander, L. T., and A. S. Cooperband. *System Training and Research in Team Behavior*. Santa Monica, CA: System Development Corp., TM 2581, 1965. A very significant monograph on team behavior that proposes an "organismic" team model to contrast with a stimulus-response model.

Altman I., "The Small Group Field: Implications for Research on Behavior in Organizations," in R. V. Bowers (Ed.), *Studies on Behavior and Organizations: A Research Symposium*. Athens: University of Georgia Press, 1966. In this incisive analysis of the state of small-group research in 1966, the author makes a strong case for opening the "black box" of small groups and of organizations, and for examining the internal processes through which system outputs are accomplished. Such analyses would permit better management of critical factors that impact upon ultimate effectiveness.

Anderson, D., and L. A. Anderson. *Beyond Change Management: Advanced Strategies for Today's Transformational Leaders*. San Francisco, CA: Pfeiffer, 2001. This unique book addresses the issue of transformation of an organization; specifically, it explores the interaction of leadership style, mindset, and the process of organizational change.

Argyle, M., G. Gardner, and I. Cioffi. "Supervisory Methods Related to Productivity, Absenteeism, and Turnover." *Human Relations*, 11, 1958, 23–40. An interesting report about supervision and its effects upon personnel. In addition, there are some interesting findings about group size, performance, and attitudes.

Argyris, C. "Human Problems with Budgets." *Harvard Business Review*, 31(1), 1954, 97–110. An analysis of budgets as one type of pressure device for increasing efficiency. The effects of pressure upon performance are examined, the opposing factors affecting performance are analyzed, and a method for improving performance without pressure is suggested.

Argyris, C. "Some Unresolved Problems of Executive Development Programs." *Journal of Educational Sociology*, 30, 1956, 20–30. This article sets forth the author's contention that a leader must be able to assess the needs of constantly shifting situations and adapt his behavior according to a realistic assessment of the situation.

Argyris, C. *Personality and Organization: The Conflict between System and the Individual.* New York: Harper & Brothers, 1957. This is a well-known and controversial analysis of the effects of formal organization and organizational practices upon the performance and attitudes of industrial personnel. Although concerned with industrial practices, this book contains many provocative ideas about leadership and organizations in general.

Argyris, C. *Interpersonal Competence and Organizational Effectiveness.* Homewood, IL: Irwin–Dorsey Press, 1962. This book analyzes interpersonal competence as a major determinant of effectiveness in high-level executive groups. It presents a model for diagnosing high-level effectiveness. It also attempts to show the impact of values held by executives about "effective human relations" upon their interpersonal relationships and administrative competence. Explanation is offered of how these values, in turn, influence organizational defensiveness, organizational structure, interdepartmental conflict and cooperation, rational decision-making, and policy formulation and execution.

Ashkanasy, N. M., C.E.J. Hartel, and W. J. Zerbb (Eds.). *Emotions in the Workplace.* Westport, CT: Quorum Books, 2000. This wide-ranging volume is an interdisciplinary effort by a number of contributors to explore the elements that evoke emotions in the workplace, their effects, and their management.

Barnard, C. I. *The Functions of the Executive.* Cambridge, MA: Harvard University Press, 1938. This book is the classic in the field of organizational theory. Although written in terms of a business organization, the theory is actually a sociological analysis and is generally applicable with only slight modification to all types of organizations, including military units. Although the concepts presented are sometimes hazy and highly abstract, the book provides valuable insights into the elements of formal organization, the relation to them of the "executive" function (that is, functions of control, management, leadership, and administration), and the place of these functions in the survival of an organization. Most present-day theories of organization owe credit to this book.

Barnard, C. I. "The Nature of Leadership," in C. I. Barnard (Ed.), *Organization and Management.* Cambridge, MA: Harvard University Press, 1948. This article discusses leadership as a function of three complex variables: the leader, the followers, and the conditions. The discussion includes a general description of what leaders have to do in four sectors of leadership behavior, thoughts concerning certain differences of conditions of leadership, remarks about the active personal qualities of leaders, notes on the problem of the deportment of leaders, and observations about the selection of leaders.

Bavelas, A., and D. Barrett. "An Experimental Approach to Organizational Communication." *Personnel*, 27, 1951, 367–71. This is a summary and general discussion of findings from a number of experiments concerned with the effects of different communication patterns upon performance in small groups and organizations.

Beckhard, R. "Optimizing Team Building Efforts." *Journal of Conemporary Business*, Summer 1972. As used in this article, the principal discussion is concerned with "Team Building" as group development but is not concerned with the development of serious teams such as fire department companies and police swat teams.

Bellin, R. M. *Management Teams: Why They Succeed or Fail*. Oxford, UK: Butterworth-Heinemann, 1996. This book presents an incisive analysis of so-called "management teams" and why they succeed or fail. Actually, the author seems to be describing ways of building cohesive groups.

Bellin, R. M. *How to Build Successful Teams*. Oxford, UK: Butterworth-Heinemann, 1998. This book gives a blueprint for developing "teams" in organizations. Mainly, "teams" refers to cohesive work groups rather than real teams.

Benne, K. D. "Case Methods in the Training of Administrators," in W. G. Bennis, K. D. Benne, and R. Chin (Eds.), *The Planning of Change: Readings in the Applied Behavioral Sciences*. New York: Holt, Rinehart & Winston, 1961. A critique of methods for training leaders of organizations. It includes a discussion of the skills required to lead an organization. It advocates training methods that confront trainees with concrete, complex behavioral situations to be diagnosed and acted upon.

Benne, K. D., and P. D. Sheats. "Functional Roles of Group Members," *Journal of Social Issues*, 4(2), 1948, 41–49. This article defines and describes the various functional roles a person may perform in a group. The actions of members are categorized into three broad classes: those that facilitate the accomplishment of a group's task, those that help build or maintain the group, and those that are concerned solely with satisfying the needs of the individual. The article is one of the earliest formulations of the concept of "task" and "maintenance" functions in groups and organizations.

Bennis, W. G. "Leadership Theory and Administrative Behavior: The Problem of Authority." *Administrative Science Quarterly*, 4, 1959, 259–301. This is an excellent review of the state of leadership theory in 1959, including a discussion of the philosophies, ideologies, and practices that identify the major conflicting movements in the field of leadership. The author also presents his explanation of leadership in terms of certain propositions based on *a priori* criteria of organizational effectiveness.

Bennis, W. G. *Changing Organizations: Essays on the Development and Evolution of Human Organizations*. New York: McGraw-Hill Book Co., 1966. This short book is a collection of addresses, articles, and essays by Warren Bennis, probably the most articulate writer on leadership, psychology, and organizations in the late 20th century. In it, he analyzes, in a very readable way, the evolution of organizational and management theory, the current state of leadership theory, and the emergence of systems concepts in relation to organizations. Very elegant but pleasurable writing about subjects that can be difficult to absorb.

Berkowitz, L., and B. I. Levy. "Pride in Group Performance and Group-Task Motivation." *Journal of Abnormal and Social Psychology*, 53, 1956, 300–306. This article is a conventional experimental study of the effects of group cohesiveness and group task motivation upon the extent to which people were motivated to perform a task. It illustrates some of the early experimental methods that have later been improved.

Blake, R. R., and L. P. Bradford. "Decisions . . . Decisions . . . Decisions!" *Adult Leadership*, 2(7), 1953, 223–24 and 233. This is a practical discussion of the psychological difficulties encountered in decision making by groups. Also discussed are ways of overcoming the difficulties. This article is a helpful guide for leaders of committees, project teams, staffs, and problem-solving groups.

Blake, R. R., and J. S. Mouton. "The Intergroup Dynamics of Win-Lose Conflict and Problem-Solving Collaboration in Union-Management Relations," in M. Sherif (Ed.), *Intergroup Relations and Leadership: Approaches and Research in Industrial, Ethnic, Cultural, and Political Areas*. New York: John Wiley & Sons, 1962. The authors develop a comprehensive theory of conflict and collaboration between groups, validated through experimental work. Although the theory is discussed in terms of union-management conflict, it is applicable to all types of intergroup situations.

Blau, P. M., and W. R. Scott. *Formal Organizations: A Comparative Approach*. San Francisco, CA: Chandler Publishing Company, 1962. This book is a sociological analysis of formal organizations. It examines the nature and types of formal organizations, the connections between them, the larger social context of which they are a part, and various aspects of their internal structure, such as peer group and hierarchical relations, processes of communication, authority, leadership, and impersonal mechanisms of control.

Boguslaw, R., and E. H. Porter. "Team Functions and Training," in R. H. Gagne (Ed.), *Psychological Principles in Systems Development*. New York: Holt, Rinehart & Winston, 1962, 387–416. In this chapter, the authors report a scheme for classifying team task situations, based upon the nature of the team's tasks and the context in which the task must be performed. They distinguish between established situations and emergent situations, which differ significantly in the coordination demands placed upon them.

Bonner, H. *Group Dynamics: Principles and Applications*. New York: The Ronald Press Company, 1959. This is a textbook for college students and for professional readers. It is a comprehensive survey of the dynamics of small groups. The analysis includes group structure, group cohesiveness, intergroup tensions, group learning, group problem solving, and group leadership. Application is made to the areas of business, community relations, political behavior, group psychotherapy, and education.

Bovard, E. W., Jr. "Group Structure and Perception." *Journal of Abnormal and Social Psychology*, 46, 1951, 398–405. This article describes the results of an experiment designed to study the effects of leadership and group structure upon how members perceive external situations, other members, and the group as a whole. The principal conclusion is that the methods a leader uses to encourage or to control interaction between group members and between him and group members exert material influence upon members' perceptions.

Bowers, D. G. *Work Organizations as Dynamic Systems*. Technical Report. Ann Arbor: Institute for Social Research, University of Michigan, 1969. This technical report was one of the early publications that addressed organizations as open systems.

Bowers, R. V. (Ed.). *Studies in Organizational Effectiveness: Contributions to Military Sociology*. Washington, DC: Air Force Office of Scientific Research (Office of Aerospace Research), 1962. This book contains reports of five studies of Air Force units dealing with significant factors in organizational effectiveness. Among the areas covered are role conflict, role ambiguity, leadership and morale, and the effects of changes in leaders upon an organization.

Bradford, L. P. "The Teaching-Learning Transaction," in L. P. Bradford (Ed.), *Human Forces in Teaching and Learning*. Washington, DC: National Training Laboratories, National Education Association, 1961, 5–15. A masterful analysis of the teaching-learning transaction.

Brannick, M. T., E. Salas, and C. Prince. *Team Performance Assessment and Measurement: Theory, Methods, and Application*. Mahwah, NJ: Lawrence Erlbaum Associates, 1997. This is a highly detailed analysis of team training, performance, assessment, measurement, and application. Here, "Team" refers to genuinely, specifically designed teams, and not the casual *ad hoc* "teams" or groups frequently found in organizations.

Brayfield, H. A., and W. H. Crockett. "Employee Performance." *Psychological Bulletin*, 52, 1955, 396–424. This rather extensive article is an analysis of performance and job satisfaction. It is concluded that job satisfaction and productivity are not necessarily complementary; that is, in some cases, they may be highly correlated, and in other cases they are not necessarily highly correlated. This is one of the first studies in which the discrepancy between job satisfaction and productivity was noted.

Burns, T., and G. M. Stalker. *The Management of Innovation*. London: Tavistock Publications, 1961. An interesting book by two of the "organizational neostructuralists," whose approach is important because they recognize that, for an organization to function effectively, both structure and functional behavior requirements must be considered.

Cantor, N. *The Learning Process for Managers*. New York: Harper & Row, 1958. In this book, the author sets out his premise of learning, which is that genuine learning requires a change in behavior. In short, trainees must behave differently if learning can be said to occur.

Carlisle, H. A. *Situational Management: A Contingency Approach to Leadership*. New York: AMACOM, 1973. This is an excellent book published by the American Management Association. It presents a new methodology called "Structural Analysis and Systems Theory."

Cartwright, D. "Achieving Change in People." *Human Relations*, 4, 1951, 381–92. Starting from the premise that the behavior, attitudes, beliefs, and values of the individual are grounded in the groups to which he belongs, the author discusses ways that group factors can be used to change people. This article includes a number of principles for achieving change in people.

Cartwright, D., and A. Zander (Eds.). *Group Dynamics: Research and Theory* (1st and 2nd eds.). Evanston, IL: Row, Peterson & Co., 1953 and 1960. These two editions of one of the definitive books on the dynamics of small groups contain selections of significant research papers in the field. Areas covered in separate sections are (a) group cohesiveness, (b) group pressures and standards, (c) individual motives and group goals, (d) leadership and group performance, and (e) the structural properties of groups. Each section includes an introduction that analyzes both practical and theoretical issues in the area under consideration.

Charters, W. W., Jr., and T. M. Newcomb. "Some Attitudinal Effects of Experimentally Increased Salience of a Membership Group," in G. E. Swanson, T. M. Newcomb, and E. L. Hartley (Eds.), *Readings in Social Psychology* (rev. ed.). New York: Henry Holt and Company, 1952. This article reports a study demonstrating that an individual's favorable attitudes toward a group and his agreement with the official values of the group are heightened as his conscious awareness of membership in that group is increased.

Coch, L., and J.P.R. French, Jr. "Overcoming Resistance to Change." *Human Relations*, 1, 1948, 512–32. This is a classical study concerned with overcoming resistance to change. It examined resistance to changes in operations in a manufacturing company and describes methods that were successful in reducing resistance to change and in obtaining acceptance of changed work procedures.

Cohen, A. R., S. Fink, H. Gadon, and R. Willits. *Effective Behavior in Organizations*. Homewood, IL: Irwin, 1980. A review and research concerned with determinants of effective behavior in organizations.

Collins, J. J. *A Study of Potential Contributions of Small Group Behavior Research to Team Training Technology Development*. Alexandria, VA: Essex Corporation, 1977. The author contends that team training technology is seriously deficient. He cites a number of serious deficiencies in military team training. The deficiencies are listed, described, and discussed.

Deal, T. E., and A. A. Kennedy. *Corporate Cultures*. Reading, MA: Addison-Wesley, 1982. This book discusses the development and effects of work contexts identified as corporate cultures.

Deutsch, M. "An Experimental Study of the Effects of Cooperation and Competition upon Group Processes." *Human Relations*, 2, 1949, 199–231. This article is a technical report of a classical experiment concerned with the effects of cooperation versus competition upon group performance and member attitudes toward the group.

Deutsch, M. "Some Factors Affecting Membership Motivation and Achievement Motivation in a Group." *Human Relations*, 12, 1959, 81–95. This is a report of another study in which no relationship was found between group cohesiveness and effectiveness.

Dubin, R. "Decision-Making by Management in Industrial Relations." *American Journal of Sociology*, 54, 1949, 292–97. This is one of the early reports in which emphasis was placed upon the way attitudes, values, and informal roles may develop within units of an organization and may conflict with structural controls.

Dyer, J. L. *Annotated Bibliography and State-of-the-Arts Review of the Field of Team Training as It Relates to Military Teams.* Alexandria, VA: U.S. Army Research Institute for the Behavioral Sciences, 1985. This is an excellent review of the literature on team training and its use in military training.

Eitington, J. E. *The Winning Trainer: Winning Ways to Involve People in Learning* (3rd ed.). Oxford, UK: Butterworth-Heinemann, 1996. This is a sourcebook for industrial trainers. A heavy emphasis is upon trainee involvement and ways of improving involvement.

Emery, F. E., and F. L. Trist. "The Causal Texture of Organizational Environments." *Human Relations*, 18, 1965, 21–32. A classical report on the effects of organizational contexts upon effectiveness and performance.

Festinger, L. "An Analysis of Compliant Behavior," in M. Sherif and M. O. Wilson (Eds.), *Group Relations at the Crossroads.* New York: Harper & Brothers, 1933. The author analyzes conditions under which individuals will comply with group standards of behavior. He distinguishes between public compliance and private acceptance of the standards and public compliance without private acceptance. He also discusses the effects upon the individual's behavior of these two types of compliance. The discussion has implications for discipline and morale.

Fiedler, F. E. "Engineering the Job to Fit the Manager." *Harvard Business Review*, 43, 1965, 115–22. In this article, the author contends that it is easier to change a managerial job to fit the individual than to try to change an individual to fit him to the job, that is, to turn him.

Fiedler, F. E. *On the Death and Transfiguration of Leadership Training*, Technical Report 70–16. Seattle: Dept. of Psychology, University of Washington, 1970. This report covers Fiedler's later research on leadership and his contention that leadership training is so difficult as to be almost impossible.

Foegen, J. H. "Should You Tell Them Everything?" *Advanced Management*, 20, 1955, 28–32. This article presents arguments for providing personnel with full information concerning matters that affect them. It discusses the pros and cons of information programs and concludes that "too much communication is impossible."

Forgas, J. P., and K. D. Williams. *Social Influence: Direct and Indirect Processes.* Philadelphia: Psychology Press, 2001. In this book, a number of social psychologists review and integrate contemporary theory and research on social influence processes.

Forsyth, D. R. (Ed.). "100 Years of Group Research." *Group Dynamics: Theory, Research, and Practice*, 4(1), March 2000. This is a review of group research past and present.

French, J.R.P., Jr. "The Disruption and Cohesion of Groups." *Journal of Abnormal and Social Psychology*, 36, 1941, 361–77. This is the report of an experiment concerned with the effects of group frustration upon the cohesion of small groups. It shows that frustration can have seriously disrupting effects upon group performance.

French, J.R.P., and B. Raven. "The Bases of Social Power," in D. Cartwright (Ed.), *Studies in Social Power.* Ann Arbor, MI: Institute for Social Research, 1959.

This article analyzes the sources of power (influence) and discusses each source in relation to its potential effectiveness.

French, R. L. "Morale and Leadership," in *A Survey Report on Human Factors in Undersea Warfare*. Prepared by the Panel on Psychology and Physiology, Committee on Undersea Warfare, National Research Council, Washington, DC, 1949. In this article, "an effort is made to outline what seem to be the major problems" concerned with group effectiveness and morale. Group effectiveness is defined, methods of measuring it are discussed, and consideration is given to a variety of factors related to it. Special attention is given to the question of leadership in relation to group effectiveness with a review of definitions and questions on the selection and training of leaders.

Gardner, B. B., and D. C. Moore. *Human Relations in Industry* (rev. ed.). Chicago: Richard D. Irwin, Inc., 1950. This well-known book is concerned with the informal social structure of work organizations, with social equilibrium and change, and with management principles and practices. Although written in the terminology of business, the book contains many observations useful to other leaders.

Gellerman, S. W. *Motivation and Productivity*. New York: American Management Association, 1963. The three stated purposes of this book are to draw together the most significant achievements in the study of motivation, to present a theory that puts most of this research into a simple understandable perspective, and to show the practical implications of all this research and theory for management policy. The book succeeds in its objectives and is recommended for anyone who desires a highly readable, understandable, and generally applicable discussion of motivation in all sorts of organizations.

Gellerman, S. W. *How People Work: Psychological Approaches to Management Problems*. Westport, CT: Quorum Books, 1998. Ten case studies are presented to demonstrate the range of managerial problems that can be solved or assisted by approaches from a psychological viewpoint.

George, C. E., G. R. Hoak, and J. Boutwell. *Pilot Studies of Team Effectiveness*. Research Memorandum No. 28. Alexandria, VA: Human Resources Research Office, 1963. This technical report concerns a field study of elements in effectiveness of small infantry teams.

Gibb, C. A. "Leadership," in G. Lindzey (Ed.), *Handbook of Social Psychology*, Vol. II. Cambridge, MA: Addison-Wesley Publishing Co., 1954. This is a survey and analysis of the social-psychological literature concerned with leadership. The major sections discuss leader behavior, group factors in leadership, psychodynamics of leader-follower relations, types of leadership, succession of leaders, and theories of leadership.

Gibb, J. "Communication and Productivity." *Personnel Administration*, 27(1), 1964, 8–13 and 45. This easily readable article presents an incisive analysis of leader communication. The merits of persuasion versus problem-solving techniques in relation to organizational effectiveness are also discussed.

Gibb, J. R., G. N. Platts, and L. F. Miller. *Dynamics of Participative Groups*. St. Louis: John S. Swift Co., 1951. This is an early analysis of participative groups, their dynamics, and procedures for training them.

Gill, D. L. "Cohesiveness and Performance in Sport Groups," in R. W. Yeeton (Ed.), *Exercise and Sports Sciences Review* (Vol. 5). Santa Barbara, CA: Journal Publishing Affiliates, 1977. This article is interesting because it describes cohesiveness and its development in sports teams.

Goetz, B. J., and W. G. Bennis. "What We Know About Learning and Training." *Personnel Administration*, 25: 1962, 20–29. An excellent analysis of training dynamics and difficulties in making adult learning successful.

Goetzinger, C., and M. Valentine. "Problems in Executive Interpersonal Communication." *Personnel Administration*, 27(2), 1964, 24–29. This article discusses some of the problems facing executives as they make decisions, implement old ideas, and create new ones, as they engage in such communication activities as receiving, analyzing, evaluating, synthesizing, and transmitting information. Twelve problems are cited that are common to most organizations, the presumed recognition of which provides a start toward the improvement of interpersonal communication and leadership.

Gordon, T. *Group-Centered Leadership*. Boston: Houghton Mifflin, 1955. An excellent presentation of the "Ethical Approach" (power sharing) to leadership training.

Gragg, C. I. "Because Wisdom Can't Be Told," in K. R. Andrews (Ed.), *The Case Method of Teaching Human Relations and Administration*. Cambridge, MA: Harvard University Press, 1960, 3–12. This chapter presents a rationale for the case method of training.

Green, T. B., and R. T. Butkus. *Motivation, Belief, and Organizational Transformation*. Westport, CT: Quorum Books, 1999. The authors contend that managing change in organizations requires building support from a highly motivated work force.

Green, T. B., and J. T. Knippen. *Breaking the Barrier to Upward Communication*. Westport, CT: Quorum Books, 1999. This book addresses problems in upward communication. It outlines more than 40 specific upper communication needs and proposes a structure for ensuring movement of ideas upward.

Greenbaum, C. W. "The Small Group Under the Gun: Uses of Small Groups in Battle Conditions." *Journal of Applied Psychology*, 15, 1979, 392–405. This article is a report of an extensive review of studies of small military units in combat (World Wars I and II, Yom Kippur War, Korean War). Greenbaum concludes that properly led individuals in combat units will develop strong bonds of identification with one another and that these bonds are functional, serving to control individual fear, and helping the individual to be effective in his work, and this leads to cohesiveness in small groups.

Griffith, J. "Measurement of Group Cohesion in U.S. Army Units." *Basic and Applied Social Psychology*, 6, 1988, 51–60. This article is concerned with the techniques for measuring group cohesiveness in U.S. Army units.

Griffith, J. "The Army's New Unit Personnel Replacement Policy and Its Relationship to Unit Cohesion and Social Support." *Military Psychology*, 1, 1989, 17–34. This article is concerned with the effect of stability in an organization and its effect upon cohesion. The Army's personnel policies for replacement were changed in the late 1980s and personnel were allowed to stay in units much longer than formerly. This resulted in higher unit cohesion and the provision of emotional support from various members to each other.

Gross, E. "Primary Functions of the Small Group." *American Journal of Sociology*, 60, 1954, 24–29. In this article, Gross reports on a study of small work groups within the Air Force and found that satisfaction with the Air Force and personal commitment to group goals were directly related to group cohesiveness.

Habbe, S. "Does Communication Make a Difference?" *Management Record*, 14, 1952, 414–16, 442–44. The author reports the results of a study of the effects of communication upon group performance by industrial workers.

Haiman, F. S. *Group Leadership and Democratic Action*. Boston: Houghton Mifflin, 1950. This is another book that advocates power sharing as a leadership tactic.

Haire, M. *Psychology in Management*. New York: McGraw-Hill Book Company, 1956. In this popular book, students and leaders are offered a "statement of a set of psychological principles and their implications for some problems of industrial management." Although written for a business audience, the basic material covered in the book is applicable to any context, is readable, and is readily understood. The book contains much useful information.

Hall, E. R., and W. A. Rizzo. *An Assessment of U.S. Navy Tactical Team Training*. Orlando, FL: Training and Evaluation Group, 1975. This is a review of U.S. Navy tactical team training, which raises many cogent issues related to training teams.

Hare, A. P. *Handbook of Small Group Research* (2nd ed.). New York: The Free Press, 1976. This book is just what it says—a comprehensive excursion through the small group literature to 1976. It contains extensive discussions of the many issues in small-group research. It also contains a 6,037 item bibliography.

Hemphill, J. K. *Situational Factors in Leadership*. Monograph 32. Columbus, OH: The Ohio State University, Bureau of Educational Research, 1949. This is the technical report of a series of experiments designed to study group factors affecting leadership.

Herbst, P. G. "Measurement of Behavior Structure by Means of Input-Output Data." *Human Relations*, 10, 1957, 335–46. In this article, it was found that middle-size groups sometimes produce better than smaller ones or larger ones.

Herzberg, F., B. Mausner, and B. B. Snyderman. *The Motivation to Work* (2nd ed.). New York: John Wiley & Sons, 1959. This book reports a study of motivation in which more than 200 industrial employees were interviewed to provide insights into the effects of attitudes upon performance. Both factors influencing attitudes and their effects are discussed along with implications of the results. A major finding was a confirmation of the hypothesis that some factors influence attitudes only in a positive direction and others only in a negative direction as contrasted to the idea that any given factor can have both a positive and negative impact upon morale.

Hinton, B. L., and H. J. Reitz (Eds.). *Groups and Organizations: Integrated Readings in the Analysis of Social Behavior*. Belmont, CA: Wadsworth, 1971. This volume contains an integrated set of readings designed to demonstrate that areas of behavioral knowledge extend from social relationships between two people to the complex relationships characteristic of large organizations.

Hite, J. *Learning in Chaos: Improving Performance in Today's Fast Changing, Volatile Organizations*. Houston: Gulf Publishing Co., 1999. The author contends that change is a functional characteristic of every organization and that it is increasingly intensive today. Under such conditions, learning is more difficult.

Hogg, M. A., and D. A., Abrams. *Intergroup Relations: Essential Readings*. Philadelphia: Psychology Press, 2001. This book, a collection of classic and contemporary readings that help define the social psychology of intergroup relations, is heavy on diversity and complexity of the topic.

Homans, G. C. *The Human Group*. New York: Harcourt, Brace and Co., 1950. This book is one of the classic sociological studies of human groups. Presented from the standpoint of a sociologist, it was one of the major books at the time of its publication.

Hunt, E. "A Cognitive Science and Psychometric Approach to Team Performance," in S. E. Goldin and E. Thorndyke (Eds.), *Improving Team Performance: Proceedings of the Rand Team Performance Workshop*. Santa Monica, CA: The Rand Corporation, 1980. This is an interesting paper, one of several appearing in the report of the 1980 Rand Corporation Conference on Team Performance. The paper describes some interesting concepts concerned with cognition and team performance.

Indik, B. P., and S. E. Seashore. *Effects of Organization Size on Member Attitudes and Behavior*. Ann Arbor: Survey Research Center, Institute of Social Research, University of Michigan, 1961. In this study, the authors report that they found no relationship between size of work group and productivity in automotive dealerships but did find that productivity was higher in small groups within a package-delivery organization. It appears that for some types of work, organization into smaller groups will lead to improved performance; for other kinds of work, size of the group may be irrelevant for productivity.

Jackson, J. M. "Reference Group Processes in a Formal Organization." *Sociometry*, 22, 1959a, 307–27. This is the report of a study concerned with factors determining the extent to which an individual will like the group of which he is a member.

Jackson, J. M. "The Organization and Its Communications Problem." *Advanced Management*, 24(2), 1959b, 17–20. This article is an excellent discussion of communication problems in organizations and some of the reasons for them. The author concludes that communication problems are often only symptomatic of other difficulties within the organization.

Jacobs, T. O. *Leadership and Exchange in Formal Organizations*. Alexandria, VA: Human Resources Research Organization, 1970. In this book, the author analyzes leadership from the standpoint of Exchange Theory.

Jacobson, E., W. W. Charters, Jr., and S. Lieberman. "The Use of the Role Concept in the Study of Complex Organizations." *Journal of Social Issues*, 7(3), 1951,

18–27. This is a discussion of the concept of "role" and its use in understanding behavior in organizations.

Jaques, D. *Learning in Groups* (2nd ed.). Houston: Gulf Publishing Co., 1992. This book is about exactly what the title says: how groups may be used as vehicles for learning.

Kahn, R. L. "Productivity and Job Satisfaction." *Personnel Psychology*, 13, 1960, 275–87. This report shows that job satisfaction and productivity are not necessarily complementary.

Kahn, R. L., and D. Katz. "Leadership Practices in Relation to Productivity and Morale," in D. Cartwright and A. Zander (Eds.), *Group Dynamics: Research and Theory*. Evanston, IL: Row, Peterson & Co., 1953. This chapter in one of the first books concerned with group dynamics is a survey of research conducted in the Survey Research Center at the University of Michigan. The authors discuss the findings of a series of studies concerned with the effects of various leadership practices in relation to productivity and morale. The conclusion is that the leadership practices have an important impact upon both productivity and employee attitudes.

The authors summarize research up to 1953 conducted in business and industry to identify the characteristics of supervisors who led relatively productive crews. Not much has changed in 50 years.

Kanter, R. M. "Power Failures in Management Circuits." *Harvard Business Review*, 74(4), 1979, 65–75. This article discusses some ways that critical organizational processes break down and how breakdowns can be prevented.

Kanter, R. M. *The Change Masters: How People and Companies Succeed Through Innovation in the New Corporate Era*. New York: Simon and Schuster, 1983. An early examination of how change in organizations can be managed without excess trauma.

Katz, D. "The Motivational Basis of Organizational Behavior." *Behavioral Science*, 9(2), 1964, 131–46. This is an interesting discussion of motivation in organizations. The author concludes that if an organization is to survive and to function effectively, it must require not one but several different types of behavior from most of its members and the motivations of these different types of behavior may also differ. The author tries to answer the basic problem: What is the nature of a person's involvement in an organization or his commitment to it?

Katz, D., and R. L. Kahn. "Some Recent Findings in Human Relations Research," in E. Swanson, T. Newcomb, and E. Hartley (Eds.), *Readings in Social Psychology*. New York: Holt, Rinehart, & Winston, 1952, 650–65. This chapter in one of the early social psychology textbooks is an excellent presentation of much of the Lewinian approach to research upon human relations in industry. Not much has changed since the publication of this chapter.

Katz, D., and R. L. Kahn. "Human Organization and Worker Motivation." In Industrial Relations Research Association, *Industrial Productivity*. Madison, WI: Author, 1953. This is a useful discussion of the ways organizational factors influence the motivations of personnel. The authors stress the importance of social-psychological factors but warn against overemphasis upon these variables at the expense of formal organizational requirements.

Katz, D., and R. L. Kahn. *The Social Psychology of Organizations*. New York: John Wiley & Sons, 1966. In this book, the authors attempt nothing more than a complete explanation of organizational behavior within Systems Theory concepts. The attempt was reasonably successful in putting into proper perspective such ideas as interchange with environments, operation by process instead of procedure, and the interrelationships among functional units.

Katz, D., N. Maccoby, G. Gurin, and L. G. Floor. *Productivity, Supervision and Morale Among Railroad Workers*. Ann Arbor: Institute for Social Research, University of Michigan, 1951. The study makes comparisons of the attitudes of railroad workers in high- and low-producing groups. The major conclusion is that leadership is as important to productivity as are the attitudes of personnel.

Katz, D., N. Maccoby, and N. C. Morse. *Productivity, Supervision and Morale in an Office Situation*. Ann Arbor: Institute for Social Research, University of Michigan, 1950. This report presents findings from a study of clerical workers in the home office of a large insurance company. Differences in group motivation are seen to be related to differences in supervisory practice and philosophy.

Katzell, R. A., R. S. Barrett, and T. C. Parker. "Job Satisfaction, Job Performance, and Situational Characteristics." *Journal of Applied Psychology*, 45, 1961, 65–72. In this study of the effects of situational characteristics upon job satisfaction and performance, it was found that smaller work unit size leads to higher productivity.

Kelley, H. H., and J. R. Thibaut. "Experimental Studies of Group Problem Solving and Process," in G. Lindzey (Ed.), *Handbook of Social Psychology*, Vol. II. Cambridge, MA: Addison-Wesley Publishing Co., 1954. This article summarizes the technical literature concerned with group problem solving. The analysis places special emphasis on the communication process and on interaction within small groups while producing solutions to various types of problems.

Kerr, W. A., G. J., Koppelmeier, and J. J. Sullivan. "Absenteeism, Turnover, and Morale in a Metals Fabrication Factory." *Occupational Psychology*, 25, 1951, 50–55. This is one of the more classical analyses of determinants of absenteeism, turnover, and morale in a heavy metals factory.

Kirkpatrick, D. L. *Managing Change Effectively*. Oxford, UK: Butterworth-Heinemann, 2001. This book is about adapting to required changes and managing change effectively. Specific approaches and methods for incorporating changes are detailed.

Kline, B. E., and N. H. Martin. "Freedom, Authority, and Decentralization." *Harvard Business Review*, 36(3), 1958, 69–75. This is an excellent discussion of freedom to act within the limits of assigned responsibility. The main focus is on the nature of freedom in an organization, its effects, and ways of fostering it among subordinates.

Knerr, C. M., D. C. Berger, and B. A. Popelka. *Sustaining Team Performance*. Interim Report. Springfield, VA: Litton Mellonics, 1979. This is an excellent analytical review of the literature on teams, team performance, and variables influencing team performance.

Knerr, C. M., L. B. Nadler, and L. E. Berger. *Toward a Naval Team Taxonomy*. Interim Report. Springfield, VA: Litton Mellonics, 1980. This report is addressed to development of a taxonomy of naval teams. It is basically a listing of factors and variables that are involved in performance of navy teams of various types.

Knickerbocker, I. "Leadership: A Conception and Some Implications." *Journal of Social Issues*, 4, Summer 1948, 23–40. This article presents the classical argument for viewing leadership in terms of what the leader does to meet the requirements of the organization and the situation rather than in terms of personal traits and characteristics. It also discusses several means by which a leader may direct the activities of people.

Knowles, M. S., E. Holton, and R. Swanson. *Adult Learner* (5th ed.). Oxford, UK: Butterworth-Heinemann, 1998. This book is claimed to be the definitive classic in the field of adult learning. It covers research on adult learning, human resource development, cognitive psychology, and educational psychology.

Landsberger, H. A. "The Horizontal Dimension in a Bureaucracy." *Administrative Science Quarterly*, 6(3), 1961, 299–332. This is a study concerned with the effects of varying amounts of communication and interaction between leaders occupying equal organizational levels.

Lawrence, P. R., and J. W. Lorsch. *Organization and Environment: Management Differentiation and Integration*. Boston: Harvard Graduate School of Business Administration, 1967. These two authors are among the writers labeled by Schein as "neostructuralists." They are concerned with design aspects of organizations in relation to the kinds of technology used and the functions served by various organizational elements.

Leavitt, H. J. "Some Effects of Certain Communication Patterns on Group Performance." *Journal of Abnormal and Social Psychology*, 46, 1951, 38–50. This article reports studies of the relationship between the behavior of small groups and the patterns of communication in which they operate. It was found that communication patterns within which groups work affect their behavior.

Leavitt, H. J. *Managerial Psychology*. Chicago: University of Chicago Press, 1958. An excellent examination of human problems within organizations. Deals with an examination of the individual and his behavior, effective influence in face-to-face situations, committees, and small groups, and the nature of business organizations, with some of the problems that seem to arise only in large organizations.

Leighton, A. H. "A Working Concept of Morale for Flight Surgeons." *The Military Surgeon*, 92, 1959, 170–80. This is an insightful discussion of morale in which the author, a well-known psychiatrist and social scientist, stresses the importance of each individual's attitudes toward his organization and its leaders.

Leonard, H. W. (Ed.). "Consulting to Team-Based Organizations." *Consulting Psychology Journal: Practice and Research*, 52(1), Winter 2000. This interesting article discusses some of the problems in developing organizations that are centered around teams and team performance.

Levinson, D. J. "Role, Personality, and Social Structure in the Organizational Setting." *Journal of Abnormal and Social Psychology*, 58, 1959, 170–80. This is a technical analysis of the psychological factors in individual functioning within an organizational setting. The article contains a useful discussion of the concept of "role."

Lewin, K. "Studies in Group Decision," in D. Cartwright and A. Zander (Eds.), *Group Dynamics: Research and Theory*. Evanston, IL: Row, Peterson & Co., 1953. This article is a summary of the famous "group-decision" experiments that demonstrate the effectiveness of group discussion and consensus upon behavior change.

Lewin, K., T. Dembo, L. Festinger, and P. Sears. "Level of Aspiration," in J. McV. Hunt (Ed.), *Personality and the Behavior Disorders*. New York: The Ronald Press, 1944. This is a technical survey of research on level of aspiration. It also contains a discussion of level of aspiration in terms of Lewin's field theory.

Lewin, K., R. Lippit, and R. K. White. "Patterns of Aggressive Behavior in Experimentally Created 'Social Climates.' " *Journal of Social Psychology*, 10, 1939, 512–32. This is the classical report of the experimental variation in leadership style and the effects of such variations upon member behavior in small groups. The senior author, Kurt Lewin, is known as the father of field theory and group dynamics in social psychology.

Likert, R. "A Motivational Approach to a Modified Theory of Organization and Management," in M. Haire (Ed.), *Modern Organization Theory*. New York: John Wiley & Sons, 1959. The author presents an understandable theory of organizational leadership and management. The theory is based on substantial research findings which show the character of the better practices and principles developed and used by managers and supervisors who the author contends are achieving the highest performance in American business.

Likert, R. *New Patterns of Management*. New York: McGraw-Hill Book Co., 1961. This is a readable book that presents a theory of organization based on research conducted mostly by the author. Although the theory is derived and discussed in terms of business and civilian governmental organizations, the book contains much that will be of use to anyone interested in leading an organization.

Likert, R. *The Human Organization: Its Management and Value*. New York: McGraw-Hill Book Co., 1967. The classic book by Rensis Likert in which he proposed a four-fold typology of organizations and concluded with extensive research that more successful organizations tend toward "System Four" management. System Four organizations are characterized by a supportive climate, group decision-making, considerable group self-control, and high performance goals. The major variables appear to be the nature of the management climate (directive versus supportive) and the individual versus group orientation. Likert also advocated an overlapping group structure, which is his well-known "linking pin" concept.

Lindzey, G. (Ed.). *Handbook of Social Psychology*. Vols. I and II. Cambridge, MA: Addison-Wesley Publishing Co., 1954. This two-volume work contains survey articles pertaining to the major areas of social psychology. Volume I deals primarily with theoretical or systematic positions and methods employed in social psychology. Volume II focuses upon the substantive findings and applications of social psychology derived from these theoretical viewpoints.

Lindzey, G., and Aronson, E. (Eds.). *The Handbook of Social Psychology* (2nd ed.). Reading, MA: Addison-Wesley Publishing Co., 1968. A review and survey of social psychology circa 1968. In 5 volumes, containing 45 chapters. Chapters that especially pertain to this book are as follows:

Cyert, R. M., and K. R. MacCrimmon. "Organizations." Vol. 1, 568–613.

Deutsch, M. "Field Theory in Social Psychology." Vol. 2, 412–87.

Gibb, C. A. "Leadership." Vol. 4, 205–82.

Sarbin, T. R. "Role Theory." Vol. 1, 488–567.

Vroom, V. H. "Industrial Social Psychology." Vol. 5, 196–267.

Lippitt, R. "Methods for Producing and Measuring Change in Group Functioning: Theoretical Problems." *General Semantics Bulletin*, 14 and 15, Winter–Spring 1954, 28–33. This article is a discussion of problems in group functioning and of theory and methods used by professional consultants when attempting to develop or direct an organization.

Ludington, C. (Ed.). *Communication in Organizations: Some New Research Findings*. Ann Arbor, MI: The Foundation for Research on Human Behavior, 1959. This is the report of a seminar on communication in organizations. It presents reports of four distinct research efforts directed toward understanding communications problems: to examine problems at the receiving end of communication systems and to study communication systems in business organizations.

McClelland, D. C., J. W. Atkinson, R. A. Clark, and E. L. Lowell. *The Achievement Motive*. New York: Appleton-Century-Crofts, 1953. A technical description of the methods used in research that identified the achievement motive as one determinant of behavior.

McClelland, D. C., and D. H. Burnham. "Power Is the Great Motivator." *Harvard Business Review*, 54(2), 1976. The senior author of this article is the well-known advocate of "Achievement Motivation." In this article, the authors concern themselves with power within organizations and the effects upon human performance.

McClelland, W. A., and J. D. Lyons. *Guidelines for Manpower Training as Developed by the Human Resources Research Office*. HumRRO Professional Paper 43–68, 1968. These authors are well-known experts in training and training methodology. In this paper, they make the important distinction between training and education.

McCurdy, H. G., and W. E. Lambert. "The Efficiency of Small Human Groups in the Solution of Problems Requiring Genuine Co-Operation." *Journal of Personality*, 20, 1952, 478–95. This report concerns one of the early studies of problem solving in small groups. It sets forth some of the issues and some of the findings that were later confirmed by other researchers.

McDavid, J. W., and H. Harari. *Social Psychology: Individuals, Groups, Societies*. New York: Harper & Row, 1968. This is an excellent textbook for introduction to social psychology. The discussions of small groups and of teamwork are especially relevant and useful in application to real life.

McGregor, D. "Conditions of Effective Leadership in the Industrial Organization." *Journal of Consulting Psychology*, 8(2), 1944, 55–63. The main theme of this article is that a subordinate is dependent for the satisfaction of many of his vital needs upon the behavior and attitudes of his superior. The author identifies and discusses several conditions essential for subordinate effectiveness.

McGregor, D. *The Human Side of Enterprise*. New York: McGraw-Hill Book Co., 1960. This highly readable book is a general discussion of some of the critical issues in leadership. The author examines the assumptions underlying conventional views of leadership and proposes an alternative approach to leadership of organizations. This book has become "the classic" in late twentieth century management literature.

McGregor, D. *The Professional Manager*. Caroline McGregor and Warren Bennis (Eds.). New York: McGraw-Hill Book Co., 1967. A collection of writings by Douglas McGregor, edited after his death by his wife and Warren Bennis. It describes McGregor's final thinking about leadership and management.

McNair, M. P. "Thinking Ahead: What Price Human Relations." *Harvard Business Review*, 35(2), 1957, 15–39. This article is an attack upon human relations training. It sets out some cogent but biased ideas about human relations training.

Mann, R. C., and F. W. Neff. *Managing Major Changes in Organizations*. Ann Arbor, MI: The Foundation for Research on Human Behavior, 1961. This is the report of a seminar concerned with accomplishing large-scale changes in organizations. Four cases of organizational change are presented and analyzed in terms of (1) the state of the organization before change, (2) the recognition of a need for change, (3) planning for the change, (4) taking action steps to make the change, and (5) stabilizing the change.

Maslow, A. H. *Motivation and Personality*, New York: Harper & Row, 1954. This book is Maslow's original presentation of his hierarchical theory of motivation, and it can be considered a landmark in the study of evolution of motivation theory.

Maslow, A. H. *Motivation and Personality* (2nd ed.). New York: Harper & Row, 1970. The second edition of Maslow's book, originally published in 1954, Maslow describes and expands upon his well-known model "Needs Hierarchy" theory of motivation. The theory is widely accepted, especially by practitioners because the concepts are simple, understandable, and make sense in the real world, especially in the world of organization.

Mayo, E. *The Human Problems of an Industrial Civilization*. New York: The Macmillan Company, 1933. The book that started it all, it discusses the famous studies at the Hawthorne Plant of Western Electric. There, researchers discovered the influence of the face-to-face informal group upon motivation and behavior in a work situation and triggered the human relations movement, which spread rapidly throughout the world.

Medelia, N. Z., and C. D. Miller. "Human Relations Leadership and the Association of Morale and Efficiency in Work Groups: A Controlled Study with Small Military Units." *Social Forces*, 33, 1955, 348–52. This is a report of research conducted on small military units. It attempts to clarify the relationship between leadership, morale, and efficiency.

Meister, D. *Behavioral Foundations of System Development*. New York: John Wiley & Sons, 1976. This book addresses the issue of system technology and systems development. It is concerned mainly with simple systems of the input-output variety.

Mellinger, G. "Interpersonal Trust as a Factor in Communication." *Journal of Abnormal and Social Psychology*, 52, 1956, 304–9. This research report analyzes the effect of interpersonal trust upon quantity and quality of communication in a government research laboratory.

Merton, R. K. *Social Theory and Social Structure* (2nd ed.). Glencoe, IL: The Free Press, 1957. This book attempts to consolidate social theory and social research with emphasis on the procedures and qualitative analysis used in sociology. It includes analyses of reference group behavior and of the breakdown of social norms.

Merton, R. K., and A. S. Kitt. "Contributions to the Theory of Reference Group Behavior," in R. K. Merton and P. F. Lazarsfeld (Eds.), *Continuities in Social Research: Studies in the Scope and Method of "The American Soldier."* Glencoe, IL: Free Press, 1950. This article was the cornerstone of research and literature on reference groups, a powerful concept that explains much about how people acquire their attitudes that are used to evaluate situations encountered in real life.

Miller, J. B. "Toward a General Theory for the Behavioral Sciences." *American Psychologist*, 10, 1955, 513–31. In this article, the author presents a general theory for the behavioral sciences. It closely resembles open systems theory and has served as one of the bases of the development of organizational theory in the direction of systems theory.

Mills, T. M. *The Sociology of Small Groups*. Englewood Cliffs, NJ: Prentice-Hall, 1967. This book describes a sociologist's approach to small groups. While somewhat different from the ordinary social psychological approach, it contains some useful ideas about how to approach small groups and their performance.

Miner, J. B. *The Management of Ineffective Performance*. New York: McGraw-Hill Book Co., 1963. This book provides a synthesis of information available in 1963 on work performance and discusses methods of dealing with individuals who are not meeting established standards of effectiveness.

Mooney, J. D. *The Principles of Organization* (rev. ed.). New York: Harper & Row, 1947. This is a discussion of certain principles of formal organization considered by the author to be the fundamental bases for effective organizational functioning. The evolution of these principles within military, church, and business contexts is traced.

Murdock, A., and C. N. Scott. *Personal Effectiveness*. Oxford, UK: Butterworth-Heinemann, 1997. This is a treatise on personal effectiveness. It presents and is centered around a Personal Competency Model.

Nadler, L., and Z. Nadler. *Designing Training Programs: The Critical Events Model* (2nd ed.). Oxford, UK: Butterworth-Heinemann, 1994. This is a source book for corporate trainers and instructors of adult learners.

Newman, W. H. "Overcoming Obstacles to Effective Delegation," in J. A. Litterer (Ed.), *Organizations: Structure and Behavior*. New York: John Wiley & Sons, 1963. This article examines some of the reasons why leaders are apprehensive about delegation and why subordinates hesitate to take responsibility.

Nieva, V. F., E. A. Fleischman, and A. Rieck. *Team Dimensions: Their Identity, Their Measurement, and Their Relationships.* Washington, DC: Advanced Research Resources Organization, 1978. This report describes the result of an attempt to develop a taxonomy of teams.

Olmstead, J. A. *Small-Group Instruction: Theory and Practice.* Alexandria, VA: Human Resources Research Organization, 1974. This is a review and analysis of the use of small groups as teaching and training methods.

Olmstead, J. A. *Leadership Training: The State of the Art.* Technical Report 80–1. Alexandria, VA: Human Resources Research Organization, 1980. This technical report presents an analysis of the current state of leadership training. The analysis includes training for military leadership, human relations, and people-related aspects of supervision and management in business and governmental organizations. The report consists of ten chapters, grouped into two parts. Part I is concerned with the present state of the field of leadership training and includes both an assessment of leader training activities and a discussion of the state of leadership training. Part II addresses considerations for improvement of leadership training through development of a leadership training technology.

Olmstead, J. A. *Battle Staff Integration.* IDA Paper P–2560. Alexandria, VA: Institute for Defense Analyses, 1992. This monograph contains an analysis of battle staff performance and identifies some critical aspects of performance and puts the concept of Organizational Competence into an analysis of battle staffs. It provides the theoretical background of "battle-staff" integration, an analysis of processes of effectiveness, and discusses implications for leadership and battle staff development.

Olmstead, J. A. *Competency-Based Organizations: Theory and Practice.* Professional Paper 97–2. West Columbia, SC: The Vanguard Research Group, 1997a. This paper describes the theoretical foundation and a conceptual model for the development and assessment of functionally competent organizations.

Olmstead, J. A. *Leadership in Organizations.* Professional Paper 97–1. West Columbia, SC: The Vanguard Research Group, 1997b. The purpose of this paper is to integrate significant research findings and to present a coherent framework for thinking about practical leadership in organizations. The effort was to present a straightforward but sound approach that could be useful to consultants and practicing leaders.

Olmstead, J. A. *Work Units, Teams, and Task Forces: Groups at Work.* Professional Paper 98–1. West Columbia, SC: The Vanguard Research Group, 1998. The current book is an expansion of this monograph. The purpose of the monograph is to present, in brief, a coherent and integrated analysis of groups at work, their dynamics, and influences that impact upon their capabilities to perform effectively. The intent was to analyze the factors that are critical for effective group performance. An additional purpose was to propose a practical framework that will be useful for understanding the dynamics of groups at work. The discussion is organized around analyses of three broad types of groups: (1) work groups (work units, sections, departments); (2) teams (work teams, crisis-management teams, project teams);

(3) operating groups (task forces, operational staffs, and high-level decision-making groups).

Olmstead, J. A. *Executive Leadership: Building World-Class Organizations.* Houston, TX: Gulf Publishing Co., 2000. This book provides an analysis of practical executive leadership and presents a workable model for use in developing functionally competent organizations. The final chapter of the book is devoted to a conceptualization of functionally competent organizations and a discussion of some of the implications for practice in executive leadership.

Olmstead, J. A. *Creating Functionally Competent Organizations: An Open Systems Approach.* Westport, CT: Quorum Books, 2002. This book presents an integrated, coherent, conceptual framework for addressing organizational performance. Some practical models are proposed for use in analyzing, assessing, and improving organizational performance.

Olmstead, J. A., and H. E. Christensen. *Effects of Work Contexts: An Intensive Field Study, Research Report No. 2, National Study of Social Welfare and Rehabilitation Workers, Work and Organizational Contexts.* Washington, DC: Department of Health, Education, and Welfare, Social and Rehabilitation Services, 1973. This report presents and describes the results of an intensive field study of the organizational contexts within which social welfare and rehabilitation work is performed. It also identifies some of the effects of those contexts upon that work.

Olmstead, J. A., H. E. Christensen, and L. L. Lackey. *Components of Organizational Competence: Test of a Conceptual Framework.* Technical Report 73–19. Alexandria, VA: Human Resources Research Organization, 1973. An empirical study of organizational competence under simulated conditions. Identified and confirmed the validity of the "adaptive-coping cycle" and its component processes as contributors to organizational effectiveness.

Olmstead, J. A., H. E. Christensen, J. A. Salter, and L. L. Lackey. *Effects of Work Contexts in Public Welfare Financial Assistance Agencies.* Technical Report 75–7. Alexandria, VA: Human Resources Research Organization, 1975. This is another report in the series concerned with social welfare and rehabilitation organizations. This study concerned the performance and effects of work contexts upon performance of public welfare financial assistance workers. It was the second in the field studies conducted by the Human Resources Research Organization for the Social and Rehabilitation Service, DHEW.

Olson, E. F., and G. H. Eoyang. *Facilitating Organizational Change: Lessons from Complexity Science.* San Francisco, CA: Pfeiffer, 2001. The authors explain how, rather than focusing on a macro (strategic) level of an organizational system, complexity theory suggests that the most powerful change processes occur at the micro level. Tips are provided for thriving in complex adaptive systems.

Otis, J. L., and W. C. Treuhaft. "Good Communication Promotes Teamwork." *Personnel Journal,* 28, 1949, 83–90. The authors discuss some of the fundamentals of communication and its relation to teamwork.

Palmer, S. *People and Self Management.* Oxford, UK: Butterworth-Heinemann, 1998. The author sets forth the skills needed by today's supervisor/team leader. The book includes some essential skills of effective self-management and the management of change.

Parsons, H. M. *Man-Machine System Experiments.* Baltimore, MD: The Johns Hopkins Press, 1972. This report is a review of machine-ascendant teams, their characteristics, and their requirements.

Parsons, T. "Suggestions for a Sociological Approach to the Theory of Organizations, I and II." *Administrative Science Quarterly,* 1 and 2, 1956, 3–85 and 225–39. This article is a precursor to Parsons' 1960 book. It sets an outline for a sociological approach to the theory of organizations. Parsons is one of the icons of sociology and the sociology of organizations.

Parsons, T. *Structure and Process in Modern Societies.* Glencoe, IL: The Free Press, 1960. Talcott Parsons sets out a systems approach to societies, governments, and organizations. It is a very understandable approach, but Parsons paints with a broad brush and, accordingly, it is sometimes difficult to apply his concepts in specific ways.

Peabody, R. L. *Organizational Authority: Superior-Subordinate Relationships in Three Public Service Organizations.* New York: Atherton Press, 1964. This is the report on a study of authority in three public organizations. It contains theory and conclusions that are particularly relevant to authority. The author concludes that authority relations are basic to the achievement of organizational objectives but that conflicting attitudes appear to be a major source of tension within organizations.

Pepitone, A., and R. Kleiner. "The Effects of Threat and Frustration on Group Cohesiveness." *Journal of Abnormal and Social Psychology,* 54, 1957, 192–200. This is a landmark article demonstrating the effects of threat and frustration on experimental groups.

Peters, T. J., and R. H. Waterman. *In Search of Excellence.* New York: Harper & Row, 1982. A wide-ranging discussion of excellence, its attributes, and its determinants.

Porter, L. W. "Role of the Organization in Motivation: Structuring Rewarding Environments." Technical Report No. 7. Irvine: University of California Graduate School of Administration, 1971. A useful discussion of some of the ways that organizations influence the motivation of their members.

Porter, L. W., and E. E. Lawler. "Properties of Organizational Structure in Relation to Job Attitudes and Job Behavior." *Psychological Bulletin,* 64, 1965, 23–51. This article is a review of research concerned with the effects of organizational structure and variations of it upon job attitudes and job behavior of personnel.

Porter, L. W., and E. E. Lawler. *Managerial Attitudes and Performance.* Homewood, IL: Richard D. Irwin and Dorsey Press, 1968. This book, among other things, sets out the authors' concepts of expectancy theory and its impact upon organizational theory. The main result is that the authors have come up with a theory concerned with expectations that people have about their work, about their work situation, and about how moderator variables impact upon the influence of climate, organizational structure, and so forth, and upon attitudes and job performance.

Pugh, D. W. "Modern Organizational Theory: A Psychological and Sociological Study." *Psychological Bulletin,* 66, 1966, 235–51. This article is an incisive critique of theoretical approaches to organizations by a noted British psychologist.

Pugh, D. S., D. J. Hickson, C. R. Hinings, K. M. MacDonald, C. Turner, and T. Lupton. "A Conceptual Scheme for Organizational Analysis." *Administrative Science Quarterly*, 8, 1963, 289–316. This article is a precursor of Pugh's 1966 article cited above.

Pugh, D. S., D. J. Hickson, C. R. Hinings, and C. Turner. "Dimensions of Organizational Structure." *Administrative Science Quarterly*, 13, 1968, 66–105. This article presents an analysis of some dimensions of organizational structure and their possible impacts upon organizational and human performance.

Rappaport, A. "A Logical Task as a Research Tool in Organization Theory," in M. Haire (Ed.), *Modern Organization Theory*. New York: John Wiley & Sons, 1959. The author of this chapter is one of the later structural theorists, who has attempted to bring internal processes into his considerations of organizational theory.

Raven, B. H., and J. Rietsema. "The Effects of Varied Clarity of Group Goal and Group Path Upon the Individual and His Relation to His Group." *Human Relations*, 19, 1957, 29–44. This study demonstrates the effects of clear and unclear goals upon relationships within a group.

Reid, M., and R. Hammersley. *Communicating Successfully in Groups: A Practical Guide for the Workplace*. Philadelphia: Psychology Press, 2000. This practical guide to communication contains practical advice and exercises.

Reitzel, W. A. *Background to Decision Making*. Newport, RI: The United States Naval War College, 1958. This interesting and helpful discussion of military decision making indicates the approaches that psychology, the social sciences generally, and the mathematical sciences in particular are developing on the general subject of decision making. It examines the ways in which military decision-making processes are similar to, or diverge from, the other types of problem situations.

Richards, C. B., and H. F. Dobryns. "Topography and Culture: The Case of the Changing Cage." *Human Organization*, 16, 1957, 16–20. This article is an excellent illustration and analysis of how the physical arrangements within an office can have important influence upon the attitudes and performance of personnel and on the development of groups within organizations.

Riecken, H. W., and G. C. Homans. "Psychological Aspects of Social Structure," in G. Lindzey (Ed.), *Handbook of Social Psychology*, Vol. II. Cambridge, MA: Addison-Wesley Publishing Co., 1954. This is a survey and analysis of technical literature concerned with groups and social organizations. It discusses critical determinants of group performance and effectiveness.

Roby, T. B. *Small Group Performance*. Chicago: Rand McNally, 1968. This book is one of the earlier discourses on group performance. Not much has changed since its publication.

Roethlisberger, F. J. "Training Supervisors in Human Relations." *Harvard Business Review*, 29(5), 1951, 47–57. This is the author's well-known critique of human relations training as often superficial.

Roethlisberger, F. J., and W. J. Dickson. *Management and the Worker*. Cambridge, MA: Harvard University Press, 1939. This is the definitive discussion of the results of the classical "Hawthorne Experiments." The authors stress that what is most significant in work environments is not conclusive answers to specific questions but development in the understanding of human situations that will help to improve personnel relations and aid in resolving the problems arising in them—when and where they occur.

Roethlisberger, F. J., and W. J. Dickson. *Management and the Worker* (2nd ed.). Cambridge, MA: Harvard University Press, 1943. An update of the original publication.

Rogers, C. R., and F. J. Roethlisberger. "Barriers and Gateways to Communication." *Harvard Business Review*, 30(44), 1952, 28–34. This article presents a discussion of interpersonal communication by two well-known experts, who are mainly concerned with removing barriers that impede understanding between people.

Rothwell, W. J., and H. C. Kazanas. *Building In-House Leadership and Management Development Programs*. Westport, CT: Quorum Books, 1999. This practical guide presents a blueprint for establishing, administering, and maintaining a planned in-house leadership and management development program.

Sarbin, T. R. "Role Theory," in G. Lindzey (Ed.), *Handbook of Social Psychology*, Vol. I. Cambridge, MA: Addison-Wesley Publishing Co., 1954. This is a technical survey of the literature concerned with roles and theories of roles.

Savell, J. M., R. E. Teague, and T. R. Tremble. Jr. "Job Involvement Contagion Between Army Squad Leaders and Their Squad Members." *Military Psychology*, 7, 1995, 193–206. This article describes a study of job involvement and the development of cohesion in small army units.

Schein, E. H. "Management Development, Human Relations Training, and the Process of Influence," in I. R. Weschler and E. H. Schein (Eds.), *Issues in Human Relations Training*. Washington, DC: National Training Laboratories, National Education Association, 1962, 47–60. This article is concerned with the impact of groups upon the attitudes and behavior of individuals and with the potential for using group influences to assist in training executives.

Schein, E. H. *Organizational Psychology* (2nd ed.). Englewood Cliffs, NJ: Prentice-Hall, Inc., 1970. This is a basic discussion of the fundamental issues in a rapidly developing new field—organizational psychology; it is an excellent discussion suitable for anyone interested in obtaining a better understanding of organizations.

Schoen, D. R. "Human Relations: Boon or Bogle?" *Harvard Business Review*, 35(6), 1957, 41–47. The article critiques and defends the "human relations" approach to leadership. The author presents some rational arguments for better understanding between superiors and subordinates.

Scott, E. L. *Leadership and Perceptions of Organization*. Columbus: The Bureau of Business Research, College of Commerce and Administration, The Ohio State University, 1956. This report presents the results of a study of naval personnel concerned with the relationship between accuracy of role perception and both morale and effectiveness.

Seashore, S. E. *Group Cohesiveness in the Industrial Work Group*. Ann Arbor, MI:

Institute for Social Research, 1954. This report describes a large-scale industrial study in which the author found that the morale of group members was related to group cohesiveness and that group influences were correlated with standards of work performance. He also found that groups of small size are more likely to have a high degree of cohesiveness than groups of larger size and the degree of cohesiveness in a group is significantly determined by manager decisions concerning the size of work groups and the continuity of membership in the groups.

Seashore, S. E. *The Training of Leaders for Effective Human Relations.* Basle: UNESCO, 1957. This publication describes a rationale for power sharing as the basis for training potential leaders.

Shepard, H. A. "Changing Interpersonal and Intergroup Relationships in Organizations," in J. March (Ed.), *Handbook of Organizations.* Chicago: Rand McNally & Co., 1965. In this chapter, the author stresses the importance of organizational leadership as the main integrating force in organizations, and he concludes that emphasis within organizations will shift from arbitration to problem solving and from delegated to shared responsibility as leaders see their organizations as organic rather than mechanistic, as adaptable rather than controlled by rigid structure.

Sherif, M. (Ed.). *Intergroup Relations and Leadership: Approaches and Research in Industrial, Ethnic, Cultural, and Political Areas.* New York: John Wiley & Sons, 1962. This is a wide-ranging collection of articles concerned with conflict between groups, societies, and nations. The various papers, although somewhat academic in approach, contain many useful contributions to understanding of intergroup conflict.

Sherif, M. "Introductory Statement," in M. Sherif (Ed.), *Intergroup Relations and Leadership: Approaches and Research in Industrial, Ethnic, Cultural, and Political Areas.* New York: John Wiley & Sons, 1962. In his introduction to an interesting book, this famous social psychologist sets forth some of the conditions leading to intergroup conflict and some fundamental causes for the resolution of such conflict.

Sherif, M., and H. Cantril. *The Psychology of Ego-Involvements: Social Attitudes and Identifications.* New York: John Wiley & Sons, 1947. This is a definitive work in the social psychology of ego-involvement. Although somewhat outdated, the book contains many useful illustrations of factors that affect the individual's involvement and identification with groups, organizations, and political systems.

Sherif, M., and C. W. Sherif. *Groups in Harmony and Tension.* New York: Harper & Brothers, 1953. This is the report of the classical "robbers cave" experiment in which groups were developed and studied under real-life conditions. It contains discussions of factors critical to the development of cohesive groups and to the development of cooperation between groups.

Sherif, M., and C. W. Sherif. *An Outline of Social Psychology* (rev. ed.). New York: Harper & Brothers, 1956. This basic textbook in social psychology contains discussions that range from the influence of single social variables upon one individual to the development of complex social groups.

Sherif, M., and M. O. Wilson (Eds.). *Group Relations at the Crossroads.* New York:

Harper & Brothers, 1953. This is a collection of technical papers concerned with various aspects of group relations.

Shills, E. A., and M. Janowitz. "Cohesion and Disintegration in the Wehrmacht in World War II." *Public Opinion Quarterly*, 12, 1948, 280–315. In attempting to determine why the German Army in World War II fought so stubbornly to the end, the authors have made an intensive study of the social structure of this army, of the symbols to which it responded, of the Nazi attempts to bolster its morale, and the Allied attempts to break it down. They found a key to many of the behavior and attitude patterns of the individual infantryman in the interpersonal relationships within the company—his primary group. The article discusses methods used by the Wehrmacht to foster high cohesion within its small units.

Simon, H. A. *Administrative Behavior: A Study of Decision-Making Processes in Administrative Organization*. New York: The Macmillan Company, 1947. This book is one of the landmarks in the evolution of decision theory. Simon retained the idea that decision behavior in organization is "intendedly rational" and that decisions are made by individuals within organizations and not by organizations as entities. He also recognized, however, the inadequacy of classical theory for understanding decisions in organizations. Accordingly, he distinguished between the role of facts and of values in decision making.

Simon, H. A. *Models of Man*. New York: John Wiley & Sons, 1957a. This book is a follow on to Simon's 1947 book. In this one, Simon contends that the decision-maker must "satisfice"—find a course of action that is "good enough"—rather than maximizing returns as would be possible if he had full knowledge of the consequences attached to every alternative. This concept of satisficing opened new vistas in theories of organizational decision making.

Simon, H. A. *Administrative Behavior: A Study of Decision-Making Processes in Administrative Organization* (2nd ed.). New York: The Macmillan Company, 1957b. This is another continuation of Simon's expansion of his theories of decision making, and he points out the contrasts between classical economic man and his administrative man, which emphasizes an important point. Rationality is central to behavior within an organization; however, if the members of an organization were capable of the kind of objective rationality attributed to economic man, theories of organization would have no purpose. Simon contended that the need for administrative theory is the fact that there are practical limits to human rationality. These limits are not static, and they depend upon the organizational environment in which the individual's decision takes place.

Simon, R. "Are We Losing Sight of Communications Principles?" *Personnel Journal*, 34, 1955, 206–9. This is a discussion of principles of written communication, with particular emphasis upon communication with personnel in large numbers. Instances of good and bad communication are cited from government and business.

Smith, C. G., and A. J. Tannenbaum. "Organizational Control Structure: A Comparative Analysis," in B. L. Hinton and H. I. Reitz (Eds.), *Groups and Organizations: Integrated Readings in the Analysis of Social Behavior*. Belmont,

CA: Wadsworth, 1971. This paper attempts to provide information concerning several aspects of organizational control through comparative analyses of a number of organizations. Some methodological refinements are called for by the authors.

Statt, D. A. *Using Psychology in Management Training: The Psychological Foundations of Management Skills*. Philadelphia: Psychology Press, 2000. This book aims to give trainers and student trainers a grounding in the ideas and research most relevant for their work.

Steiner, I. D. *Group Process and Productivity*. New York: Academic Press, 1972. This book is an excellent analysis of group processes and their effects upon performance and group productivity.

Stogdill, R. M. "Leadership, Membership, and Organization." *Psychological Bulletin*, 47, 1950, 1–14. In this article, the author outlines some of the critical factors in organizational functioning and in leadership. He contends that leadership must be viewed from the standpoint of influence upon organizational activities.

Stogdill, R. M. *Individual Behavior and Group Achievement*. New York: Oxford University Press, 1959. This book presents a theory for describing both the structure and the achievements of groups. Variables are developed using personality and group constructs. Research findings are cited to support the theory.

Stogdill, R. M. *Handbook of Leadership: A Survey of Theory and Research*. New York: The Free Press, 1974. This detailed survey of theory and research on leadership to 1974, conducted by Ralph Stogdill, one of the icons in the field of leadership, contains all you would ever want to know about leadership at that time.

Strauss, G. "Some Notes on Power-Equalization," in H. J. Leavitt (Ed.), *The Social Science of Organizations*. Englewood Cliffs, NJ: Prentice-Hall, 1963. This article is an incisive and unbiased critique of the so-called "human relations movement" that increasingly exercised potent influence upon thinking about leadership and organizational practices. The author identifies the fundamental issues and discusses the pros and cons of each. This article will be helpful to anyone who wishes to understand more about the practical issues involved in the question of "democratic" versus "authoritarian" leadership.

Swanson, G. E., T. M. Newcomb, and E. L. Hartley (Eds.). *Readings in Social Psychology* (rev. ed.). New York: Henry Holt and Company, 1952. This book of readings presents illustrative selections of the ways in which the influence of social conditions upon psychological processes have been studied. Topics include influence and interpersonal relationships, collective problem solving, recurring interaction patterns, effects of interaction patterns on individual participants, and some social psychological approaches to public issues.

Tannenbaum, R. "The Manager Concept: A Rational Synthesis." *The Journal of Business*, 22(4), 1949, 225–41. This article differentiates "managerial" services from "nonmanagerial" services by isolating those functions performed exclusively by "managers." The author defends the thesis that "managers are those who use formal authority to organize, direct, or control responsible subordinates so that all contributions will be coordinated in the attainment of an organization's purpose." As used in this article, the term "manager" might equally apply to leaders in any type of organization.

Tannenbaum, R. "Managerial Decision-Making." *The Journal of Business*, 23(1), 1950, 22–39. This is an analysis of decision making in organizations. The inter-individual and intergroup relationships that make it possible for the decisions of one person to affect the behavior of another are explored. Some conclusions are presented concerning the work of managers (leaders), indicating how managers affect the behavior of their subordinates and how other people affect the behavior of managers.

Tannenbaum, R., and F. Masserik. "Leadership: A Frame of Reference." *Management Science*, 4(1), 1957, 1–19. The frame of reference described in this article takes into account three separate aspects of leadership: the leader and his psychological attributes; the follower with his problems, attitudes, and needs; and the group situation in which followers and leaders relate to one another. Leadership is treated as a process or function rather than as an exclusive attribute of a prescribed role.

Tannenbaum, R., and W. H. Schmidt. "How to Choose a Leadership Pattern." *Harvard Business Review*, 36(2), 1958, 95–101. This article discusses the apparent conflict between two ways of leading an organization: the democratic, participative approach and the authoritarian, one-man method. The authors contend that no such conflict should exist. They believe there is a large spectrum of possible leadership attitudes and that different approaches are appropriate for different situations. The successful leader is described as the man who recognizes the nature of the particular problem with which he is dealing and adapts his methods of leadership to it.

Taylor, D. W. "Decision Making and Problem Solving," in J. G. March (Ed.), *Handbook of Organization*. Chicago: Rand McNally & Company, 1965. This article is an excellent presentation within March's handbook in which the author provides an excellent analysis of decision making and problem solving within complex organizations. This is an excellent article.

Thelen, H. A. *Dynamics of Groups at Work*. Chicago: University of Chicago Press, 1954. This book is a comprehensive analysis of the dynamics of problem solving and work groups. It contains many practical comments upon the functioning of small groups. The book is divided into a section of theory and a section illustrating the application of theory in various practical situations.

Thorndyke, P. W., and M. G. Weiner. *Improving Training and Performance of Navy Teams: A Design for a Research Program*. Rand Report R-2607-ONR. Santa Monica, CA: Rand Corporation, 1980. This discourse on ways to improve training of navy teams is useful in designing team training.

Triandis, H. C. "Similarity in Thought Processes in Boss-Employee Communication," in C. Ludington (Ed.), *Communication in Organizations: Some New Research Findings*. Ann Arbor, MI: The Foundation for Research on Human Behavior, 1959. The study reported in this article was concerned with the relationship between communication and similarity in thinking between superiors and subordinates. Findings and a discussion of their implications are reported.

Tyler, T. R., and S. Blader. *Cooperation in Groups in Procedural Justice, Social Identity, and Behavioral Engagement.* Philadelphia: Psychology Press, 2000. This book explores the motives that shape the extent and nature of cooperative behavior in groups, organizations, and society.

Urwick, L. *Leadership in the Twentieth Century.* London: Sir Isaac Pitman and Son, Ltd., 1957. In this short book, a well-known management consultant, writer, and retired British Army officer discusses the need for leadership, the psychological basis of leadership, what the leader does, and the development of leaders.

Vaill, P. B. "Toward a Behavioral Description of High Performing Systems," in M. McCall and M. Lombard (Eds.), *Leadership: Where Else Can We Go?* Durham, NC: Duke University Press, 1976. This article is a behavioral description of high performance groups and addresses leadership aspects of such groups.

Van Zelst, R. H. "Sociometrically Selected Work Teams Increase Production." *Personnel Psychology,* 5, 1951, 175–85. This article is a good example of how people whose attitudes are favorable toward each other work more productively and with better performance than those who do not like each other.

Vecchio, R. P. *Leadership.* Notre Dame, IN: University of Notre Dame Press, 1998. This book sets out one of the latest approaches to leadership. It is fairly comprehensive in its coverage of the subject.

Viteles, M. S. *Motivation and Morale in Industry.* New York: W. W. Norton & Company, 1953. This is a basic work on motivation and morale in industry. It contains wide-ranging discussions of factors affecting attitudes and performance.

Vroom, V. H. "Industrial Social Psychology," in G. I. Lindzey and E. Aronson (Eds.), *The Handbook of Social Psychology* (2nd ed.). Vol. V, *Applied Social Psychology.* Reading, MA: Addison-Wesley Publishing Co., 1969. This is an excellent chapter on the issues involved in industrial social psychology in the late 1960s. The issues have not changed much since the chapter was printed.

Wagner, H., N. Hibbits, R. D. Rosenblatt, and R. Schultz. *Team Training and Evaluation Strategies: State of the Art.* Alexandria, VA: Human Resources Research Organization, 1977. This technical report sets forth the most advanced methods for training teams and proposes an advanced model for both designing and evaluating all types of training.

White, R., and R. Lippitt. "Leader Behavior and Member Reaction in Three 'Social Climates,' " in D. Cartwright and A. Zander (Eds.), *Group Dynamics: Research and Theory.* Evanston, IL: Row, Peterson & Co., 1953. This was the famous original study of the ways democratic and authoritarian degrees of control affect group life. The study examined the effects upon individual and group behavior of three variations in social atmosphere labeled "democratic," "authoritarian," and "laissez-faire." Leadership behavior is described from the viewpoint of both the leader and the members of the group.

Whyte, W. F. *Man and Organization*. Homewood, IL: Richard D. Irwin, 1959. This book is one of Whyte's earliest and is very well known. It considers the effects of the place of man in organizations and the effects of the organization upon his performance.

Whyte, W. F. *Men at Work*. Homewood, IL: The Dewey Press, and Richard D. Irwin, 1961. This comprehensive book presents research cases, the analysis of cases, and a theoretical scheme to explain them. There is discussion of such questions as What factors account for conflict or cooperation in organizational relations? What conditions lead to high morale among organizational members? What conditions lead to high productivity? What does the job mean to the worker? What conditions account for the cohesion of work groups? and How do people in organizations react to changes?

Williams, H. B. "Some Functions of Communications in Crisis Behavior." *Human Organization*, 16, 1957, 15–19. This is an excellent article and one of the few that discusses crisis behavior. Here, the impact of faulty communication in crisis situations is emphasized; but what happens to organizations in crises is an important aspect of this article.

Zaleznik, A., C. R. Christensen, and F. L. Roethlisberger. *The Motivation, Productivity, and Satisfaction of Workers: A Prediction Study*. Boston: Graduate School of Business Administration, Harvard University, 1958. This is one of the better known studies to come out of the Harvard Business School concerned with motivation, productivity, and satisfaction of personnel.

Zaleznik, A., and D. Moment. *The Dynamics of Interpersonal Behavior*. New York: John Wiley & Sons, 1964. This book is concerned with interpersonal relations within organizations. Somewhat in conflict with the group dynamics writers and with the descendants of Lewin, it is a semi-sociological report of human behavior.

Zander, A. F. "Resistance to Change—Its Analysis and Prevention." *Advanced Management*, 15–16, 1950, 9–11. This is an analysis of the factors leading to resistance to change. The article also gives suggestions for preventing and overcoming such resistance.

Zander, A. F. *Effects of Group Goals Upon Personal Goals*. Technical Report No. 12 (Factors Determining Defensive Behavior in Groups). Washington, DC: Group Psychology Branch, ONR, National Training Laboratories, 1961. This survey report reviews various findings relevant to a member's acceptance of a goal provided him by his group. Level of aspiration is analyzed in relation to personal and group objectives. The nature and origin of efforts to cope with demands that are higher than the individual can fulfill are also discussed.

Author Index

Subject Index

About the Author

JOSEPH A. OLMSTEAD is Vice President, Product Development, at the Vanguard Research Group, Columbia, S.C. He earned a doctorate in psychology from the University of Texas, and served as Senior Staff Scientist and Program Director at the Human Research Office of the George Washington University. Earlier, he was Chief of Training and Management Development at Eli Lilly and Co. Among his more than 50 papers, monographs, and technical reports is another book published by Quorum, *Creating the Functionally Competent Organization* (2002).

Communication
Theory:
Eastern
and Western